How to Report Economic News

Since the global financial crisis in 2008, economics has dominated the news agenda, with issues such as migration, growth, trade and unemployment remaining hotly debated in the media. *How to Report Economic News* is an accessible introduction to our contemporary economic landscape and journalistic approaches to economic news coverage.

Nicola Walton, an experienced financial journalist, presents a comprehensive guide to important economic indicators and how to report on them, as well as giving advice on identifying essential facts needed for any economic news story. The author also offers useful tips on journalistic writing that can help ensure articles are written clearly, concisely and with precision. To provide readers with further guidance, each chapter concludes with assignments to test your knowledge, a resource list for further reading and a glossary of key terms.

Chapters cover key topics including inflation, monetary policy, labour markets, fiscal policy and residential property markets. The book takes the UK economy as its main focus, but also explores European, US and Japanese markets. In addition, the title explores other major global topics such as the rise of the Brazil, Russia, India, China (BRIC) economies and the role of multinational organisations such as the International Monetary Fund.

By combining an overview of current financial systems and economic developments with instruction on economic reporting, this title is a valuable resource for students of journalism, trainee journalists, as well as anyone interested in learning more about modern economics.

Nicola Walton has worked as a financial journalist in broadcast and print media for many years. She was a visiting lecturer at City University's School of Journalism in London from 2010–2014, where she taught an economic reporting module on the Financial Journalism MA course.

How to Report Economic News

Nicola Walton

LONDON AND NEW YORK

First published 2017
by Routledge
2 Park Square, Milton Park, Abingdon, Oxon OX14 4RN

and by Routledge
711 Third Avenue, New York, NY 10017

Routledge is an imprint of the Taylor & Francis Group, an informa business

© 2017 Nicola Walton

The right of Nicola Walton to be identified as author of this work has been asserted by her in accordance with sections 77 and 78 of the Copyright, Designs and Patents Act 1988.

All rights reserved. No part of this book may be reprinted or reproduced or utilised in any form or by any electronic, mechanical, or other means, now known or hereafter invented, including photocopying and recording, or in any information storage or retrieval system, without permission in writing from the publishers.

Trademark notice: Product or corporate names may be trademarks or registered trademarks, and are used only for identification and explanation without intent to infringe.

British Library Cataloguing in Publication Data
A catalogue record for this book is available from the British Library

Library of Congress Cataloging in Publication Data
A catalog record for this book has been requested

ISBN: 978-1-138-93350-7 (hbk)
ISBN: 978-1-138-93351-4 (pbk)
ISBN: 978-1-315-67853-5 (ebk)

Typeset in Bembo
by RefineCatch Limited, Bungay, Suffolk

For Freddie and Matthew

Contents

List of figures	viii
List of tables	ix
Preface	x
Acknowledgements	xi
1 Monetary policy	1
2 Inflation	25
3 Economic growth	45
4 Labour markets	74
5 Fiscal policy	98
6 Trade	119
7 Emerging markets	146
8 The International Monetary Fund and World Bank	167
9 Residential property markets	188
10 Surveys	224
Index	240

Figures

1.1	Federal Reserve Chairwoman Janet Yellen participates in the Inaugural Michel Camdessus Central Banking Lecture on financial stability at the IMF Headquarters in downtown Washington, DC on 2 July 2014	7
2.1	Harvesting combine in the field	31
3.1	Shale oil platform	51
4.1	Job centre in England	76
5.1	The Rt Hon George Osborne MP Former Chancellor of the Exchequer speaks to conservative candidates and supporters at Saunton Sands Hotel, Devon	101
6.1	Jaguar Landrover assembly line in Halewood, Merseyside	122
7.1	Real, Brazilian currency	159
8.1	Thessaloniki, Greece, 20 January 2015. Alexis Tsipras, leader of Greece's Syriza main opposition party spoke at a pre-election campaign rally, in Thessaloniki, northern Greece, ahead of Sunday's crucial general elections	169
9.1	Northern Rock Building Society queues	190

Tables

1.1	Inflation targets	6
2.1	Most important categories in the UK CPI (2016)	27
3.1	IMF 2016 GDP growth forecasts	48
4.1	Unemployment rates	74
7.1	IMF GDP growth forecasts	146
8.1	IMF quota shares	175
9.1	Largest mortgage lenders by gross lending market share	191
9.2	UK house prices since 1952	196

Preface

The scale and duration of the financial crisis of 2008 meant that financial news became *the* news. Stories about the consequences of the financial crash continue to be headline news, whether that's the twists and turns of the Greek debt negotiations or speculation as to how far and how fast the US authorities will be able to raise interest rates after years of unnaturally loose monetary policy.

The growth of the mobile technology market means that increasingly people, particularly the under 30s, get large amounts of information from their phones and tablet computers.

Whilst the means of news distribution may have changed over the years what has not is the need for journalists to be able to communicate often complex matters in an informative and engaging manner. This book, which assumes no prior knowledge of economics, aims to provide the information needed to help you understand some of the issues that are setting the economic news agenda.

Acknowledgements

I would like to express my gratitude to Steve Schifferes, Marjorie Deane Professor of Financial Journalism at City University, who in 2010 appointed me, despite my having no prior teaching experience, as one of the inaugural visiting lecturers, on what was then the new MA Financial Journalism course. It was the lack of a textbook to accompany the economics course that I was teaching that prompted me to write this book.

I am also grateful to Professor Roger Goodman of Oxford University and Dr Liz Fisher of Oxford University for their insights into academic publishing.

Thanks must also go to my dear friends Helen, Matthew, Paul, Kieron, David and John for their support and encouragement.

I am grateful to the editorial staff at Taylor & Francis, particularly Niall Kennedy and Katherine Imbert. Finally, I hope my late husband David, who died in 2006, would be proud of what I have done.

1 Monetary policy

Quantitative easing, forward guidance . . . what do they mean and why should you care? Find out this, why America has consciously uncoupled its interest rate policies from that of the Eurozone and other major economies such as Japan, and who the people are who decide interest rate policy in the UK and US.

The financial crash of 2008/2009 has changed the parameters of discussion of **monetary policy**. Historically, as an economic reporter one would have been expected to be writing about changes in interest rates and the impact that might have on **mortgage** rates, the stock market, etc. However, the shock waves emanating from the 2008/2009 financial crisis were such that interest rates were slashed to historic lows – 0.5% in March 2009 in the case of the UK – to try to stave off an economic slump and they have yet to be raised.

Monetary policy is the government policy relating to the quantity of money in the economy, the rate of interest and the exchange rate.

The **bank base rate** is the rate of interest around which the main UK banks and building societies fix their lending and borrowing rates.

The majority of homebuyers take out a mortgage when they want to buy a property, which is a loan linked to the property which could last 25 years. There are several different types of mortgage depending on whether one wishes to have fixed or variable interest payments. We will look at these in more detail in the global property chapter. However, variable loans change when the **Bank of England** alters interest rates.

In the UK, monetary policy has been the responsibility of the Bank of England (also known as the Old Lady of Threadneedle Street, a reference to the street on which the Bank is located in the City of London) since 1997 when it was given independence by the then Labour government. The aim was to prevent monetary policy suffering from the short-term time horizons of politicians, who are often tempted to look to the nearest election rather than focus on what is in the best long-term interests of the economy.[1]

The objective of the Bank of England is to deliver price stability – low inflation – and to support the government's economic objectives including those for growth and employment.[2]

From the mid-1980s up until the financial crisis of 2008/2009, the Bank of England used interest rates as its main instrument of monetary policy.

The direction of interest rates tends to be similar in the developed economies reflecting the interdependence of global economies. However, given the severity of the financial crisis economies have recovered at differing speeds and so there has been a divergence in interest rate policy. Any change in interest rates is a major news story for an economic reporter and news of such a change is likely to top the news bulletins on the day it happens.

Box 1.1 Reporting interest rate changes

- What was the rate change – to what level, was it expected? What's the likely future trend of interest rates?
- Include comment on likely impact . . . If rates rise variable mortgage rates increase and consumer confidence is likely to fall.
- Stock market reaction: shares, bonds, sterling.
- Quote from economist/politician/housing market researcher.

Box 1.2 The effect of an increase in Bank of England interest rates

- Will increase the rates charged by other banks.
- Encourages saving and reduces consumption spending.
- Signals intention to control inflation. Discourages inflationary wage claims.
- More demand for sterling from overseas investors. UK exports relatively more expensive so lowers demand and helps reduce inflation.

The decision to alter interest rates is not made by just one person. In the UK, the **Monetary Policy Committee** (MPC) is involved.

Monetary Policy Committee (MPC)

Box 1.3 Monetary Policy Committee (MPC)

- Nine member committee including the Governor of the Bank of England, Mark Carney, three deputy governors, chief economist and four external appointees.
- Two-day monthly meeting to set the interest rate.
- Minutes published two weeks after the interest rate decision, including any differences of opinion.

The outcome of the monthly meeting, even if there is no change to interest rates, is always reported in the press as a news story.

> **Journalistic practice**
>
> In a news story, any differences of opinion between the MPC members should be highlighted and explained, as this can give an indication of the mood music in the MPC and signal the future direction of interest rates. The views of a City economist should be sought to get an opinion on whether the action taken is supported by practitioners in the financial markets. End the report with the reaction (or not) of the FTSE 100 index and sterling's value against the dollar and euro.

When the Bank of England changes the interest rate, it is attempting to influence the overall expenditure in the economy.

When the amount of money grows more quickly than the volume of output produced inflation is the result.

Inflation

Changes in interest rates are used to control inflation but before any change is made various factors are taken into account.

> **Box 1.4** Economic indicators taken into account
>
> - House prices
> - Rate of increase in average earnings
> - Exchange rate
> - Output gap
> - Lending by banks and building societies
> - Consumer confidence surveys.

House prices

There is regular concern expressed about a housing market 'bubble' in London and the south-east of England. House prices are widely thought to have risen to an unsustainable level.[3]

Journalistic practice

In reporting on house prices, comparisons can be made with prices in London and for a similar size property in north-east England, which has some of the cheapest property in the UK. Graphs can be included of the annual change in house prices. These can be obtained from the Office of National Statistics (ONS). Such reports are easy to illustrate with shots of streets, and for sale signs in the case of London.

If house prices are increasing rapidly, it can encourage more borrowing thereby boosting overall expenditure in the economy. News stories can be written on booming retail sales picking out notable features such as cars or leisure spending with associated photographs.[4]

One consequence of the financial crash was a prolonged squeeze on real income — that is incomes adjusted for inflation. Wages were either frozen, particularly in the public sector, or rose by less than inflation. The opposition Labour Party in the UK made much of problems facing the 'squeezed middle' section of the population during the 2015 General Election campaign.[5]

The Oxford English Dictionary defines the squeezed middle as 'the section of society regarded as particularly affected by inflation, wage freezes, and cuts in public spending during a time of economic difficulty, consisting principally of those people on low or middle incomes'.

Rapid wage growth could feed through to higher costs for firms. They then seek to pass these on to customers which would be inflationary. If the pound is weak relative to other currencies then exports become more competitive, because firms can sell their goods cheaper, increasing overall demand. Foreign buyers need less currency to buy the same quantity of UK goods.

The **output gap** is the difference between actual demand and what economists estimate is the potential level of output of the economy. When there is spare capacity in the economy, such as slack in the labour market — where there are more people looking for work than there are available jobs — there is less inflationary pressure.

Even with the UK economy recovering strongly from the financial crisis, banks with their fingers burnt during the financial crisis are, perhaps not surprisingly, more cautious.

Bank lending has been less than the government would like particularly to small businesses hence the introduction of its **Funding for Lending** (FLS) scheme.

Funding for Lending (FLS)

This programme was launched by the Bank of England and the UK Treasury in July 2012 to encourage banks and building societies to increase lending to businesses and non-financial companies.[6]

Funds were made available at below the existing elevated market rate. The price and quantity of funding provided is linked to their lending performance. The Bank and Treasury announced an extension to the scheme in April 2013, which was amended in November 2013, December 2014 and November 2015. This allows participants to borrow from the FLS until January 2018, with incentives to boost lending skewed towards small and medium-sized enterprises (SMEs).

> **Journalistic practice**
>
> An introductory comment can set the scene, detailing the figures showing a decline in bank lending over a specific timescale before and after the financial crisis. This can be illustrated graphically.
>
> Various angles can then be taken to illustrate FLS. The Chancellor of the Exchequer can be interviewed on what the government hopes the scheme will achieve. This can be coupled with a view from a representative of small business such as the Federation of Small Business on what they think of the scheme.
>
> An alternative approach can be interviewing a representative from one of the big four UK banks on their lending policy to small business. This can be contrasted with what's actually happening on the ground. Interview a small business owner on the problems they have faced securing financing and how this has constrained growth of the business. The report can end with a mention of the growth of alternative financing channels such as crowd funding and peer-to-peer lending.

FLS is still a work in progress and is likely to be the subject of news reports for some time as the scheme is fine-tuned in an attempt to achieve the desired objective.

How people are feeling about their personal financial circumstances, 'consumer confidence', very much influences the actions of the Bank of England, which is keen not to derail the economic recovery. Research by Professor Ben Jacobsen, Chair in Financial Markets at University of Edinburgh Business School, has shown that women tend to be more pessimistic about the future than men and so they worry more about a rise in interest rates.[7]

'For the first time, by collating all available data on gender differences in consumer confidence and opinion, we've been able to comprehensively prove men are more optimistic about their own, their families and their countries' future prospects,' he said.

There are various problems facing the MPC when making their assessment of the state of the economy at any one given time. Economic data can be very volatile from month to month. Judgements have to be made about how much weight to attach to the data provided.

6 Monetary policy

It is not often that all the economic data points to the same conclusion due to lags in the economy. For instance, unemployment can continue rising even when an economy is recovering from a downturn. Some economists attach more importance to, for example, an increase in wage inflation than others.[8]

The Bank of England has 12 agencies located around the UK. Their primary role is to assess economic conditions affecting businesses in their area. Each agency provides a monthly assessment to the MPC about business conditions, helping the Bank form a view on the likely path of the economy and inflation. In addition, members of the MPC make regular visits to different parts of the UK explaining how they make their policy decisions.

Box 1.5 Inflation report

- First published by the BOE in 1993.
- Published every quarter.
- Sets out detailed economic analysis and inflation projections on which the Bank bases its interest rate decisions.
- Also forecasts output growth.
- BOE government-set inflation target is 2%.

Inflation target

The Bank of England's inflation target is announced each year by the Chancellor of the Exchequer in the Budget.[9] The 2% inflation target is thought to be the most likely to deliver price stability and maximum employment over the long term. A lower inflation rate runs the risk of the economy falling into deflation with prices and possibly wages falling and is symptomatic of a very weak economy. A higher inflation rate makes it harder to make long-term economic and financial decisions.

If the target is missed by more than 1% either side i.e. if the annual rate of consumer price inflation is more than 3% or less than 1%, the Governor of the Bank of England must write an open letter to the Chancellor explaining the reasons why inflation has increased or fallen to such an extent and what

Table 1.1 Inflation targets

UK	2%
ECB	2%
US	2%
Japan	2%

the Bank proposes to do to ensure inflation comes back to target within a reasonable time frame, without creating undue instability in the economy.

John McDonnell, current Shadow Chancellor, thinks the Bank of England's remit needs to be larger. He believes the Bank's policymaking should take into account other factors such as economic growth and long-term investment in infrastructure.[10]

If the opposition Labour Party wins power then it will carry out a review of the Bank of England's mandate, whilst maintaining its independence.

> **Journalistic practice**
>
> Comment pieces can be produced on the desirability or not of inflation targets and how well they have been met. Depending on the audience, more detailed economic analysis can be provided with input from academic economists.

US Federal Reserve

In the US, the **Federal Reserve** (widely referred to as the Fed) is in charge of monetary policy. Dr Janet Yellen has been Chair of the Federal Reserve since February 2014.[11] She has a four-year term of office and is the first woman to head the US central bank.

Figure 1.1 Federal Reserve Chairwoman Janet Yellen participates in the Inaugural Michel Camdessus Central Banking Lecture on financial stability at the IMF Headquarters in downtown Washington, DC on 2 July 2014. Image courtesy of Kristoffer Tripplaar/Alamy.

The appointment of a new central bank governor in the major economies is a major news story.

Journalistic practice

In writing a profile of a new head of a central bank, there are various key facts that should be included. Obviously there will be an interest in basic biographical details such as education and previous relevant jobs. However, what the financial markets are interested in is what implications the appointment might have in terms of the future direction of monetary policy.

There are various questions one can aim to answer in the course of the profile. What has the appointee said in the past about monetary policy? Are there any clues as to what their priorities might be in office? Is the appointee a 'Hawk' or a 'Dove' in terms of monetary policy? This means are they in favour of strict adherence to the inflation target and accordingly tight monetary policy, or the opposite. Do the financial markets like the new appointment? If so, then this is usually reflected by a jump in the stock market indices. Is the appointee likely to have to respond to any major financial news announcements in the near future which may give some pointers to their future policy stance?

The US is the world's largest economy so what the Fed does in terms of policy has ramifications around the world. Janet Yellen is thought to be more concerned about growth than inflation. At the time of her appointment in January 2014 that seemed the right priority given the mixed messages coming out of the US economy. Even with the US economy leading growth amongst the industrialised Western economies, Janet Yellen has not rushed to tighten US monetary policy.

In testimony before the Senate Banking Committee in February 2015, she said 'too many Americans remain unemployed or underemployed, wage growth is still sluggish and inflation remains well below our longer-run objective'.[12]

A highly influential previous chair of the Fed was Alan Greenspan whose views are still sought today. He served from 1987–2006, after several re-appointments, the second-longest tenure in the position.

The chief decision making body of the Fed is the **Federal Open Market Committee** (FOMC). This is a 12-member group of representatives of regional reserve banks and federal appointees.

During the course of and in the aftermath of the financial crisis, concerns about inflation took a back seat to promotion of economic growth. Policy makers were desperate to avoid the world economy slipping into a 1930s-style depression.

Delivering his penultimate Inflation Report in February 2013, when UK inflation was 2.7% and expected to rise further, the then Bank of England Governor Sir Mervyn King said attempting to bring inflation back to target sooner would risk 'derailing the recovery'.[13]

The financial crash of 2008 has made several technical financial terms commonplace, one of them being **quantitative easing** (QE).

Quantitative easing

QE is the electronic printing of money to buy assets, mainly government bonds (gilts in the case of the UK) from banks and insurance companies. These organisations then use the money raised from the sales to purchase other assets such as corporate bonds and shares.

Buying **bonds** pushes up the price and lowers the **yield** (see glossary for definitions of a bond and yield), which should lead to lower borrowing costs for businesses and consumers.

QE was the co-ordinated response of policy makers in mature industrialised economies to stagnant growth. QE was introduced largely because interest rates could not be reduced much further, having been slashed to just 0.5% in the immediate aftermath of the financial crash. QE had never been done prior to the financial crash.

Journalistic practice

There has been a huge amount of coverage of QE. This includes explanation of what it is, why it is being done and the likely impact on the financial markets. A number of other angles can be taken. These include detailing the winners – shares, property, commodities and higher-risk bonds and losers from QE, such as savers and pensioners. The possible long-term economic consequences of QE also provide fertile ground for opinion and comment pieces.

When a central bank announces a change in its QE policy, any news report should quote the statement with the reasons for the decision. Include an opinion from a financial analyst or economist with a mention of what the share price reaction was to the announcement. The report can be brought bang up to date with the latest economic data that vindicates the action taken by the central bank e.g. better economic growth or unemployment figures.

A wider global perspective can be taken by charting the negative impact on emerging markets such as India and Brazil of a reversal of QE in the larger mature markets. Such reports can include details of movements in the associated emerging stock and currency markets and critical comments from politicians and central bankers in these countries. In 2010, Brazil's finance minister Guido Mantega complained about what he saw as the start of an international currency war as a result of the Fed's bond-buying programme which he said unfairly weakened the dollar and boosted the real (Brazil's currency), thereby reducing Brazil's competitiveness.

Journalists will continue to debate whether it has been a good thing in what were dire circumstances. In January 2009, before the Conservative Party formed part of the UK's coalition government, Shadow Chancellor George Osborne described QE as 'the last resort of desperate governments when all other policies have failed'.[14]

In 2009, as Chancellor of the Exchequer, Mr Osborne authorised the Bank of England to set up an asset purchase facility (APF) to buy high quality assets financed by the issue of Treasury Bills and the Debt Management Office's (DMO) cash management operations. The aim of the facility was to improve liquidity in credit markets. On 4 August 2016, the MPC voted to increase the stock of purchases of UK government bonds by the APF to £435bn. In addition, the MPC voted to make up to £10bn of purchases of corporate bonds over 18 months.[15]

How successful has QE been? Even the Bank of England itself is not entirely sure. Charlie Bean, the then Bank of England chief economist, said:

> The truth is that we will probably never know exactly how effective the policy of quantitative easing has been, for the simple reason that we can never know with precision what would have happened in its absence. My only confident prediction is that academic economists and their PhD students will be poring over the topic for decades to come.[16]

However it is widely believed by the markets to have declined in effectiveness over time. The Bank of England estimates that its first round of QE, when £200bn ($300bn) worth of bonds, equivalent to about 14% of GDP, were purchased between March and November 2009, helped to boost the UK's annual economic growth by 1.5–2%. In the words of the Bank this was deemed to be 'economically significant'.[17]

The value of a whole range of assets has been affected by QE from UK house prices to inflation, pension annuities and gold in dollar terms.[18]

There are widespread concerns about the possible adverse long-term effects of the unorthodox monetary policy, even amongst those carrying out the policy. Spencer Dale voiced his worries in a speech in 2012. The former chief economist at the Bank of England and member of the MPC said that having a sustained loose monetary policy over a long period of time 'could lead to increases in the risk taking of investors and financial institutions in a way that could store up problems for the future'.[19]

Commenting on the limits of monetary policy in 2012, Mr Dale added that '[prolonged and aggressive monetary accommodation] may also delay some of the rebalancing and restructuring that our economy needs to undertake'. This has led to the emergence of the phrase 'zombie' companies, unprofitable companies that are able to stay alive on a steady drip of low credit. In a mature industrialised economy, innovation and with it the emergence of new improved technologies and companies are deemed to be the best route to future economic prosperity.

William White, influential former chief economist to the Bank for International Settlements, the international body that represents the world's central banks, believes that QE is doomed to fail in Europe because 'Europe has a far greater reliance than the US on small and medium-sized companies and they get their money from banks, not from the bond market'.[20]

The UK was the fastest growing of the G7 industrialised nations in 2014 and 2015, despite a turbulent economic and geo-political climate. Post-Brexit uncertainty prompted the International Monetary Fund (IMF) to lower its 2016 UK GDP forecast to 1.8%, down from 2.2% in 2015.[21]

Speaking at the International Monetary Fund's spring conference in Washington in April 2015, Christine Lagarde, managing director of the IMF, praised the management of the UK economy saying the authorities had managed to provide the right balance of spending cuts and revenue-raising. 'When we look at the comparative growth rates delivered by various countries in Europe it's obvious that what is happening in the UK has actually worked,' she said.[22]

However, the whole principle of QE is not without its critics. In the US, some Republican politicians are calling for more political oversight of the Federal Reserve's (Fed's) discussions and policies. They are concerned that the Fed's policies may destabilise financial markets and eventually lead to higher inflation.

Box 1.6 Criticisms of QE

- Pension income reduced by lower yields.
- No guarantee it will have desired effect of boosting the economy.
- Increased commodity price inflation with bank speculators using the spare cash.
- Enabled Chancellor to 'borrow' £35bn to make public finances look better.

Box 1.7 Criticisms of the Bank of England

- Slow to act during the 2008 financial crisis.
- Bank of England Court not rigorous enough in oversight of policy.
- The Bank does not understand how markets work in reality given its academic economic profile.
- Printing money makes the BOE no better than 1920s Germany or Zimbabwe and risks hyperinflation.
- Unelected and unaccountable which is undesirable in a democracy.

Anti-austerity protests

The debate on the balance of power between unelected banking officials and the electorate became very heated during the depths of the financial crisis. People took to the streets to protest about the dire effects of austerity measures in a number of countries including Greece, Italy and Spain.

Public frustration and fatigue with austerity were instrumental in the election of Alexis Tsipras's left wing Syriza party in the Greek parliamentary election in January 2015.[23] The established parties in Spain are being given a run for their money by Pablo Iglesias, the charismatic leader of the anti-austerity Podemos movement. Following historic elections in December 2015 the incumbent Spanish Conservatives won but with no majority.[24] The political uncertainty unsettled the financial markets with a slump in Spanish bonds and shares.

Elsewhere in Europe, a coalition of left wing parties in Portugal pooled their votes to unseat the Conservative government after an inconclusive election in October 2015. In the UK, the membership of the opposition Labour Party elected the veteran left wing anti-austerity MP Jeremy Corbyn as party leader.

The UK was not alone in taking the QE medicine. The US, Japan and **European Central Bank** (ECB) have all introduced their own versions of QE. The US started its asset purchase programme in 2009 during the financial crisis when US interest rates were almost zero, so there was little room for further easing of monetary policy in the traditional sense. The US Federal Reserve focused on buying government debt in the form of Treasury bonds and assets backed by home loans. A total of three separate QE programmes were carried out, adding more than $3.5 trillion to the Fed's balance sheet. Has the seed been sown for the next financial crisis?

The US called a halt to its QE programme in October 2014 amid encouraging inflation and unemployment data. Just a hint that the US QE programme might be scaled back was enough to prompt investors in emerging markets to switch back to US assets, attracted by the prospect of higher US interest rates. At the end of 2013, the so-called 'tapering' of the QE programme had a negative impact on a number of emerging markets with particular shock waves recorded in those economies with large current account deficits such as Brazil and Turkey.[25]

South Africa is also amongst the list of what investment bank Morgan Stanley refers to as the 'fragile five' emerging markets economies, said to be most at risk from higher US interest rates.[26]

It was already an area of concern because of its domestic political and economic troubles. There is speculation that the ratings agencies will remove South Africa's investment grade status, relegating its bonds to junk.[27]

Brazil and South Africa face the double negative of also being vulnerable to weaker global demand for commodities in the wake of the slowdown in the Chinese economy. These economies suffered large capital outflows and a sharp drop in the value of their currencies and stock markets.

Like the UK a softly, softly approach is being taken to US interest rate rises given the apparent slack in the US labour market and continuing problems in parts of the US housing market. The jury is still out on whether QE worked in the US given the recovery in the US economy has been weaker than that which followed many previous recessions.

QE was effectively invented by Japan's central bank in the 1990s to try to stave off a period of deflation and recession. However, despite spending trillions of yen since 1990 on various stimulus programmes including infrastructure projects, Japanese GDP has barely grown. After his re-election in December 2012, Prime Minister Shinzo Abe launched a huge economic stimulus package that became known as **Abenomics**.

Abenomics

The stimulus programme included a massive fiscal stimulus, aggressive monetary easing by the Bank of Japan and structural reforms to boost Japan's competitiveness. Although the jury is still out on the long-term ability of the programme to defeat the perennial problem of Japanese deflation, there have been short-term benefits.

Box 1.8 Abenomics

- Negative interest rates and a large asset purchase programme.
- Inflation target of 2%.
- Raise consumption tax in April 2014 from 5–8% to tackle huge debts, equivalent to more than 200% of GDP.
- Reduce excessive regulation.
- Weaker yen.
- Encourage foreign inward investment.

The yen weakened by around 30%, particularly versus the US dollar, boosting exports and tourism. The Tokyo stock market rose, companies reported record profits and unemployment fell to a 20 year low at 3.1%.[28] International tourism in Japan continues to grow. In July 2016, there were 2.29 million visitors, up 19.7% from a year earlier.[29]

The Bank of Japan (BOJ) shocked the global financial markets in October 2014 when it announced an expansion in its annual asset purchase programme, from Y60–70trn to Y80trn (about £447bn).[30]

Commenting on the day that the extra stimulus was announced, BOJ Governor Haruhiko Kuroda said 'Now is a critical moment for Japan to

14 *Monetary policy*

emerge from deflation. Today's step shows our unwavering determination to end deflation'.[31]

Following the announcement the Nikkei stock index jumped to a seven year high but the yen dropped to a six year low versus the dollar. The BOJ's announcement was widely seen as an admission that the programme to date had failed given poor domestic consumer confidence and weak demand.

In December 2015, the BOJ again surprised the markets with the announcement that it would start buying government bonds with longer to run until maturity and add Y300bn ($2.4bn) a year to its purchases of equities. The BOJ insisted that the actions were not symptomatic of a further easing of policy. Like the US Federal Reserve's Operation Twist in 2011, buying longer-term bonds should exert downward pressure on longer-term rates.

Meanwhile Japan remains the most indebted country amongst advanced industrialised nations in comparison to the size of its economy with public debt that has exceeded 230% of gross domestic product (GDP).

Journalistic coverage

Feature reports on Abenomics inevitably should include some of the history of the government's attempts to revive the economy over many years. Detail can then be given on how successful the various elements of the latest programme have been including quotes from financial analysts or economists.

Market stories should look at the impact of Abenomics on the value of the yen, which can be illustrated graphically. Reporters can also look at the political dimension of a possible currency war with various countries competing to devalue their currency in the hope of achieving a competitive advantage in international trade. Such reports should include a quote from a central banker or politician.

European Central Bank

The European Central Bank (ECB) is in charge of monetary policy for all the countries that use the euro, the European Union's single currency. Based in Frankfurt, its governing council defines Eurozone monetary policy and fixes the interest rates at which commercial banks can obtain money from the ECB. The governing council includes six members of the executive board plus the governors of the 19 national central banks in the Eurozone.

The ECB's objective is to maintain price stability. Its president is the well-regarded Mario Draghi. Credibility is important if central bankers are to be respected by the markets. Mr Draghi's comments in July 2012 that the ECB would do 'whatever it takes to preserve the euro' have been widely credited with preventing financial meltdown at the height of the Eurozone crisis.

There was a controversial bond-buying programme during the financial crisis with critics arguing against a bail out of indebted nations such as Greece and Spain. However in January 2015, Mario Draghi formally announced that the ECB would inject at least Euro 1.1 trillion to try to shake the Eurozone economy out of its torpor.

Just the expectation that the ECB would introduce QE had the desired effect of lowering bond yields. In September 2016, the ECB QE programme was Euro 80 billion a month, with the central bank buying euro-denominated public sector securities. A programme on this average scale is intended to be carried out until the end of March 2017. However it may be extended, as the governing council of the ECB will want to see visible signs that European inflation is likely to move close to its medium term target of 2%.

The hope is that inflation will rebound towards a level below, but close to the ECB's 2% inflation target. However this is likely to take longer than the ECB originally anticipated given the wider deflationary environment. Inflation has not been at the ECB's 2% target since the start of 2013.

In March 2016, Mr Draghi signalled his determination to stimulate the Eurozone economy with a package of measures including a cut in the ECB deposit rate to −0.4%, more QE in the form of corporate bond buying and incentives to banks to increase lending with the provision of cheaper short-term loans and longer-term liquidity at negative interest rates. Mr Draghi said interest rates would stay low for 'an extended period' and he kept open the option of a further cut.[32]

He has expressed his concern about the impact of negative rates on banks. However ECB chief economist Peter Praet has said the ECB would be prepared to slash rates further if economic prospects deteriorated. It could pump cash directly into the real economy through so-called 'helicopter drops'.[33]

Journalistic practice

The ECB came latterly to the QE party so many journalists have questioned whether it has been too late or whether it should have joined in at all. What do City investors think of the strategy? Include market expectations for Eurozone inflation plus yields on German government bonds. The views of the respected head of the ECB Mario Draghi, who has earned the moniker 'Super Mario', should also be included.

Forward guidance

Forward guidance is another relatively new phenomenon in the lexicon of economic commentators. In August 2013, the MPC issued a guidance statement saying that the UK base rate would not be raised 'at least until the

Labour Force Survey headline measure of the unemployment rate has fallen to a threshold of 7%'.[34]

Along with many commentators, the Bank's own economists were not expecting the UK economy to recover as strongly and as quickly as it has and so the goal posts were shifted with forward guidance amended in February 2014, when it became clear that unemployment would reach the 7% target sooner than anticipated.

The MPC said 'Despite the sharp fall in unemployment, there remains scope to absorb spare capacity further before raising Bank Rate'. Even when the economy has returned to what are deemed to be normal levels of capacity and inflation is close to its 2% target, any interest rate rises are expected to be gradual and according to the MPC are 'likely to be materially below the 5% level set on average by the Committee prior to the financial crisis'.[35]

In the aftermath of the financial crisis, the US has also had its own version of forward guidance. In August 2011, the FOMC stated that it 'anticipates that economic conditions . . . are likely to warrant exceptionally low levels for the federal funds rate at least through mid-2013'. This statement prompted US economists and financial commentators to change their expectations of when US interest rates would rise thereby prompting a drop in the yields on US Treasuries (fixed price bonds).

Subsequent statements were made in the following years so that effectively the hands of the financial markets were held whilst the economy stepped gingerly out of recession.

Journalistic practice

The introduction of forward guidance was a major news story in its own right with journalists explaining what it meant and interviews with Mark Carney. Comparisons were made between the UK and US versions of forward guidance. Interviews were done with City practitioners such as currency traders and City economists on how useful they thought forward guidance would be in determining the timing of any policy change.

In future months, journalistic coverage can continue to monitor whether economic indicators are signalling that action might be taken imminently in line with the forward guidance. Past coverage reported the apparent moving of the goal posts. When UK unemployment figures appeared in reach of the stated target earlier than expected, the Bank of England announced that it was not the only indicator that was looked at in determining when interest rates might rise.

Mixed messages from central bankers on when interest rates might rise confuse the markets and prompt comment pieces on how good a grasp said banker has of their brief.

Even with the US economy seeming to recover well relative to other major economies, policy makers were cautious. In March 2015, Janet Yellen said in a speech to the San Francisco Federal Reserve that although a rate increase 'may be warranted later this year', any move towards a normal Fed funds rate 'was likely to be gradual'.[36] A number of reasons were cited including the fact that the US economic recovery was weak by historic standards.

Forward guidance is meant to reassure businesses and consumers that interest rates will stay low so they have the confidence to invest and go out and spend respectively. Once 'normal' monetary conditions return then forward guidance will probably change again.

Speaking in Paris in March 2015, Cleveland Federal Reserve President Loretta Mester said, 'Whilst explicit forward guidance was used as a policy tool during the recession and earlier in the recovery, in more normal times, away from the zero lower bound, I believe forward guidance should be viewed more as a communications device'.[37]

On 16 December 2015, Janet Yellen announced a quarter point rise (also known as a 25 basis point hike) in the target range for US interest rates to 0.25–0.5%, the first US rate rise in nine years.[38] Ms Yellen was keen to emphasise that future increases would be 'gradual'. Despite widespread expectations that the rate would increase stock markets around the world moved higher, expressing relief that the era of super low interest rates was over.

> **Journalistic practice**
>
> A wide range of angles can be taken to cover a US interest rate hike. These include the financial market reaction, the likely medium/longer implications for other economies and comment pieces on the likely future direction of US monetary policy with quotes from economists and market participants. A personal financial angle can be covered looking at the likely impact of the rate rise for investors with expert predictions on the outlook for equities.

The US rate rise announcement was taken as a positive sign that the US economy was growing and monetary policy could start to be normalised. In the aftermath of the financial crisis even the most pessimistic forecaster would not have predicted that interest rates would remain as low as they did for as long as they did. The trajectory for US rates is seemingly upwards but at a slower rate than seen in the past.

In December 2015 four US rate rises were expected to occur in 2016 but there may be only two. A number of external negative factors including weaker global economic growth and sharp falls in commodity prices, notably oil, prompted the US authorities to scale back their tightening ambitions.[39] Ms Yellen is keen not to blow the US economy off course.

In any case the US action is out of synch with most of the rest of the world with some other central banks operating with negative interest rates. In March 2016, the Hungarian central bank reduced its deposit rate by 15 basis points to −0.05%. Its move into negative rate territory follows similar action taken by the central banks of Japan, Switzerland, Denmark, Sweden and the ECB.[40]

Ms Yellen has not ruled out in principle the possibility of having negative interest rates. However, fears about the negative impact on the money market fund industry prevented the Federal Reserve from going down the road of negative interest rates during the financial crisis.

Ms Yellen is optimistic about the overall long-term prospects of the US economy. However, fluctuations in monthly US jobless figures, coupled with ongoing vulnerabilities in overseas economies such as China and the Eurozone, mean that caution is likely to be the watchword in decision making regarding US monetary policy.

Journalistic practice

There was detailed scrutiny of Janet Yellen's statement accompanying the December 2015 rate rise to ascertain the pace and scale of future rate increases. The views of economists, market traders, fund managers and ex members of the Fed were sought on the Fed's future actions. The results of polls of economists on the timing of the next rate rise were reported.

In order to illustrate the impact of higher interest rates an interview can be done with a small business owner. In terms of coverage account should be taken of what the rate rise means for emerging markets, and general consumers. What impact will it have on the actions of other central banks?

In the UK, there has been some criticism that forward guidance has been anything but that. Exactly when interest rates should rise is a difficult call for the MPC to make, balancing as it must the situation in the domestic economy against the global economic backdrop.

Central bankers

In the past, central bankers did not feel it necessary to explain their actions. However it is now accepted that a greater understanding of why certain actions have been taken makes unpalatable monetary medicine easier to swallow by both the financial markets and general public.

The merits of this approach are summarised well by Alan Blinder writing in his book *Central Banking in Theory and Practice*. He said, 'In a democratic society, the central bank's freedom to act implies an obligation to explain itself to the public. Thus independence and accountability are symbiotic, not in conflict'.[41]

In the process of explaining their actions central bankers have become 'celebrities'. Indeed in the coverage of the appointment of Mark Carney to the governorship of the Bank of England in July 2013, there was much comment on his rock star good looks alongside analysis of what positions he may take in terms of monetary policy.[42]

Box 1.9 Mark Carney

- Mark Carney was appointed Bank of England governor in July 2014 for a five-year term.
- First foreigner to hold the post.
- Well-regarded ex-Bank of Canada governor and head of G20 Financial Stability Board.
- *Forward guidance* – explicit guidance regarding future conduct of monetary policy.

Mr Carney is widely admired for steering Canada through the worst of the financial crisis relatively unscathed. He is a skilful media operator as shown early on in his tenure in an interview with Jeremy Paxman on 23 January 2014 on one of the BBC's flagship current affairs programmes, 'Newsnight'.[43]

The softly, softly approach to interest rate rises outlined in the interview has been the governor's approach despite the apparent strength of the UK economy. Slow wage growth, prolonged relatively weak UK **productivity** coupled with a collapse in domestic inflation has extended the time horizon for an increase in the UK base rate.

On the basis of its 2015 official staff visit, known as a mission, to the UK, the IMF said there was 'a strong case for the Bank of England to maintain the policy rate at 0.5% and the stock of QE assets at £375bn until signs of stronger inflationary pressures emerge'.[44]

However, a spanner was thrown in the works when Britain voted to come out of the European Union following the referendum in June 2016. The ensuing chaos on financial markets and a collapsing pound prompted Mr Carney to issue a statement the morning after the referendum aimed at reassuring the markets. Mirroring comments by Mario Draghi on a different occasion, Mr Carney said 'The Bank will not hesitate to take additional measures as required as those markets adjust and the UK economy moves forward'.

He emphasised that UK banks were much stronger than during the financial crisis in terms of their capital base. In addition, the Bank stood ready to provide more than £250bn of additional funds and also had large foreign currency reserves it could use if necessary.[45]

20 Monetary policy

Fellow central bankers, the US Federal Reserve and the European Central Bank, were quick to rally round offering the Bank of England support to inject more liquidity (which basically means more funds for the banking system), if necessary.

The Bank of Japan governor Huruhiko Kuroda was paying particular attention to the currency markets as the yen soared in value as a perceived safe haven. He said the central bank stood ready to ensure market stability. 'The BOJ, in close cooperation with relevant domestic and foreign authorities, will continue to carefully monitor how the EU referendum would affect global financial markets'.[46]

In the acrimonious campaign run-up to the referendum, the neutrality of Mark Carney was questioned by a senior member of the Vote Leave team, Bernard Jenkin MP. In an angry rebuttal, Mr Carney said any comments made regarding issues related to the referendum 'have been limited to factors that affect the Bank's statutory responsibilities and have been entirely consistent with our remits'.[47]

The power of central bankers to move the markets was amply demonstrated in January 2015 when the Swiss National Bank (SNB) shocked the financial markets by unilaterally scrapping its currency ceiling against the euro, without any prior notice. The Swiss National Bank introduced its ceiling against the euro in 2011.[48]

Journalistic practice

News stories were written about the losses suffered by foreign exchange brokers across the world and the soaring value of the Swiss currency. Quotes from the IMF's managing director Christine Lagarde and retail currency investors were included. Feature reports included an assessment of the likely adverse effect of the SNB's action on parts of the Swiss economy such as tourism, exports, watchmakers, banks and healthcare companies. Many commentators also outlined why the Swiss franc is seen as a safe haven for investors in a volatile financial world.

Assignments

Write a 200 word profile of Mark Carney, Governor of the Bank of England.
Produce a feature report on the US quantitative easing programme. This should include the scale of it, why it was done, impact on the financial markets and whether it has been a success.

Glossary of key terms

Abenomics: the three-pronged economic stimulus package launched in 2012 in Japan by Prime Minister Shinzo Abe.

Bank base rate: the rate of interest around which the main UK banks and building societies fix their lending and borrowing rates.

Bank of England (BOE): the UK central bank that sets interest rates. It was founded in 1694 and is also known as the 'Old Lady of Threadneedle Street', referring to its location in the City of London.

Bonds: loans with fixed interest payments. They are used for government financing.

Bond yields: these measure the interest return on fixed interest securities. They are an indicator of interest and inflation expectations and creditworthiness.

European Central Bank (ECB): central bank in charge of monetary policy for all the countries that use the euro, the European Union's single currency.

Federal Open Market Committee (FOMC): 12-member group of representatives of US regional reserve banks and federal appointees who determine the US monetary policy.

Forward guidance: a central bank steer to the financial markets as to the likely future direction and pace of change of interest rates.

Funding for Lending (FLS): a programme that was launched in 2012 by the Bank of England and UK Treasury, to encourage banks and building societies to increase lending to businesses and non-financial companies. It has been extended a number of times and amended. The current scheme, which runs until January 2018, favours lending to small and medium enterprises (SMEs).

Monetary policy: central government policy on the quantity of money in the economy, rate of interest and exchange rate.

Monetary Policy Committee (MPC): the nine-person committee of the Bank of England charged with setting UK interest rates. The committee consists of the Bank's governor, the two deputy governors, two other bank officials and four economists nominated by the government.

Money supply: the stock of liquid assets in an economy that can freely be exchanged for goods and services. This includes sterling notes and coins in circulation and bank and building society deposits.

Mortgage: a loan provided to purchase a property over a certain time period.

Output gap: the difference between the actual level of activity in an economy and what economists estimate to be the potential level of sustainable output of the economy. It is measured as a percentage of the level of gross domestic product (GDP).

Productivity: a measure of the amount of output of goods and services produced by a unit of labour input. It is calculated by dividing output by the number of hours worked, so-called 'output per hour'.

Quantitative easing (QE): the electronic printing of money by central banks to buy assets from banks and insurance companies to help stimulate economic growth.

US Federal Reserve: US central bank in charge of monetary policy.

Resource list

Bank of England website: www.bankofengland.co.uk
Federal Reserve website: www.federalreserve.gov
European Central Bank website: www.ecb.europa.eu
Bank of Japan website: www.boj.or.jp
Balls, Ed, James Howat and Anna Stansbury (2016) 'Central Bank Independence Revisited: After the financial crisis, what should a model central bank look like?' Harvard University Kennedy School. www.hks.harvard.edu/centers/mrcbg/publications/awp/awp67

Recommended reading

Blanchard, Olivier, David Romer, Michael Spence and Joseph Stiglitz (eds) (2012) *In The Wake Of The Crisis Leading Economists Reassess Economic Policy*. Cambridge, MA and London, UK: The MIT Press.
IMF (3 December 2015) *Monetary Policy in Developing Countries: The Way Forward*. www.imf.org/en/News/Articles/2015/28/04/53/sopol120315a

Notes

1 '1997: Brown sets Bank of England free.' (6 May 1997). news.bbc.co.uk/onthisday/hi/dates/stories/may/6/newsid_3806000/3806313.stm
2 'What we do.' (n.d.). www.bankofengland.co.uk/about/Pages/onemission/default.aspx
3 Rachel Blundy (2 November 2015). 'Is London heading for another property price bubble as soon as 2017?' www.standard.co.uk/news/london/london-faces-risk-of-housing-bubble-by-2017-report-warns-a3104941.html; Christopher Williams (3 January 2016). 'Odey flags up threat of UK house bubble in fears for global economy.' www.telegraph.co.uk/finance/markets/12079046/Odey-flags-up-threat-of-UK-house-bubble-in-fears-for-global-economy.html
4 Ray Massey (5 March 2015). 'UK car boom as sales rise 12% while consumer confidence shows signs of an upturn.' www.thisismoney.co.uk/money/cars/article-2981525/UK-car-boom-sales-rise-12-consumer-confidence-shows-signs-upturn.html
5 Nicholas Watt (14 January 2014). 'Ed Miliband vows to give hope to "squeezed middle class".' www.theguardian.com/politics/2014/jan/14/ed-miliband-makes-overtures-to-middle-class-voters
6 'Funding for Lending Scheme.' (n.d.). www.bankofengland.co.uk/markets/pages/fls/default.aspx
7 Ben Jacobsen (13 November 2014). 'Business school research suggests men more optimistic than women on economy.' www.business-school.ed.ac.uk/blogs/school-blog/2014/11/13/business-school-research-suggests-men-more-optimistic-than-women-on-economy/
8 Matthew West (18 June 2014). 'No wage rises until jobless rate falls to 5% says MPC member'. www.bbc.co.uk/news/business-27901454
9 George Osborne (18 March 2015). 'Chancellor George Osborne's Budget 2015 speech.' www.gov.uk/government/speeches/chancellor-george-osbornes-budget-2015-speech. This speech was published under the 2010 to 2015 Conservative and Liberal Democrat coalition government.

10 'McDonnell orders Bank of England review.' (19 October 2015). labourlist. org/2015/10/mcdonnell-orders-bank-of-england-review/
11 Q. Ylan Mui (6 January 2014). 'Janet Yellen confirmed as Federal Reserve chairman.' www.washingtonpost.com/business/economy/janet-yellen-confirmed-as-next-fed-chief/2014/01/06/14b38582-76f2-11e3-8
12 Binyamin Appelbaum (24 February 2015). 'Fed's Janet Yellen, in testimony, counsels patience on interest rate increase.' www.nytimes.com/2015/02/25/business/economy/fed-chief-yellen-testifies-before-congress.html?_r=0
13 Bank of England Inflation Report (February 2013). 'The Policy Discussion', p.8. www.bankofengland.co.uk/publications/Documents/inflationreport/2013/ir1301.aspx
14 Graham Hiscott (10 February 2012). 'Easy money: George Osborne lets Bank of England print £50bn more cash to stave off recession.' www.mirror.co.uk/news/uk-news/george-osborne-lets-bank-of-england-680062
15 For more information on the Quantitative Easing Asset Purchase Programme visit www.bankofengland.co.uk/markets/Pages/apf/default.aspx
16 Charlie Bean (13 October 2009). Speech. www.bankofengland.co.uk/archive/Documents/historicpubs/speeches/2009/speech405.pdf
17 Michael Joyce, Matthew Tong and Robert Woods (2011). 'The United Kingdom's quantitative easing policy: design, operation and impact.' *Quarterly Bulletin*, Q3.
18 Andrew Oxlade (3 March 2016). 'How QE affected your wealth: a snapshot.' www.telegraph.co.uk/investing/news/how-qe-affected-the-value-of-everything---in-one-snapshot/
19 Spencer Dale (8 September 2012). 'Spencer Dale warns on QE: full speech.' www.telegraph.co.uk/finance/economics/9530138/Spencer-Dale-warns-on-QE-full-speech.html
20 Ambrose Evans-Pritchard (20 January 2015). 'Central bank prophet fears QE warfare pushing world financial system out of control.' www.telegraph.co.uk/finance/economics/11358316/Central-bank-prophet-fears-QE-warfare-pushing-world-financial-system-out-of-control
21 IMF (October 2016). 'World Economic Outlook. Subdued Demand: Symptoms and Remedies.' www.imf.org/external/pubs/ft/weo/2016/02
22 Mehreen Khan (17 April 2015). 'Christine Lagarde heaps praise on UK economy.' www.telegraph.co.uk/finance/economics/11544245/Christine-Lagarde-heaps-praise-on-UK-economy.html
23 Gavin Hewitt (26 January 2015). 'Greece election: anti-austerity Syriza wins election.' www.bbc.co.uk/news/world-europe-30975437
24 Alistair Dawber (20 December 2015). 'Spain election: Conservatives win but Podemos are stars of the show with fifth of vote.' www.independent.co.uk/news/world/europe/spain-election-conservatives-win-but-fall-short-of-parliamentary-majority-a6780871.html
25 Fernanda Nechio (3 March 2014). 'Fed tapering news and emerging markets', *FRBSF Economic Letter*. www.frbsf.org/economic-research/publications/economic-letter/2014/march/federal-reserve-tapering-emerging-markets/
26 Mamta Badkar (24 September 2013). 'Morgan Stanley presents: "The Fragile Five" – the most troubled currencies in emerging markets.' www.businessinsider.com/morgan-stanley-fragile-5-emerging-markets-2013-9?lR=T
27 Maria Levitov (11 October 2016). 'South Africa Junk-Rating Risk Surges on Gordhan Fraud Charge.' www.bloomberg.com/news/articles/2016-10-11/south-africa-junk-rating-risk-surges-on-gordhan-fraud-charges
28 'The impact of Abenomics on Japan's economy.' (19 July 2013). www.nippon.com/en/features/h00033/

24 *Monetary policy*

29 Japan National Tourism Organization (JNTO) (n.d.). 'Number of visitors to Japan.' www.japanmacroadvisors.com/page/category/economic-indicators-gdp-and-business-activity/number-of-visitors-to-japan/
30 Angela Monaghan and Graeme Wearden (31 October 2014). 'Bank of Japan to inject 80 trillion yen into its economy.' www.theguardian.com/business/2014/oct/31/bank-of-japan-80-trillion-yen-economy
31 'Bank of Japan expands monetary stimulus measure.' (31 October 2014). www.bbc.co.uk/news/business-29845466
32 Claire Jones (11 March 2016). 'ECB cuts rates and boosts QE to ratchet up Eurozone stimulus.' www.ft.com/cms/s/0/9a45a960-e6ac-11e5-a09b-1f8b0d268c39.html
33 Szu Ping Chan (18 March 2016). 'ECB's bazooka has not run out of ammunition, says chief economist'. www.telegraph.co.uk/business/2016/03/18/ecbs-bazooka-has-not-run-out-of-ammunition-says-chief-economist/
34 'Forward guidance.' (7 August 2013). www.bankofengland.co.uk/monetarypolicy/pages/forwardguidance.aspx
35 Listen to the BOE Governor Mark Carney's BBC Radio 4 Today programme interview on 8 August 2013 on forward guidance on the Bank of England's website: www.bankofengland.co.uk/publications/Pages/interviews/default.aspx
36 Ann Saphir and Michael Flaherty (27 March 2015). 'Fed's Yellen sees gradual rate hikes starting this year.' www.reuters.com/article/us-usa-fed-yellen-idUSKBN0MNidISL2NOWT22420150327
37 Reuters (23 March 2015). 'Fed's Mester urges shift in forward guidance role.' www.reuters.com/article/2015/03/23/us-economy-fed-mester-idUSKBN0MJ0ND20150323
38 Patrick Gillespie (16 December 2015). 'Finally! Fed raises interest rates.' money.cnn.com/2015/12/16/news/economy/federal-reserve-interest-rate-hike/
39 Sam Fleming and Robin Wigglesworth (17 March 2016). 'Global risks bring Fed into line with markets on next rate rises.' www.ft.com/cms/s/0/a69ca30a-eba0-11e5-bb79-2303682345c8.html
40 Reuters with CNBC.com (22 March 2016). 'Hungary central bank cuts deposit rate into negative territory.' www.cnbc.com/2016/03/22/hungary-central-bank-cuts-deposit-rate-into-negative-territory.html
41 Alan S. Blinder (1999). *Central Banking in Theory and Practice*. Cambridge, MA: The MIT Press.
42 Heather Stewart (26 May 2013). 'Mark Carney: Canada's rock-star banker faces four bars to success.' www.theguardian.com/business/2013/may/26/mark-carney-rock-star-banker-four-bars
43 See www.youtube.com/watch?v=0Pw0HkWLne4
44 International Monetary Fund (11 December 2015). 'United Kingdom-2015 Article 1V Consultation Concluding Statement of the Mission.' www.imf.org/external/np/ms/2015/121115.htm
45 'Statement from the Governor of the Bank of England following the EU referendum result.' (24 June 2016). www.bankofengland.co.uk/publications/Pages/news/2016/056.aspx
46 Karishma Vaswani (24 June 2016). 'Brexit: Asian shares fall sharply as UK votes to leave EU.' www.bbc.co.uk/news/business-36613890.
47 Kamal Ahmed (16 June 2016). 'Carney and Vote Leave clash over EU battle.' www.bbc.co.uk/news/business-36546302
48 Alice Baghdjian and Silke Koltrowitz (16 January 2015). 'Swiss central bank stuns market with policy U-turn'. www.reuters.com/article/us-swiss-snb-cap-idUSKBN0KO0XK20150116

2 Inflation

This chapter explains what inflation is, how it is measured and its causes. After reading this chapter you should be able to produce an inflation news report following publication of monthly statistics or the Bank of England's quarterly inflation report and comment on the success of inflation targeting. You will also be able to discuss the effects of inflation on food and commodity prices.

Inflation or rather the lack of it has been the noteworthy feature of inflation data throughout much of the industrialised world in recent years. Inflation is very much a hot news topic given its effect on the necessities of modern life namely fuel, housing and importantly food.

What is inflation?

Inflation is a general sustained rise in price levels.

The **inflation rate** is the change in average prices in the economy over a given period of time.

The price level is measured in the form of an index. So if the price index were 100 today and 110 in one year's time, then the rate of inflation would be 10%.

> **Journalistic practice**
>
> The publication of the latest UK inflation data is always big news in the financial markets with analysts using the data to try to second-guess what it might mean for monetary policy.
>
> News articles focus on the data itself. Did it meet expectations, were there any particular features e.g. lower petrol prices, what is the outlook in the months ahead and what influence might the data have in terms of the timing of any interest rate changes?
>
> Feature articles can give a historic timeline of a particular country's inflation data highlighting flash points and discussing the responses of the relevant politicians and policy makers. Such articles can include inflation forecasts, for example those given by the Bank of England in its quarterly inflation report.
>
> *(Continued)*

Inflation in a particular market can be the focus of comment and analysis e.g. in the case of commodities such as gold which is widely viewed as a hedge against inflation. Such an article can include forecasts and graphics from the World Gold Council.

Editors are usually keen for any coverage of rising house prices. In such articles, outline the underlying factors pushing up inflation in that market, illustrate with graphs and discuss what measures can be taken to try to combat it. Include opinion from an industry outsider who can give an indication of what the future might hold for that particular market within a certain time frame.

Journalistic practice – reporting on UK inflation data

Always include both the RPI and CPI figure and the change on the month.

Were there any special factors influencing the data such as rises in fuel prices?

How does the CPI figure compare with the Bank's target inflation rate?

Include political and City reaction and any stock market response in sterling or bonds.

Were the figures as expected? Higher than forecast inflation could be expected to lead to a fall in the value of gilts, UK government bonds, as the authorities may decide to increase interest rates to try to tackle inflation.

What is the inflation outlook?

In order to get an index the prices of a representative range of goods and services are recorded on a regular basis. Changes in the price of food are more important than changes in the price say of tobacco because a larger proportion of total household income is spent on food.

In the UK, the two main measures are the **Retail Price Index (RPI)** and the **Consumer Price Index (CPI)**.

Consumer Price Index

> **Box 2.1** Consumer Price Index
> - Based on an average basket of goods bought by all households, *excluding* housing related items such as mortgage interest payments and council tax.
> - CPI is used by the Bank of England to measure inflation and set state benefit payments.
> - CPI is the most common measure of inflation in advanced economies e.g. USA and Japan.

This is a measure developed by the European Union to be used across all countries in the EU. It has only been calculated in the UK since January 1996. It has been used by the Bank of England to measure inflation against its target since 2003, and is therefore now the key indicator for monetary policy. The CPI is the most common measure of inflation throughout the developed world. It is used in the USA and Japan, for example.

The CPI is based on the average basket of goods bought by all households but it *excludes* a number of housing related items such as mortgage interest payments and council tax.

Consumer Prices Index Housing (CPIH) is a measure of UK consumer price inflation that includes owner occupiers' housing costs.[1] These are the costs associated with owning, maintaining and living in one's own home. It does not include costs such as utility bills which are already included in the index. It also does not seek to reflect rising house prices.

Table 2.1 Most important categories in the UK CPI (2016) (%)

Transport	15.30
Recreation and culture	14.80
Restaurants and hotels	12.30
Food and non-alcoholic beverages	10.30
Miscellaneous goods and services	9.60
Clothing and footwear	7.10
Furniture and household goods	5.90
Housing and household services	12.00
Alcohol and tobacco	4.20
Health	2.80
Communication	3.20
Education	2.5[2]

Retail Price Index

> **Box 2.2** Retail Price Index
>
> - Measures average price of the typical basket of goods bought by the average household.
> - Basket of goods is regularly reviewed to ensure it matches current spending patterns so included are e-cigarettes and craft beer.
> - RPI used in setting wage agreements, rents and rail fares.

The RPI measures the average price of the typical basket of goods bought by the average household. It therefore measures average consumer prices.

The RPI is the traditional measure used in the UK and is called the headline rate of inflation. It has been used to calculate index-linked gilts, a form of long term government borrowing, and, until 2011, increases in public sector pensions, tax credits and other state benefits.

The government's switch to the CPI measure for increases in non-pension benefit payments was controversial because CPI tends to be lower than RPI so benefit payments will rise less in future. Annual differences between the two measures are small but increase over time.

Trade unions and firms may use the RPI in wage agreements and property management companies use it to calculate increases in rents on properties.

Inflation is also used in the calculation of some services, such as rail fares.

The RPI excludes high income households, defined as the top 4% by income of households, and pensioner households which derive at least three-quarters of their total income from state pensions and benefits. These two types of household are considered to have atypical spending patterns and so would distort the overall average.

The basket of goods

> **Box 2.3** Basket of goods
>
> - Around 110,000 prices collected each month for 700 consumer goods and services from shops across the UK and online.
> - Added in 2016: computer game downloads, coffee pods and pouches of microwave rice.
> - Removed in 2016: nightclub entry and rewriteable DVDs.

The shopping basket of items used in compiling the Consumer Price Index and Retail Price Index have been reviewed each year since 1947 to make sure that they match current spending patterns. In total the Office for National Statistics (ONS) collects around 180,000 prices each month for a 'shopping basket' of around 700 consumer goods and services in around 140 areas throughout the UK.

Updates to the basket in 2016 reflect developments in technology. Computer game downloads were added as more money is being spent on them. Also appearing in the basket were coffee pods, pouches of microwave rice, cream liqueur, nail varnish and multipacks of meat-based snacks, the latter representing the market for buffet-type food.

Items that left the basket in 2016 included rewriteable DVDs which are being overtaken by streaming services and personal video recorders (PVRs) and nightclub entry, as fewer people visit nightclubs.

Inflation targeting

This was first introduced in the 1980s in New Zealand and spread rapidly in the 1990s including to the UK. The idea is for the government to set an inflation target, usually a range of 0–3% per annum and ask an independent central bank to use interest rate policy to achieve it. The Bank of England, US Federal Reserve and European Central Bank all have a 2% inflation target.

The Bank of England Governor must write to the UK Chancellor every time the target is missed by 1% on either side. He has had a lot of writing to do. Higher commodity prices propelled UK inflation to 5% in 2011.

The UK inflation rate averaged 2.67% from 1989 until 2015, reaching an all-time high of 8.5% in April 1991 and a record low of −0.1% in April 2015. This was the first time the British economy had entered negative inflation territory since 1960. Core inflation has been weaker than the bank had been expecting due to some external factors. Significant downward pressure on inflation is coming from cheaper food prices partly due to supermarket price wars in the UK and lower fuel prices. Diesel slid to 99.7p per litre in January 2016, its cheapest price since 2009.

Low commodity prices are expected to persist for some time exerting continued downward pressure on UK inflation. By the end of 2017, Bank of England Governor Mr Carney hopes to have 'returned inflation to target sustainably'.

Two per cent is seen as a good rate because it is thought to be consistent with long term price stability and maximum employment. A small level of inflation makes it less likely that the economy will suffer deflation if economic conditions worsen.

Andy Haldane, chief economist at the Bank of England, made the front pages of the financial press when he mooted the idea that it might be desirable to raise the UK's inflation target from 2% to 4%. His thinking goes that back in the 1990s when world real interest rates averaged around 4%, an inflation target of 4% meant that nominal interest rates averaged around 6% over the course of a typical cycle.

However since the financial crisis, world real interest rates have dropped from 2% to around zero. With a 2% inflation target, that would put nominal interest rates on average over the cycle at 2%. 'That would mean there is

30 *Inflation*

materially less monetary policy room for manoeuvre than was the case a generation ago,' he said in a speech given at the Portadown Chamber of Commerce, Northern Ireland.[3]

Critics of such an increase in the inflation target cite the negative effects of higher inflation on the poor and those on fixed incomes and the likely negative impact on the value of sterling. Mr Haldane himself acknowledged strong concern about inflation amongst the general population. 'The public's preferences appear, if anything, to be for inflation below rather than above current targets,' he said.

Inflation report

Box 2.4 Inflation report

- Bank of England publishes a quarterly inflation report.
- Includes detailed economic analysis and inflation forecasts.
- By mid 2018, UK inflation is expected to rise above its 2% target, to 2.75% due to weaker sterling.
- UK interest rate rises will be gradual and limited.

This quarterly report was first published in the UK in 1993. It sets out detailed economic analysis and inflation forecasts on which the Bank's monetary policy committee bases its interest rate decisions. Within the report there are sections on the global economy and financial developments, demand and output, supply and the labour market, costs and prices and the prospects for UK inflation.[4]

Watch the Governor's press conference for the November 2016 Inflation Report at www.bankofengland.co.uk/publication/Pages/inflationreport/2016/nov.aspx.

Box 2.5 Inflation causes

- Too much demand in the economy
- Rising costs.

Four major causes of rising costs

- Government raising indirect taxes e.g. VAT
- Higher commodity prices
- Firms raising prices to boost profit margins
- Higher wages and salaries.

Inflation can be caused by two main factors: too much demand in the economy, known as *demand-pull inflation* or rising costs, known as *cost-pull inflation*.

If total demand rises but there is no increase in total supply then demand-pull inflation is likely to occur.

When there is too much demand in the economy, the average level of prices in the economy will rise. Increases in demand can come from a number of areas; steep rises in consumer spending, firms substantially increasing their investment spending, government spending may be increasing or taxes may have been cut, world demand for UK exports may be rising because of a boom in the world economy.

Cost-push inflation occurs because of rising costs. There are four major sources of increased costs:

- Wages and salaries account for roughly 70% of national income so increases in wages increase the costs of production.
- Imports can rise in price.
- Profits can be increased by firms when they raise prices to improve profit margins.
- Government can raise indirect tax rates.

Commodity prices have boosted inflation in certain time periods, most recently in the 2000s, in what has been referred to as a **commodity supercycle**. Increased demand from fast growing emerging economies notably China coupled with weather related supply disruptions led to huge jumps in the price of soft commodities. These are items such as cocoa, wheat and cotton.

Figure 2.1 Harvesting combine in the field. Image courtesy of Small_Frog/iStock.

32   *Inflation*

Between April and July 2012 wheat prices jumped 30% due to a major drought in the US 'corn belt' and poor wheat harvests elsewhere. Rice prices in July 2012 were 22% more than in the same period a year earlier.

Ultimately, increased commodity prices feed through to higher prices that consumers will have to pay for finished goods such as bread, a bag of flour or box of cereal. Commodity traders describe this phenomenon as **agflation**. The financial sector's involvement in speculative commodity trading has greatly increased compared to previous cycles, which exacerbates volatility.

That famous stock market adage that 'prices can go down as well as up' also applies to commodity prices. In July 2012, the price of rice was 43% lower than it was in 2008.

The slowdown in the Chinese economy has reduced demand for commodities and prices started to slide in the summer of 2014. This has had a particularly negative effect on several emerging economies such as Russia, Brazil and Venezuela that have a heavy reliance on commodity-related export earnings. Commodity prices declined sharply in the three years to 2015.

It is difficult to predict when prices will stabilise given the numerous uncertainties affecting the global economy. In the last commodity sell-off, prices took a decade to recover and looking out to 2017/2018 the economic outlook does not appear to provide scope for an aggressive rebound in prices. Research by the IMF estimates that the weak commodity price outlook subtracts almost one percentage point annually from the average rate of economic growth in commodity exporters over 2015–2017 as compared with 2012–2014. In exporters of energy commodities, the drag is estimated to be larger, about 2.25% on average over the same period.[5]

Journalistic practice

Market stories can be written charting the volatility of various commodity prices with forecasts from industry analysts on future prices. The impact on the FTSE-100 index of leading shares can also be included given its high component of commodity shares such as Anglo American and Vedanta Resources. Graphs of movements in the FTSE 100 index and specific shares can be included for illustrative purposes.

Articles on specific commodities can begin with the main news item such as a sell-off in the market. The news can be put in context with comment on historical price movements/supply issues. Finish off the report with prospects for the price. Illustrate the report with a graph.

Features can be written on specific companies exposed to commodity prices. For example, mining group Glencore saw its shares fall dramatically in volatile trading in 2015 hit by concern about how it would service its huge corporate debts against a background of declining commodity prices. Include analyst comment on how low the share price might fall, illustrated with a graph. Are other similar mining companies affected? If so, how have their shares responded?

Petrol is another example of goods whose price is closely linked to commodity prices. Supply disruptions such as those caused by war or sabotage can prompt a sharp rise in oil prices which feeds through to higher prices on petrol forecourts. This in turn hits firms' margins, reduces consumers' spending power and exerts upward pressure on inflation. Brent crude is the London benchmark oil.

The slump in oil prices since 2014 has led to a welcome drop in the price of petrol and diesel for consumers. In January 2016, Brent crude fell below $30 a barrel for the first time since 2004.[6]

> **Journalistic practice**
>
> Petrol price movements are an important consumer story and often headline main news reports. In the run-up to the UK budget there is always speculation on what changes may occur in the fuel levy.

Food inflation

Disruption in commodity markets can lead to social consequences as we saw during the 2007/2008 food crisis which led to riots in Haiti and Bangladesh. A combination of sanctions and a steep fall in the oil price has severely damaged the Russian economy. Oil is Russia's main export. Food inflation in Russia averaged 9.28% from 2010 until 2016, peaking at 26.1% in February 2015. In 2014, Moscow banned many Western food imports of items such as beef, fish, milk and vegetables. This was in retaliation for the sanctions imposed on Russia by the US and European Union following Russia's hostile actions in Ukraine.

Countries across Africa and the Middle East who are heavily dependent on food imports are particularly exposed to rising global food prices. In terms of vulnerability to higher food prices, the International Monetary Fund says there are significant variations across regions. It identifies the African, Central American, Caribbean and Middle Eastern regions as 'the most exposed to rising food prices amid low inventory buffers and high dependence on the global market for their food supplies'.[7]

Typically, households in developing countries spend a significantly higher proportion of their income on food than those in industrialised nations. For example, in India around half of total household consumption is on food. As China, the world's most populous country, shifts its economy in favour of increased domestic consumption, household demand for food is likely to increase.

Countries most vulnerable to food price inflation

China
India
Mexico
Indonesia

Russia
Saudi Arabia
Hong Kong
Egypt
Nigeria
Pakistan
Bangladesh
Algeria
Philippines.

Source: Nomura[8]

In compiling its list Nomura takes into account nominal GDP per capita in dollars, the share of food in total household consumption and net food exports as a percentage of GDP.

Box 2.6 Higher world food prices

- Countries benefiting: large net exporters such as New Zealand, Uruguay, Netherlands and Argentina.
- Countries disadvantaged: those who spend a higher proportion of their income on food. This includes Bangladesh, Algeria, Egypt, Nigeria and Pakistan.

Source: Nomura Research

It is thought that a steep rise in global food prices may have several negative effects in vulnerable countries: reductions in GDP growth, higher CPI inflation, worsening trade and fiscal positions, higher interest rates, currency depreciation and widening credit spreads.

World food prices are tracked by the United Nations. They show a dramatic decline since 2009 due to bumper global harvests of a number of crops including soybeans and corn. The UN's Food and Agriculture Organisation (FAO) produces a **Food Price Index**. This is a measure of the monthly change in international prices of a basket of food commodities. It consists of the average of five commodity group price indices, weighted with the average export shares of each of the groups for 2002–2004.

The FAO Food Price Index began 2016 with another decline, averaging 150.4 points in January, down almost three points from December, and as much as 29 points (16%) below January 2015. The prices of all the commodities tracked by the index fell, with sugar and dairy products registering the steepest decline.[9]

In August 2015, global food prices, as measured by the FAO Food Price Index, fell by 5.2%, the fastest rate in seven years. The FAO attributed this to 'ample supplies, a slump in energy prices and concerns over China's economic slowdown'.[10]

Farmers across Europe protested about the threat to their livelihoods with dairy farmers particularly badly hit. They suffered a 20% decline in European wholesale milk prices in a year. Slowing demand in China and a Russian embargo on Western food imports in retaliation for EU and US sanctions over the crisis in Ukraine are hitting food producers.

Prices are monitored for 73 food products and surged to records in 2008 and 2011 after crop shortages. During the commodity price boom of 2008 consumer food price inflation peaked at 23% in Africa compared to a rise of only 7% in the OECD countries. In the 2009 recession, food prices in the US and Japan fell but they jumped by 21% in India, partly due to increased demand and rising incomes. In low-income countries, any additional money tends to be spent on buying more food.

> **Journalistic practice**
>
> News stories are often written when the UN's food price index is released.[11] Market reports regularly reflect movements in commodity prices by highlighting the impact on the share price of companies such as Cargill, the world's biggest agricultural trader.[12]

Weather plays a crucial role in food pricing with adverse weather disrupting supplies and causing prices to surge. For example, drought in Midwest America can boost the price of soya beans, corn and wheat, as America is the world's leading producer and exporter of these soft commodities.

In a study published in March 2016, 'El Niño Good Boy or Bad,' the International Monetary Fund noted that El Niño-induced drought in Indonesia harmed its economy and agricultural sector, 'pushing up world prices for coffee, cocoa, and palm oil'. In southeast Australia it is said to increase the frequency and severity of bush fires, 'reduces wheat export volumes, and drives up global wheat prices, leading to a drop in the country's real GDP growth'.[13]

Farming is an energy intensive industry and so higher oil prices also impact on global agriculture. Periodically the International Monetary Fund (IMF) does a special report on food. Energy prices feed into global food prices through two main channels: cost push and demand pull. Energy intensive inputs such as ammonia-based nitrogen fertilisers and power provide a transmission mechanism from energy prices into food prices. Second, the diversion of crops from food to fuel production has become an important factor in recent years – corn and sugar have been increasingly used for ethanol production and soybeans and other oilseeds for biodiesel production.[14]

Longer term, there is a food supply and demand imbalance as the world's population continues to grow, particularly in developing countries, but agricultural productivity growth has not kept pace and arable land supply is

36 *Inflation*

under pressure for a number of reasons including the growth in demand for biofuels. Collectively, this will put upward pressure on food prices.

Gold

The precious metal has historically been seen as a safe haven in times of economic volatility. 'Gold bugs' believe it is one of the few assets with intrinsic value. However it is out of favour. The general trend is thought to be one of decline in the medium term. Despite all the negative economic and political headwinds buffeting the world, gold traded around $1000 an ounce in December 2015, not far above the lows last seen in 2009. At its peak in the summer of 2011, the gold price shone above $1,900 an ounce.[15]

Many major industrialised countries are mired in mountains of debt following the financial crisis, economic recovery has been anaemic in many cases and deflation is spreading its net wider. The rising trend for US interest rates will also take the shine off gold. Non-yielding commodities such as gold tend not to respond positively to rate increases, which boost income-generating assets. Rate rises also tend to increase demand for the dollar, against which gold is negatively correlated.

Box 2.7 Negative factors for gold

- Rising interest rates
- Stronger dollar
- Low inflation/deflation
- Weak physical demand for the yellow metal
- It is technically expensive relative to other precious metals.

Exchange Traded Funds (ETFs) allow investors to invest in gold more cheaply than buying the physical metal. There are no storage or insurance costs associated with ETFs and they are a more accurate way of tracking the gold price than buying gold-mining shares. ETFs have grown enormously in popularity with both private and institutional investors, partly because of concerns about political interference in some unstable gold-producing countries. Alongside greater investment in ETFs has come greater volatility in the underlying gold price.[16]

Journalistic practice

Regular comment features are done on the supposed safe haven status of gold, with illustrations of its volatile price. Gold analysts are quoted on the prospects for the yellow metal in the months ahead. The performance of the gold price is a regular feature of daily financial market reports, alongside movements in the pound and dollar. Personal finance coverage can look at how private investors can invest in gold, the launch and performance of specialist gold funds and include the views of market watchers and fund managers.

Box 2.8 Producer prices

- Good forward indicator of inflation.
- Output Price Indices measure change in the price of goods produced by UK manufacturers – *factory gate prices*.
- Input price indices measure change in the prices of materials and fuels bought by UK manufacturers for processing.

Producer prices are a good forward indicator of inflation. The *Producer Price Index* (PPI) is a monthly survey that measures the price changes of goods bought and sold by UK manufacturers. The PPI is conducted by the Office for National Statistics.[17]

The *output* price indices measure change in the prices of goods produced by UK manufacturers. These are often called 'factory gate prices'.

The *input* price indices measure change in the prices of materials and fuels bought by UK manufacturers for processing. These are not limited to just those materials used in the final product, but also include what is required by the company in its normal day-to-day running. Lower input prices will reduce the pressure on companies to raise their prices to protect their margins.

You can also get an indication of the price pressures on manufacturers from the influential *Confederation of British Industry's Industrial Trends Survey*. This monthly survey of manufacturing industry is published before the official Producer Price Index.[18]

Inflation is bad for several reasons:

Greater uncertainty feeds through to *higher borrowing costs*. Savers and borrowers, uncertain about how prices will develop in the future, demand an insurance against a reduction in the future value of their money. This insurance is called a *risk premium* and results in higher interest rates. Higher interest rates make it more expensive to borrow, which can dampen investment and thereby activity in the economy.

It reduces the *purchasing power* of a currency within its economy; it reduces its internal value. If prices are increasing in the UK then one pound will not be able to buy as much as it did before the price increase.

The real rate of return on savings (the return adjusted for inflation) will be lower with higher rates of inflation. It is less profitable to save in a bank account since the money deteriorates in value. This is particularly bad news for those living on a fixed income such as pensioners. People on lower incomes spend a higher proportion of their money on gas, electricity and food, the cost of which has risen sharply in recent years.

The position in the UK is exacerbated by historically low interest rates of just 0.5%. There are very few savings accounts that beat inflation for basic rate taxpayers.

The ability of an employee to bargain for higher wages in line with inflation depends on the extent to which they are in demand in the economy and/or whether they are represented by trade unions. Tube drivers have a very strong union and so they were able to negotiate a special bonus for working during the London Olympics despite already earning £50,000 per annum.

Inflation will therefore have a *redistributive effect* on real incomes with the earnings of some groups able to keep pace with inflation, and others not. In recent years, UK wages have shown little or no growth which has led to the longest decline in the real value of take-home pay in the UK since the 1920s. This so called cost of living crisis was a key political battleground in the 2015 UK general election. This sustained period of below-trend wage growth is expected to continue. By comparing how fast the cost of living is increasing with the speed at which households' incomes are rising, one can calculate the rate at which a society's standard of living is improving.

Britain suffered a bigger fall in real wages since the financial crisis than any other advanced country apart from Greece. A TUC report found that between 2007 and 2015, UK real wages – income from work adjusted for inflation – fell by 10.4%.[19]

Internationally, if the prices of firms in the UK are increasing faster than their trading partners this may make the country's products uncompetitive compared to those of foreign firms. This may reduce the earnings from exports and increase the spending on imports. This will negatively affect the *balance of payments*. Domestically, the UK may struggle to compete because imports will be relatively cheaper.

If UK goods and services are relatively expensive then this is likely to reduce demand for the products, and therefore for pounds. With less demand for the *currency* it will *fall in value*, all other things being unchanged.

High, fluctuating inflation may *damage business confidence* because of fears about the future impact on costs such as wages. This may reduce levels of investment in new products and machinery.

Box 2.9 Why is inflation bad?

- It reduces purchasing power of the currency.
- Real return on savings is reduced – bad news for people on fixed incomes e.g. pensioners.
- Redistributive effect on real incomes – some people suffer cost of living crisis.

- Negatively impacts the balance of payments as British goods become uncompetitive.
- Damages business confidence and investment.

Benefits of inflation

Politicians tend to like a little bit of inflation as it encourages people to spend rather than save because it slowly erodes the value of money in one's pocket. This is good for consumer driven economies such as the UK.

Inflation also erodes debt so indebted governments often let inflation move higher, effectively reducing the amount of money they owe.

How can inflation be controlled?

Central bank independence has helped the cause of low inflation. Double digit inflation is now a rarity. In the 1970s, oil crises led to inflation of over 20% in the US and UK.

Up until 2007, the monetary policy committee of the Bank of England was deemed to have done a good job. In the aftermath of the global financial crisis in 2007, UK interest rates were cut to 0.5%. Attention was focused on avoiding a deep recession rather than rigidly maintaining CPI inflation at 2%. In 2008, then governor of the Bank of England Mervyn King said the bank had 'a difficult balancing act' in juggling a slowing economy and accelerating inflation.[20]

Definitions

Box 2.10 Different types of inflation

- *Stagflation*: high and rising cost of living coupled with poor economic growth.
- *Hyperinflation*: inflation that has spiralled out of control e.g. Zimbabwe in 2008. Often associated with wars and political upheaval.
- *Deflation*: sustained reduction in the general level of prices – worries about Eurozone. Japan suffered for many years.

In the aftermath of the financial crisis in 2008, the UK suffered from **stagflation**. This is when you get a high and rising cost of living, combined with poor or non-existent economic growth.

Hyperinflation is the term used to describe inflation that has spiralled out of control. Under hyperinflation the general price level could rise by 5 or 10%

or even more every day. Hyperinflation is visible when there is an unchecked supply of money. This was seen in Zimbabwe in 2008, when annual inflation reached 11 million per cent.

Hyperinflation is often associated with wars and political or social upheaval. Germany suffered from hyperinflation after World War I.

Deflation is a sustained reduction in the general level of prices. This has been a major concern of central bankers in the aftermath of the 2008 financial crisis. However, speaking in 2015, Dr Ben Broadbent, Deputy Governor Monetary Policy, Bank of England, said he thought 'the chances of a sustained and widespread deflation are in any case low'.[21]

Deflation occurs when the inflation rate drops below 0% (a negative inflation rate). This may reflect recession or, in the case of some consumer electronics markets, supply is increasing rapidly due to developments in technology.

Deflation increases the real value of money. This allows one to buy more goods with the same amount of money over time. Deflation is seen as a problem in modern economies because it destabilises economies. There is a danger of a deflationary spiral, namely lower production, leading to lower wages and demand, leading to further decreases in prices.

However deflation in 'good' areas like fuel prices frees up cash for consumers to spend on other items thereby boosting consumption. Alongside retailers, falling oil prices are also good news for a number of sectors including cars, leisure, airline and transport.[22]

There is a positive correlation between rates of home ownership and inflation. Low inflation favours renting because the real burden of mortgage debt stays high and rents cannot increase much if wages and prices are not rising. Countries that have experienced high inflation in the last 50 years, such as Spain and Italy, tend to have higher rates of home ownership than low inflation countries such as Switzerland and Germany.

Deflation is often, though not inevitably, accompanied by declines in output and employment. The US and much of the world suffered from deflation during the Great Depression in the 1930s.

The most obvious policy response to deflation is to stimulate spending and borrowing, via lower interest rates to get demand up so that prices stop falling and the economy stabilises. However Eurozone rates are already at record lows. Fear of the consequences of deflation prompted the European Central Bank to launch a programme of quantitative easing (QE) in March 2015 but inflation is still some way off its official target of 2%. Some economists think that lower Eurozone inflation is a sign that wages are falling in countries like Spain and Greece, where labour costs had become too high for companies to compete in the international marketplace.

The European Central Bank (ECB) expects Eurozone inflation to remain 'very low' for some years against a background of growing threats to economic growth. The ECB's inflation target is below but close to 2%. Eurozone inflation in October 2016 was 0.5% and was below 1% for more than two years previously. The expectation of continued weak oil prices will exert downward pressure on inflation.

Speaking in Germany in January 2016, ECB president Mario Draghi said:

> There are forces in the global economy today that are conspiring to hold inflation down. Those forces might cause inflation to return more slowly to our objective. But there is no reason why they should lead to a permanently lower inflation rate.[23]

To counter the low inflation the ECB could carry on its QE programme for longer than originally envisaged, in larger monthly amounts and it could be extended to other assets. Originally, the programme was expected to end in September 2016.

There are some economists calling for a different approach, namely for central banks to overtly print money to finance increased fiscal deficits with large scale public spending e.g. on infrastructure projects. Such a policy is referred to as the printing of 'helicopter money'. Lord Adair Turner, Chairman of the Institute for New Economic Thinking, thinks that in some circumstances helicopter money may be 'the only certain way to stimulate nominal demand'.[24]

US inflation is below the 2% Federal Reserve target, and has been for much of the time since the global economic downturn in 2008.[25] Similar to the debate in the UK, some commentators are calling for a higher inflation target in the US to give the Federal Reserve more monetary ammunition to fire up the economy. A figure of 4% has been mooted but a change is unlikely any time soon given the 2% consensus in the major industrialised economies. Right-leaning politicians would also be hostile to higher inflation.

Some researchers think that globalisation has changed the inflation process, so that global rather than domestic slack is now the key determinant of inflation rates. However in 2015 Mark Carney, Governor of the Bank of England, said 'the evidence of domestic monetary sovereignty is remarkable given the ever stronger cross-country links via commodity markets, goods and services trade, and financial channels'.[26]

What is irrefutable is that in many of the major developed economies, inflation rates are below target. In addition to the US, this is the case in Japan, Canada, the Eurozone, Sweden and New Zealand.

Abenomics is the name given to the economic revival programme implemented by the Japanese Prime Minister Shinzo Abe. Japan is a very visible example of a deflationary economy. On 29 January 2016, the governor of the Bank of Japan (BOJ) surprised markets by announcing a negative interest rate. The aim of this being to further stimulate the economy by charging private sector lenders a penalty of 0.1% to hold onto their excess cash or reserves.

In theory, negative rates encourage banks to lend more and consumers to spend rather than save. They can also weaken a country's currency, helping exporters. The BOJ's action was given the thumbs down by the financial markets, seen as recognition that Abenomics had not succeeded in all its aims. Following news of the negative interest rate, the yield on Japanese 10 year bonds, the benchmark of government borrowing, slid below zero for the first time. In addition, the strong yen dragged Japanese stocks down more than 5%.[27]

Countries have been keen to avoid falling into a similar economic trap. Since 1997, Japan has endured a sustained slump with a negative output gap (actual output below potential output). It imports a lot of consumer goods and raw materials from low cost China so its domestic producers have to match those prices to remain competitive. Japan also has a major demographic problem of an ageing population with around a quarter of the population over the age of 65.

Assignments

What are the top ten items in your typical shopping basket each week? How do you think this might vary with people in other countries or differ from a typical shopping basket 10 years ago?

The jury is still out on Abenomics. Write 800 words on the current state of the Japanese economy with reference to some of its financial history.

Glossary of key terms

Abenomics: name given to economic revival programme of Prime Minister Shinzo Abe centred on boosting Japan's inflation rate.

Agflation: the phenomenon of rising prices for agricultural commodities such as wheat leading to more expensive foodstuffs such as bread, a box of cereal or bag of flour.

Commodity supercycle: decades-long price movements in a wide range of commodities. This phenomenon has been seen since the late 1800s.

Consumer Price Index (CPI): compares the price of a typical basket of goods and services for all households with the price a year earlier. It excludes housing related items such as mortgage payments.

Deflation: a sustained reduction in the general level of prices.

Food Price Index: United Nation's Food and Agriculture Organisation's (FAO) measure of the monthly change in international prices of a basket of food commodities.

Hyperinflation: large increases in the price level.

Inflation: a persistent increase in the general level of prices.

Inflation hedge: an investment such as gold that is widely thought to provide protection against the decreased value of a currency. The hedge is expected to maintain or increase its value over a specified time period.

Inflation rate: the change in average prices in the economy over a given period of time.

Inflation target: an explicit level of inflation, the achievement of which governs the actions of monetary policy.

Retail Price Index (RPI): measures the average price of a typical basket of goods bought by the average household. Therefore it measures average consumer prices. It is also referred to as the headline rate of inflation.

Stagflation: high and rising cost of living combined with poor or non-existent economic growth.

Resource list

Bank of England Quarterly Inflation Report. Read the governor's opening remarks and access the webcast and podcast: www.bankofengland.co.uk

Food Statistics Pocketbook is published annually by Defra, the Department for Environment, Food & Rural Affairs. Among the topics included are food prices and expenditure, global and UK supply and the environment: www.gov.uk/government/collections/food-statistics-pocketbook

IMF World Economic Outlook (WEO) (October 2015). *Adjusting to Lower Commodity Prices:* www.imf.org

UK inflation statistics – Office for National Statistics (ONS): www.ons.gov.uk

World Gold Council: www.gold.org

Notes

1. Consumer Prices Index Housing (CPIH). Office for National Statistics (n.d.). 'Introducing the new CPIH measure.' www.ons.gov.uk/ons-guide-method/userguidance/prices/cpi-and-rpi/introducing-the-new-cpih-measure-of. . . .
2. Philip Gooding (2016). 'Consumer Price Inflation. The 2016 basket of good and services.' www.ons.gov.uk/releases/consumerpriceinflationbasketofgoodsandservices2016
3. Andrew Haldane (18 September 2015). 'How low can you go?' www.bankofengland.co.uk/publications/Pages/speeches/2015/840.aspx
4. 'Bank of England Inflation Report.' (February, 2016). www.bankofengland.co.uk/publications/Pages/inflationreport/2016/feb.aspx
5. 'World economic outlook: adjusting to lower commodity prices.' (October 2015). www.imf.org/external/pubs/ft/weo/2015/02/pdf/c2.pdf
6. Mehreen Khan (14 January 2016). 'Oil price crash means petrol could become cheaper than bottled water'. www.telegraph.co.uk/finance/economics/12098469/Oil-price-crash-means-petrol-could-become-cheaper-than-bottled-water.html
7. 'World economic outlook: coping with high debt and sluggish growth'. (October 2012). www.imf.org/external/pubs/ft/weo/2012/02/pdf/text.pdf
8. Nomura (13 October 2015). 'Nomura Research cautions about El Niño, food price surge.' www.thestar.com.my/Business/Business-News/2015/10/13/nomura-research-cautions-about-el-nino-food-price-surge/
9. 'FAO Food Price Index.' (4 February 2016). www.fao.org/worldfoodsituation/foodpricesindex/en/

10 Food and Agriculture Organization of the United Nations (2015). 'FAO Food Price Index registers sharpest fall since December 2008.' www.fao.org/news/story/en/item/327815/icode/
11 Robert Miller (5 June 2015). 'Food prices stumble to six-year low'. *The Times*, p.32.
12 Jamie Nimmo (18 November 2015). 'Market report: falling food price piles pressure on Glencore'. www.standard.co.uk/business/market-report-falling-food-price-piles-pressure-on-glencore-a3117646.html
13 Paul Cashin, Kamiar Mohaddes, and Mehdi Raissi (March 2016) 'El Niño Good Boy or Bad?' www.imf.org/external/pubs/ft/fandd/2016/03/cashin.htm
14 'World economic outlook: coping with high debt and sluggish growth.' (October 2012). www.imf.org/external/pubs/ft/weo/2012/02/pdf/text.pdf, p.37, special feature Commodity Markets Review, 'Supply concerns in food markets'; IMF Survey (8 October 2012). 'IMF survey: policy options for riding out food, fuel price spikes.' www.imf.org/external/pubs/ft/survey/so/2012/INT100712A.htm
15 Matt Egan (17 December 2015). 'Gold tumbles to six-year low'. www.money.cnn.com/2015/12/17/investing/gold-prices-fed-rate-hike/
16 'Why gold ETFs are gaining popularity among investors.' (n.d.). www.moneycontrol.com/master_your_money/stocks_news_consumption.php?autono=737468
17 'Summary of producer price inflation, December 2015.' (19 January 2016). www.ons.gov.uk/ons/rel/ppi2/producer-price-index/december-2015/summ-ppi-december-2015.html
18 'Industrial trends survey.' (n.d.). www.cbi.org.uk/business-issues/economy/business-surveys/industrial-trends-survey/
19 Katie Allen and Larry Elliott (27 July 2016). 'UK joins Greece at bottom of wage growth league.' https://www.theguardian.com/money/2016/jul/27/uk-joins-greece-at-bottom-of-wage-growth-league-tuc-oecd
20 'UK inflation woe set to worsen.' (14 May 2008). www.news.bbc.co.uk/1/hi/business/7400074.stm
21 Ben Broadbent (27 March 2015). 'The economics of deflation.' www.bankofengland.co.uk/publications/Pages/speeches/2015/813.aspx
22 Sarah Gordon (15 January 2015). 'Eurozone's slide into deflation need not be a negative thing.' www.ft.com/cms/s/0/d1529150-9bdc-11e4-a6b6-00144feabdc0.html
23 Claire Jones (1 February 2016). 'ECB's Draghi says weak inflation justifies further loosening.' www.ft.com/cms/s/0/a6091bcc-c908-11e5-be0b-b7ece4e953a0.html
24 Jeremie Cohen-Setton (5 January 2015). 'Permanent QE and helicopter money.' www.breugel.org/2015/01/permanent-qe-and-helicopter-money/
25 Lucia Mutikani (20 January 2016). 'Weak US inflation, housing data lower March rate hike chances.' www.reuters.com/article/us-usa-economy-inflation-idUSKCN0UYILH
26 Mark Carney (29 August 2015). 'How is inflation affected by globalisation?' Economic Policy Symposium, Federal Reserve Bank of Kansas City, Jackson Hole,Wyoming.www.weforum.org/agenda/2015/08/how-is-inflation-affected-by-globalisation
27 Jonathan Soble (9 February 2016). 'Japan bond yield slides below zero and stocks fall.'www.nytimes.com/2016/02/10/business/international/japans-bond-yields-follow-interest-rates-into-negative-territory.html?_r

3   Economic growth

What's the definition of a recession? You will know once you have read this chapter. You will also be able to discuss the rise of China to be the world's second biggest economy, why the UK's decision to leave the European Union is bad news for the global economy and learn about the 'productivity conundrum'.

Britain's shock decision on 24 June 2016, to leave the European Union after four decades, so-called 'Brexit', dealt a serious body blow to global economic prospects at a time when economic recovery was already fragile.

The financial markets were swift to signal their displeasure at the announcement. The pound plunged 10% to a 30 year low in volatile trading on international markets. It dropped to levels not seen since 1985 against the dollar. Its decline was more than seen when sterling left the European Exchange Rate Mechanism (ERM) on 'Black Wednesday', 16 September 1992. It also suffered a bigger fall than that seen during the 2008 financial crisis.

The FTSE 100 index of 100 leading UK shares opened 8% lower, wiping £200bn off share values.[1] The UK stock market slump was the biggest one-day fall since the collapse of Lehman Brothers during the financial crisis in October 2008. The Brexit result reverberated around the world with the Euro Stoxx bank index down 17% to levels last seen during the depths of the Eurozone crisis in August 2012. US shares fell by more than two per cent but the perceived safe havens of the US dollar and gold moved sharply higher.[2]

Asian stock markets also tumbled with traders likening the rout to the 'Great Fall of China's stocks' in the summer of 2015.[3]

Although UK bank shares were in a much stronger financial position compared to the financial crisis of 2008, they are viewed as a mirror on the economy and the reflection is not good. Bank profitability will be hit as they do less business in an economy where both business and consumer confidence has taken a massive blow. They will also make less money on loans if UK interest rates are cut to stave off fears of **recession**.

There were also concerns in the markets about the repercussions of the Brexit vote on the Euro currency and fears the Eurozone debt crisis could be reignited. Greek and Italian bank shares were punished heavily by the markets, losing almost a third of their value in some cases.

Commenting on the Brexit decision, Christine Lagarde, managing director of the International Monetary Fund, said 'We urge the authorities in the UK and Europe to work collaboratively to ensure a smooth transition to a new economic relationship between the UK and the EU'.[4]

China was also concerned about the repercussions of the UK's decision to leave the EU. Finance Minister Lou Jiwei said the fallout would 'emerge over the next five to ten years'. Huang Yiping, a member of China's central bank monetary policy committee, said the Brexit could mark a 'reversal of globalisation'. If so, he said, it would be 'very bad' for both the world and China.[5]

Economic uncertainty was compounded by the high level of political uncertainty generated when Prime Minister David Cameron announced his resignation shortly after the referendum result. There was also a loss of confidence in the opposition Labour Party after a wave of Shadow Cabinet resignations following the Brexit vote. Markets dislike uncertainty. No major country has left the European Union before which means that no one knows with any certainty what the future holds.

Many international businesses use their UK operations as an entry point into the larger European single market. There are fears that a Brexit will encourage firms to transfer their business to Continental Europe to safeguard their commercial interests. This would jeopardise thousands of UK jobs and investment thereby reducing economic growth.[6]

Post-Brexit, the Confederation of British Industry (CBI), the business lobby group, is keen that a loud and clear message is given by the UK government that Britain remains open for foreign investment.[7]

Large foreign banks and multinational companies are amongst those expected to scale back their UK operations in favour of locations such as Frankfurt, Amsterdam and Dublin.[8]

According to Deutsche Bank, German business leaders are concerned about industries vulnerable to Brexit and a downturn in the UK economy.[9]

Standard & Poor's, the credit rating agency, downgraded Britain to AA. The UK has enjoyed the coveted maximum triple AAA rating since 1978.[10]

Negative implications of the vote leave as far as the credit rating agencies are concerned include:

- the risk to Britain's large financial services sector, exports and growth in the wider economy;
- harm to sterling's role as a global reserve currency;
- uncertainty in the wake of the referendum will deter investment. Such uncertainty may make it harder for the UK to fund its large current account deficit;
- the possibility of a constitutional crisis if there is a second Scottish independence referendum.

The credit rating downgrade is effectively an early warning indicator of the stormy times ahead for the economy and sterling.

The UK's international standing has undoubtedly been compromised by *Brexit*. Britain's momentous historic decision to leave the EU made news headlines around the world.

> **Journalistic practice**
>
> Accompanying news reports of the Brexit decision was the statement by Mark Carney, Governor of the Bank of England, seeking to calm market turmoil,[11] and the Chancellor George Osborne.[12]
>
> Reports were done from the trading floors of City firms documenting the turmoil in the financial markets both in London and overseas. Graphs of sterling's value against the dollar, the FTSE 250 index gold price and overseas indices such as the Euro Stoxx 600 were given to illustrate the shock to the markets. Bond market reports highlighted the rush to the safety of US Treasuries and German bonds with comment and prices.
>
> In addition to market reports, features on how specific sectors, such as property, banks, airlines and retail, might be affected were produced with share price movements highlighted.[13]
>
> Reaction to the Brexit decision was garnered from a wide range of interested parties including large businesses, City economists, commercial lawyers, union leaders and politicians both at home and abroad.[14]
>
> Comment pieces speculated on what the decision would mean for future trading relationships with the EU, Britain's largest trading partner. There are all sorts of feature angles that can be taken given the UK's entry into unchartered territory. These include the mechanics of how new trade deals might be established, and debate about the uneven distribution of the benefits of globalisation. Attempts were made to quantify the likely hit to the UK economy in terms of foregone **GDP** growth and potential job losses.
>
> Personal finance coverage focused on what the Brexit decision might mean for pensions, investors, savers and home buyers.[15]

The twists and turns of the world economy since the financial crisis have been and continue to be well documented in the media. The extent of the slowdown in China, the world's second largest economy, is still a topic of intense debate.

The World Economic Outlook, WEO, published twice a year by the International Monetary Fund, is the go-to guide as to general expectations of economic performance.

Listen to what Maurice Obstfeld, IMF economic counsellor and director of research, had to say on the prospects for the global economy at an

IMF press conference in October 2016: www.imf.org/external/pubs/ft/weo/2016/02/

Table 3.1 IMF 2016 GDP growth forecasts (%)

US	1.6
China	6.6
Japan	0.5
Germany	1.7
France	1.3
Brazil	−3.3
UK	1.8
India	7.6
Russia	−0.8

Source: World Economic Outlook, October 2016

Journalistic practice

Growth forecasts from respected bodies such as the International Monetary Fund (IMF) or the **Organisation for Cooperation and Development** (OECD) often provide the lead for an economic news story. Such reports should include the new and previous forecasts together with comment on the reasons for the change in outlook and the likelihood of any policy changes e.g. a reduction in interest rates. Include quotes from an economist or central banker and record the reaction in the financial markets to the announcement.

Given the importance of the Chinese economy to the wider global world economy, and the fact that its transition to a mature diversified economy is ongoing, financial data releases in China are closely monitored by the world's financial press and analysts. Typically, publication of economic growth figures leads to comparisons being made with the historic growth rates. There is also commentary on the desire by the Chinese authorities for a move away from cheap export-led growth to increased domestic consumption in China fuelled by a growing middle class. Note should be made of reaction in the financial markets, such as movements in the value of the Chinese currency, the renminbi.

When reporting on the Eurozone economies it is usually a case of Germany performing better than its neighbours. Give statistics to back this up such as manufacturing output data, new orders, consumer and business surveys and include a forward looking forecast on the outlook. Include examples of comparable statistics in other European countries

> to illustrate the diverse economic performance. Might the data prompt a policy response? Include a comment from Mario Draghi, President of the European Central Bank (ECB).
>
> Specific factors affecting economic growth can be singled out for comment and analysis, for example the prolonged decline in UK productivity despite strong economic growth.

World economic growth in 2015 was a tale of two halves with advanced economies showing a modest pick-up in growth. In contrast developing and emerging economies experienced their fifth consecutive year of slower growth.

The collateral damage from China rebalancing its economy coupled with moves to normalise monetary policy in the US contributed to the more pessimistic mood. The global economy ended the year with growth of 3.1%.

With several negative headwinds such as financial market volatility, political instability and continuing worries about China's economic slowdown, the IMF expects anaemic growth at best in 2016. It advocates a three-pronged approach to boost economic growth encompassing structural, fiscal and monetary measures. For example, there is thought to be scope to boost spending on infrastructure and research and development in a number of countries.

As 2016 unfolded, the OECD also became more pessimistic about the growth prospects for the world economy. The sharp falls in commodity prices and a significant slowdown in global trade growth were cited as negative factors for growth, which is not expected to be higher than in 2015. This would be its slowest pace in five years.[16]

OECD chief economist Catherine Mann issued a rallying cry:

> Given the significant downside risks posed by financial sector volatility and emerging market debt, a stronger collective policy approach is urgently needed, focusing on a greater use of fiscal and pro-growth structural policies, to strengthen growth and reduce financial risks.[17]

Maybe low growth is the new normal and we will all have to get used to that and adjust our expectations accordingly. What are the implications of a low growth world? This and other questions are addressed in *Prosperity without Growth. Economics for a Finite Planet*, by Tim Jackson, Professor of Sustainable Development at the University of Surrey.[18]

He argues that advanced economies have been slowing down since the 1960s in terms of productivity per annum. This is ascribed to the growth of the labour-rich service sector, 'an economy of craft, care and culture'. He thinks low growth coupled with the well documented rise in inequality is storing up potential trouble for governments. Speaking in London in May

2016, he said 'Social stability depends on economic stability' and called for the creation of 'a new macroeconomics'.[19]

US economy

Despite all the hype about emerging markets in recent years, the US economy in 2015 was still the largest in the world. You will come across the phrase 'When America sneezes everyone else catches a cold', which means that given the size of the US economy anything that happens there has repercussions for other economies. We saw that with the fallout in emerging markets from the FED's decision to tighten US monetary policy by reducing the amount of money it pumps into the economy.

However with one eye on the consequences of their actions on emerging markets, US central bankers have been at pains to stress (like their UK counterparts) that any rise in interest rates will be gradual given the fragility of the economic recovery.

Despite the fact that rates are on a gradual upward trajectory, there is a risk that emerging markets could react sharply with currency depreciations, rising bond spreads, reduced capital inflows and tighter liquidity.

Against a backdrop of weaker than expected economic data both at home and in China, the timescale for the US Federal Reserve to tighten monetary policy was extended. There had been a widespread expectation that US rates would rise in September 2015.

However the first US rate rise in nine years, of 0.25%, did not occur until December 16 2015. It was seen as a vote of confidence in the US economy with solid annual growth of 2.1% and US unemployment at 5%, the lowest level in seven and a half years. The US dollar had been marked higher a few months earlier in anticipation of the rate rise.

Janet Yellen has been criticised in some quarters for poor communication and for being too reactive rather than proactively taking a long view, looking 1–2 years ahead.

The opening months of 2016 saw a slew of economic data that disappointed the markets and reduced optimism in the world's economic growth prospects. This was reflected in the financial markets with bond markets forecasting recession. In Germany, the average yield on all government debt was negative and in the US the 10-year Treasury yield headed south.[20]

Ahead of the UK referendum, Janet Yellen said a Brexit 'could have significant economic repercussions'. Ms Yellen told the Senate Banking Committee that a split would lead to uncertainty that could create market instability. However she did not think it was likely to send the US economy into recession.[21]

The IMF cited improving government finances and a stronger housing market as supportive of US domestic demand. These will help offset the negative effect on net exports from a strong dollar and weaker manufacturing.[22]

Figure 3.1 Shale oil platform. Image courtesy of Ramon Perez/iStock.

The future prospects of the US economy have been enhanced by the discovery of significant quantities of cheap shale gas.[23]

Shale gas refers to natural gas that is trapped in fine-grained sedimentary rocks known as shale formations. A combination of horizontal drilling and hydraulic fracturing has allowed access to large volumes of shale gas that were previously uneconomical to produce.

> **Journalistic practice**
>
> Much has been written about the transformative effects of shale gas on the prospects for the US economy. Reports should describe what shale gas is, how much is available and what contribution it makes to US energy requirements. Profiles can be done of the major producers. Comment and analysis pieces can be produced on the wider implications of the growth of shale gas. Will it exert downward pressure on global energy prices?

Energy security is very important in these times of increasing global political instability. The availability of cheap local energy in the US has transformed people's assessments of the long-term prospects for that economy.

Lower energy costs make American manufacturing industry more competitive. The IMF is expecting it to grow by 1.6% in 2016. In the US, jobs are being created, consumers are spending, debt is being repaid and businesses are investing. However the US economy is not immune from sluggishness elsewhere. Therefore in 2016 and 2017 the IMF is expecting US growth to be lower than the 2.6% seen in 2015.

Chinese economy

The rapid emergence of China on the world economic stage has been *the* major economic news story in recent years. A fast rate of growth is often achieved by economies that are industrialising quickly and starting from a relatively low base.

During the financial crisis China picked up the baton for global economic growth and has been running with it ever since albeit at a slower pace. The rebalancing of the Chinese economy away from an export-led manufacturing model towards a domestic consumer and services-led one has not followed a smooth path.[24]

The authorities have occasionally resorted to what appear to be panic measures – such as cutting interest rates and slashing bank reserve requirements thereby freeing up more funds for lending – when data emerges suggesting slower than expected economic growth. On several occasions Chinese financial markets have demonstrated their lack of confidence in the Chinese economy.[25]

In January 2016, a weaker than expected purchasing managers index signalling a contraction in the Chinese economy, prompted a 7% drop in the Chinese stock market triggering a temporary government suspension of trading. The authorities are keen to maintain stability within the financial markets.

Previous to this, the markets were unsettled when third quarter growth statistics in 2015 came in at 6.9%, slightly lower than the 7.0% target of the Chinese government and the weakest rate since the global financial crisis. Investment, which includes construction of new houses and factories, contributed 43%. Services share of output is more than half and is growing faster than the industrial sector.

Consumption accounted for 58% of the growth with spending thought to have increased in telecoms, education, travel, elderly care and the financial services sector, the latter despite steep declines in the local stock market in the second quarter.

Against a backdrop of challenging economic conditions, the Chinese National People's Congress approved lowering the GDP target for 2016 to 6.5–7%. Growth in 2015 was the slowest in 25 years at 6.9%, compared with 7.3% a year earlier.[26]

Volatility in the financial markets raises concerns about financial turmoil and potential social unrest in China.

The third quarter growth figure in 2015 added to the roll call of disappointing data releases with manufacturing, imports and inflation figures all seemingly pointing to a harder than desired landing for the world's second biggest economy.

There is some market scepticism about the quality of Chinese financial reporting given that growth figures are produced quickly and are never revised.[27]

Some analysts think that based on indicators such as industrial production, electricity use and credit growth, China's real growth rate might be as low as 3%. This suggests that the economy requires additional stimulus from investment spending.

Gross domestic product indicates the amount of economic production taking place in an economy, calculated as the total output within a specific year.

Box 3.1 Gross domestic product (GDP)

- GDP measures a country's total income and total spending.
- Most widely recognised measure of a country's economic strength. Used by IMF, OECD and World Bank to compare countries.
- The EU uses GDP estimates to determine countries' contributions to the EU budget.

Box 3.2 How is GDP measured?

- Usually GDP data is published quarterly. i.e. every three months.
- Growth rate is the key figure *not* the total amount.
- Real GDP figures exclude inflation effects.
- Nominal GDP figures include inflation effects.

Box 3.3 Reporting on GDP

- Give quarterly change relative to the previous three months.
- How does data compare with expectations?
- Put data in context of whole economy performance – unemployment, CBI surveys.
- Include political comment – Chancellor.
- Economist reaction and forward forecasts.
- Financial market reaction, £, bonds, equities.

As recently as 2011, Chinese GDP was 9.3%. For 30 years China grew at around 10% per annum. A major boost came from government spending on infrastructure, particularly in the aftermath of the global financial crisis.

It is widely accepted that the days of annual double-digit economic growth are over. China's transition from an export-led manufacturing economy to an economy focused more on services and spending by Chinese consumers is illustrated starkly in a regular stream of statistics showing lower manufacturing activity.

It is not all doom and gloom as retail sales are growing strongly and the property market appears to be stabilising. Chinese banks are expanding and are expected to increase their international activity. They are well represented in London helping to facilitate trade by Chinese companies. Eventually they are expected to provide finance for non-Chinese business.

Relative to the economies of Europe and the US, as Martin Jacques notes in his book *When China Rules the World*, 'The Chinese, buoyed by huge foreign exchange reserves, large trade surpluses and a high level of savings, can look forward to many more years of fast economic growth'.[28]

Concern that the slowdown in China would impact growth prospects elsewhere in the region was a major factor in the World Bank reducing its growth forecasts for the Asia Pacific region in 2015 and 2016.

The Bank is expecting Chinese growth of 6.6% in 2016, down from 6.9% in 2015. According to the World Bank, East Asia accounts for almost two-fifths of the world's economic growth.[29]

Key facts

- China's contribution to world GDP has risen from below 2% in 1990, to around 17% in 2015.
- Even with slower GDP growth in 2015, China represented around a quarter of global growth.

Source: HM Treasury[30]

The Chinese authorities have an economic and financial reform plan that aims to open up sectors monopolised by state-owned enterprises to private and foreign firms. The telecoms, oil, gas, electricity and transport markets are expected to benefit. Financial reforms are to be made in a number of areas including interest rates, exchange rates and insurance. London is seen as a base for internationalising the renminbi.[31]

The Chinese authorities are looking to move the economy up the value chain by focusing on achieving a leading position in sectors such as semiconductors, robotics and healthcare.

Anecdotal evidence suggests that since 2009, investment has been a greater contributor to Chinese economic growth than consumption.

The government has done various things to try to boost growth in other ways such as the launch of free trade zone in Shanghai. Within this area, foreign firms are now allowed to enter some previously closed markets such as the provision of home internet access and manufacture of gaming consoles.[32]

Efforts are being made to boost innovation. A $690m facility was opened in 2011 close to Beijing, housing hundreds of animation, film and computer game companies.

In the past China's export-led manufacturing growth was based on cheap copies of existing products.

There is some concern, even amongst the Chinese authorities, that long-term growth prospects may be harmed by bad loans made by the banking sector, often in property resulting in large numbers of empty properties in ghost towns. There is also the growth of the unregulated shadow banking sector – covering everything from private individuals lending their own money to off balance sheet loans from banks.[33]

As people become less optimistic about the prospects for China, domestic investors are voting with their feet and moving into other markets such as global real estate.

Europe

The Eurozone was severely impacted by the financial crisis and its associated recession. Subsequently, it has struggled to make a sustained recovery and is still overshadowed by problems in its banking system.

However there were some encouraging signs in the first three months of 2016 with a better than expected rebound in Eurozone household consumption and business investment. Eurostat data showed Euro area GDP rose by 0.3% in the third quarter of 2016.

Eurozone industrial production hit a six-year high in January 2016. Ireland, Estonia and Germany led the way with a striking 42.7% uplift in Irish industrial production compared with the same period of 2015. Eurostat official data showed monthly rises in output in manufacturing, mining and utilities.[34]

However, a pessimistic note was sounded in May 2016 with the publication of financial data from Markit, showing a slowdown in its activity index. Its survey of private sector firms in the single currency bloc indicated the slowest pace of growth for 16 months. This was deemed a disappointing outcome by the financial markets given the concerted efforts of the European Central Bank to stimulate the Eurozone economy.[35]

The European Central Bank expects inflation in the Eurozone to remain 'very low' for some years. It downgraded its economic growth forecasts for 2016 from 1.9% to 1.7% recognising the adverse impact of muted global growth.[36]

In 2015 the economies of Spain and France showed signs of recovery after a prolonged period in the doldrums with hopes that this would feed through to a sustained upturn in job creation.[37]

Despite an unstable domestic political environment, the Spanish economy is expected to grow by around 2.7% in 2016. Retail sales and business and mortgage lending are rising. Spain grew by 3.2% in 2015, the fastest pace of growth since 2007, before the financial crisis.

The French economy is the second biggest in the Eurozone after Germany. Private sector investment and consumer spending are recovering. However in 2016 unemployment was still high at around 10%. Close to three million people are without work, many of them young people. The government finances are weak.

A relatively resilient *Germany*, Europe's biggest economy, has helped underpin what recovery there has been in the wider Eurozone.

However, there was widespread shock in September 2015 when Volkswagen, Germany's largest car manufacturer, confessed that for years it had cheated on its environmental tests for diesel emissions in the US. The full impact on the company, both in financial terms and reputational damage, is difficult to quantify.[38]

In June 2016, Volkswagen agreed to pay $10.2bn to settle some claims from diesel car owners in the US.

The German car industry has been widely admired across the world for its engineering excellence and integrity, key planks of successive marketing campaigns. Around one in seven of all German jobs are thought to be connected in some way to the car industry.

Journalistic practice

A wide range of angles were covered from basic who knew what and when at VW, reporting the associated suspension of key personnel, investigations launched and legal action taken by various countries through to whether the scandal has damaged brand Germany as a whole. There was speculation as to how long it would take for VW to repair its reputational damage. The severe impact on the VW share price was also noted – the shares crashed more than 30% in the two days following the announcement.

Broader comment pieces looked at whether the scandal was symptomatic of the integrity deficit between the general public and big business which has been growing for a while following the financial crisis and rigging of various financial markets. There were also attempts to quantify the total monetary cost of the scandal to VW.

UK economy

Britain grew faster than any other major advanced economy in 2015, at 2.6%. However, in February 2016, the Bank of England announced a significant lowering in its forecast for overall economic growth to 2.2% from 2.5% in its November forecasts.[39]

Growth in 2017 was forecast to be lower at 2.4%, down from 2.7%. Bank of England governor Mark Carney cited turbulence in financial markets and the tough global economic backdrop as reasons for the downgrades.[40]

Given the deteriorating outlook for the UK economy and public finances, it was not a surprise that in the March Budget, the independent watchdog, the Office for Budget Responsibility, reduced its 2016 estimate for GDP to 2% from 2.4% in November.

These downgrades were before the shock announcement of Britain leaving the EU. Prior to the referendum vote, the International Monetary Fund had warned that EU exit represented the 'largest near-term risk' to the British economy. It warned that the net economic effects would probably be 'negative and substantial' and that the UK could miss out on up to 5.6% of GDP growth by 2019.[41]

Under its least adverse scenario for Brexit, by 2019 UK GDP would be 1.4% below what it would have been before Brexit.

Pre-referendum analysis by the Treasury suggested the UK 'could be 6% smaller' by 2030, after an EU exit. The 200 page report said the reduction in GDP would cost each household the equivalent of £4,300 a year.

The analysis found that the negative impact on the economy would result in a total reduction in tax receipts of £36bn, equivalent to around an 8p increase in the basic rate of income tax.[42]

Against a backdrop of hostility from some of his European counterparts, Chancellor George Osborne stuck to his economic plan of cost reduction in the aftermath of the financial crisis. Speaking after the Brexit result Mr Osborne said 'our economy is about as strong as it could be to confront the challenge our country now faces'.

He noted employment was at 'a record high', the budget deficit had declined from 11% of national income to an estimated 3% in 2016 and growth had been robust.[43]

In December 2015, the IMF gave Mr Osborne an early Christmas present by delivering an upbeat assessment of the UK economy. In its annual update on the UK economy it 'saluted' the country's growth. Christine Lagarde, the head of the IMF said Britain had 'managed to repair the damage of the crisis' achieving this milestone along with 'very few other countries'.[44]

The nation's 'recent economic performance has been strong, and considerable progress has been achieved in addressing underlying vulnerabilities', the report added. Ms Lagarde also said that rapid falls in UK unemployment would mean that higher wage growth would be here to stay.

Confidence amongst British consumers was underpinned by real wage growth and record employment. Looking at specific industries, construction and manufacturing were not as strong as the service sector.[45]

Box 3.4 Service sector

- Accounts for roughly three-quarters of UK GDP.
- Includes consumer businesses e.g. restaurants, and business and professional services such as banking and legal. UK accounts for 40% of European financial services.
- CBI Services Survey covers 40 sectors. Done in February, May, August and November. Includes business optimism, costs and profits, and employment.

58   *Economic growth*

For many years, the service sector has dominated the UK economy with areas such as financial services, petroleum refining, and TV and film production performing particularly strongly.

Blockbuster movies such as *Bridget Jones's Baby* and *Wonder Woman* helped London's TV and film-making industries generate a record £649m in 2015. London ranks alongside New York and Los Angeles as one of the busiest and most popular places for film and television production.[46]

Out of nearly 2.5 million new jobs created since the end of 2009, over 2.2 million have been created in services. The UK is the second biggest exporter of services in the world behind the United States.

In 2015, total UK exports of services were £226bn, equivalent to around £8,400 per UK household, and only just behind the value of manufactured exports at £229bn.

Productivity

One conundrum facing the UK economy is the seeming disconnect between productivity – output per worker per hour – and economic growth. France and Italy are more productive than the UK even though their economic growth is less. Only Japan is worse than us.

There are calls for a cross-party commission on productivity and a new improved Productivity Plan from the Treasury.[47] It is important to make the UK economy more productive so that sufficient revenues can be generated to reduce the budget deficit.

The financial crisis appears to have caused lasting damage to the UK economy. Some estimate that 7–8% of national output was permanently lost during the crisis. Productivity has remained below trend in Great Britain since the 2008 financial crisis despite relatively strong economic growth and record employment. This so-called *productivity conundrum* has exercised some of the wisest minds in economics but no definitive answer has been found.

Investment spending grew steadily between 2010 and 2015, with 2013 and 2014 recording new all-time highs. However, productivity in 2013 and 2014 was disappointingly low at 0.4% and 0.5% respectively.

Possible reasons for low productivity growth

The nature of the UK labour market has changed with many of the people who have recently joined the labour market working in low paid, irregular employment, for example on zero-hour contracts. Many of the new employees have been immigrants and with social and political pressure growing to restrict their numbers, productivity could slip back even more.

'When the UK economy grows faster than its neighbours, as has been the case over the past couple of years, you'd expect to see greater inward migration and a disproportionate rise in the supply of low-skilled labour in particular,' said Dr Ben Broadbent, Deputy Governor Monetary Policy at the Bank of England.[48]

The fallout from the financial crisis of 2008 led to large job losses in the highly productive financial services sector. Not all of those jobs have returned. Productivity in financial services and insurance was rising before the crisis at an annual 4.1%. The financial services sector affects the productivity of the rest of the economy because of its role in providing finance for business investment.

Increased regulation in the banking sector in the aftermath of the recession could also be impeding productivity growth.

More people are self-employed or working part-time rather than full-time.

The long distances large numbers of people commute to work, particularly to jobs in London and south-east England, has also been cited as a negative drag on productivity.

There is also an argument that at least part of the problem might be the failure of small and medium enterprises (SMEs) to export new products and services. This may be due to the difficulties many SMEs faced in accessing credit to grow during the recession.

Against a background of many years of low wage growth, employers retained more staff than they needed during the recession. This enables them to avoid having to pay for expensive hiring and training of new staff when market conditions improved.

It matters because ultimately in the long-term strong productivity growth is needed to maintain the UK's competitiveness in the global economy and raise domestic living standards. If productivity rises it takes fewer hours of work for the economy to produce the same amount of output. That allows firms to increase pay, leading to higher living standards.

> **Journalistic practice**
>
> Comment pieces can be produced speculating on the possible causes of low productivity growth. This can be illustrated with interviews with people on zero-hour contracts with background information provided on the scale of cutbacks in the City of London during the financial crisis.

The government is keen to see a rebalancing of the British economy towards exports rather than domestic consumption.

Infrastructure

It is not just the Chinese authorities that see infrastructure spending as a major means of boosting the economy. The British government also hopes that infrastructure investment will help boost the UK economy.

The Chinese have already invested in Heathrow and Manchester airports and controversially in the Hinkley Point nuclear power station in Somerset. Confirmation of the landmark agreement to build a new generation of power stations in the UK came during the China President's state visit to the UK in October 2015.[49]

In the largest inward investment ever in the UK, EDF Energy and China General Nuclear Power Corporation (CGN) are expected to spend a total of £18bn with the Chinese having a one-third stake. Two other new nuclear power stations are included in the deal. In July 2016, Prime Minister Theresa May delayed giving final approval for the project on security grounds. However on 15 September 2016, approval was given with the introduction of a 'golden share' to protect national security. The UK government will be able to stop EDF selling its controlling stake in the project and will have more influence over future developments in 'critical infrastructure'.

Journalistic practice

What are the terms of the deal? Discuss pros and cons of the deal including criticisms from security experts, environmentalists and consumer groups.

More than £30bn of deals between the UK and China were struck during the President's four day UK state visit. Among them Chinese investment group SinoFortone announced a £2bn investment in Orthios Eco Parks to develop waste power and food production in Wales. It is also investing in developing an amusement park in Kent.

In the past, the Chinese premier Li Keqiang has expressed an interest in investing in the biggest and most controversial UK infrastructure project, the £32bn High Speed rail network.[50]

George Osborne was keen to secure Chinese investment in the HS2.[51]

The project aims to narrow the gap between the economic performance of the north and south of England – the so-called north-south divide – by helping to promote economic growth in regions of Britain such as the midlands and north-west England.

The benefits are expected to come from quicker travel times and job creation. Government estimates 40,000 jobs created in phase 1 from growth around the high-speed stations, construction of the line and operation of the trains.

Leaving aside concerns about the environmental impact of HS2, critics say there are better ways to spend £32bn to stimulate growth. Academics say experience of similar lines overseas such as Seville to Madrid does not provide the economic regeneration benefits.

Japan

Despite the aggressive attempts by the Japanese government under Prime Minister Shinzo Abe to reflate the Japanese economy, it continues to bounce along the bottom. Consumer spending took a hit from a rise in sales tax in April 2014. There are fears that another increase from 8% to 10% will further depress consumer sentiment.

Higher government spending is helping to offset some of the weakness in business investment and exports. The world's third largest economy has fallen into recession four times since the global financial crisis.

In 2015, a 30% devaluation of the Japanese yen boosted exports and tourist numbers with the Chinese out in force. Around a quarter of the 14 million arrivals in 2015 were from China despite the political tensions between the two countries.[52]

As Japan's population ages the country's high savings rate will fall prompting fears that the Japanese public will no longer be able to finance the country's high level of government debt. As the world's third largest economy this could prompt a fiscal crisis in the years ahead with an adverse knock on effect on the global economy.[53]

Turmoil in the financial markets following the UK's decision to leave the European Union saw the Japanese yen acquire the status of a safe haven. It surged in value against the US dollar. This is not good news for Japanese exporters such as Toyota and Panasonic.

There are various ways in which GDP can be recorded.

Box 3.5 Measurement of GDP

- Output measure: the value of goods and services produced by all sectors of the economy.
- Expenditure measure: the value of the goods and services purchased by households and government, investment in machinery and buildings and value of exports minus imports.
- Income measure: the value of income generated mostly in terms of profits and wages.

In theory all three approaches should produce the same number.

The UK produces the earliest estimate of GDP of the major economies, around 25 days after the quarter in question.

This provides policy makers with an early 'flash' estimate of the real growth in economic activity. However, it is only based on the output measure which accounts for around 40% of the total so the figure is revised as more information becomes available. There are two subsequent revisions at monthly intervals.

Shadow/underground/informal/parallel economy

> **Box 3.6** Hidden/informal economy
>
> - Certain industries have a big presence in the hidden economy e.g. gardeners, taxi drivers, cleaners and builders.
> - Tax evasion is motivating factor.
> - Cash transactions.
> - In the UK 7–15% of GDP, Greece, Spain and Italy estimated as high as 30%. Developing countries could be as much as 80%.

The shadow economy encompasses both illegal and legal activities. Illegal activities include drug dealing and manufacturing, prostitution, gambling, smuggling, fraud and trade in stolen goods.

Taxes such as VAT, income tax and national insurance contributions, and government regulations such as health and safety laws, impose a burden on workers and businesses. Some people are tempted to evade taxes and operate in the shadow economy.

In the building industry, it is common for workers to be self-employed and to under-declare or not declare their income to all the tax authorities. Tax evasion is the dominant motive for working in the hidden economy but some people also claim welfare benefits to which they are not entitled.

Income earned overseas and repatriated in cash outside the banking system is thought to be a factor inflating the informal economy of the Philippines by as much as 20%.

Variable rates of tax collection are a problem for some southern European countries such as Greece and Italy and Latin American economies. The hidden economy in Greece is estimated to account for 25% of GDP compared to 15% in Germany.

Although tax revenues are rising in Latin American countries they are lower as a proportion of their national income than in most OECD countries. However, there has been a marked improvement in the tax to GDP ratio since 1990. There is a varied picture across countries with Argentina and Brazil above the OECD average with the likes of Guatemala at the lower end.

Effects on the official economy

Lower tax receipts inevitably mean governments have to impose higher tax rates or cut public spending, including welfare benefits which is likely to encourage more people to work in the shadow economy, thereby perpetuating a vicious circle.

As the shadow economy grows, the official growth rate of the economy may appear to be depressed because of the larger number of people seeming to move out of the official economy. However, around two-thirds of the income earned in the shadow economy is thought to be spent immediately in the official economy. This could lead to an increase in overall economic growth although by its nature it is hard to quantify this effect.

Cash is king in the shadow economy and so rising activity in the shadow economy is likely to be reflected in a higher demand for currency.

The shadow economy has grown steadily across the world with higher incidences seen in developing nations. For example in Egypt and Nigeria, the shadow economy is thought to account for as much as 75% of GDP. However even in Denmark, the share of the total labour force engaged in the shadow economy is estimated to be around 20%.

The IMF has researched the shadow economy and concluded that 'countries with relatively low tax rates, fewer laws and regulations, and a well-established rule of law tend to have smaller shadow economies'.[54]

Many studies have shown that more corruption, the abuse of public power for private benefit, results in a larger shadow economy. Macroeconomic and microeconomic modelling studies based on data from several countries suggest that the major driving forces behind the size and growth of the shadow economy are an increasing burden of tax and social security payments, combined with rising restrictions in the official labour market. Wage rates in the official economy also play a role.

Enforced reductions of work in the official economy, for example, through restrictions on working hours, may push people into the shadow economy.

Growth promoters

Non-renewable natural resources such as oil, zinc and tin, are important contributors to national incomes in countries such as Brazil, Mexico and Venezuela.

Some countries have experienced large growth rates almost solely because they have plentiful *natural resources*, oil in the case of Saudi Arabia and Norway.

Oil

The UK received a windfall when it discovered oil and gas in the North Sea, off the coast of Scotland in 1969. Oil production peaked in 1999 at 2559 million barrels. There were boom years in the 1970s and again in 2013 but the collapse in world oil prices during the course of 2015 – down more than 60% – means that North Sea oil and gas production has become uneconomic.

The manufacturing supply chain has been battered leading to cutbacks in investment and jobs. It is estimated that up to 150 North Sea platforms may close. The trade body Oil and Gas UK said that 65,000 jobs were lost in the 10 months to September 2015, principally in Scotland, north-east and Eastern England.

64   *Economic growth*

In February 2016, BP announced its biggest-ever annual loss and Shell reported an 80% drop in profits to a 13 year low. The companies' revenues were decimated by the slump in the oil price from $115 a barrel in the summer of 2014 to around $35 in February 2016.[55]

A study carried out by Company Watch showed that half of the 22 UK-listed companies with operations in the North Sea – one of the world's most mature oilfields – are making losses of over £6bn. While costs have been reduced, relatively high tax and staffing costs along with strict safety laws make the North Sea the world's most expensive oilfields. Net debt amongst smaller North Sea oil companies has risen sharply as they struggle to keep afloat.[56]

Efforts by Saudi Arabia to bolster its market leading position in the face of competition from US shale gas has been blamed for the steep decline in oil prices. In December 2015, oil prices dropped to a nine year low.[57]

In the financial markets, geopolitical considerations are overriding the economic benefits of lower oil prices.[58]

The lifting of some sanctions against Iran will add to the downward pressure on oil prices. At the end of November 2015, Iran overhauled the way in which it offers contracts to foreign energy companies in a bid to attract up to $30bn of new investment, with a view to increasing output by 500,000 barrels a day. Iran has some of the biggest oil and gas reserves in the world.

In the years ahead, Iran would like to increase oil production from around three million barrels a day now, to five million by the end of the decade.[59]

Worsening political relations between Saudi Arabia and Iran saw the oil price gain 2% on 4 January 2016 on fears about supply disruption.

As of November 2015, stockpiles of oil stood at a record three billion barrels, enough to supply all the world's needs for more than a month.[60]

Such a huge stockpile will take time to unwind, exerting continuing downward pressure on oil prices for the foreseeable future. This in turn will exert particular pressure on countries such as Algeria and Nigeria.

Venezuela, another casualty of the collapsing oil price, has proposed a price band with an automatic floor for prices at $70 a barrel. It would like to see a mechanism put in place within OPEC for progressive production cuts to control prices with an eventual target of $100 per barrel. In the meantime it has set a target price of $40 per barrel for oil in its 2016 budget.

Relative to other oil producers, Saudi Arabia's huge reserves and ability to borrow mean that that it is better able to handle the pain from a prolonged period of low oil prices. However even it must have been taken aback by the scale and speed of the collapse in oil prices. This is reflected in cuts to domestic spending and plans for privatisation of some state-run companies, including oil producer Aramco.[61]

Within some Gulf states, export revenues are sharply down, budget deficits are rising and there is the possibility of the introduction of VAT to increase non-oil tax revenues.

Pros and cons of a lower oil price

On the plus side lower oil prices are good for the global economy as a whole as they make manufacturing costs cheaper and consumers have more money to spend as the price of petrol falls.

The £1 a litre price on UK forecourts will keep inflation lower for longer enabling the Bank of England to delay the day of reckoning when it raises UK interest rates, albeit gradually and in small amounts. France and the Republic of Ireland were ahead of the UK with petrol prices in November 2015, of less than £1 per litre.

Industry also benefits from lower oil prices and this is reflected by increased business investment. Despite the scaling back of North Sea operations, UK business investment in 2015 was up over 6% compared with a 4.6% rise in 2014.

Advanced economies that are not solely reliant on oil and commodity revenues have been boosted by lower oil prices.

In contrast, the decision by Royal Dutch Shell to halt oil exploration in the Arctic in September 2015 was blamed on high costs relative to the oil price. Around 350,000 people are employed in the UK oil industry. An estimated 65,000 jobs were lost in the two years to December 2015 as investment was reduced.

Gulf nations tightened their belts with their sovereign wealth funds withdrawing sizeable amounts of money out of global fund management houses.

Aside from the economic woes for specific companies and nations, there is concern that lower oil revenues in countries such as Iraq and Algeria will make it harder for them to fund the fight against Islamic extremists within their borders.

Stock markets around the world fell as oil and gas shares are large constituents of the indices, particularly in the UK. Shares in Shell and BP moved lower.

What is the outlook for oil prices?

The Paris-based International Energy Agency (IEA) forecasts that lower production in the North Sea, US and Russia will lead to output outside OPEC dropping to 57.7m barrels per day (bpd) in 2016. Following a thaw in diplomatic relations, Iran is keen to get its oil back on the world market adding to the oversupply.

Iran has some of the biggest oil and gas reserves in the world. It plans to increase oil production from around three million barrels a day in 2015 to about five million by the end of the decade. This will help economic growth, which has been hit by a number of factors including economic sanctions and corruption.

In November 2015, Iran sought to attract $30bn of new oil contracts with foreign investors offered more favourable terms than in the past. Foreign energy companies are now able to retain a stake in the oil field leading to more lucrative longer-term contracts.[62]

OPEC itself is predicting increased demand for its oil in 2016. However, the International Energy Agency (IEA) thinks it will take months to clear the glut and growth in global demand for oil will fall in 2016 as the allure of lower prices fades.

Oil price boosters

- Reduced output by OPEC members.
- Strong world economic growth.
- Supply disruption or the threat of interruption of supplies e.g. due to conflict in the Gulf region or political unrest in Nigeria.
- Comments by oil ministers on price targets.
- Lower oil stockpiles.

Journalistic practice

Explanatory reports can be produced on the structure of the global market. Who are the big players and why are prices falling? Against a backdrop of falling or low oil prices, news reports can be written on how various companies in the sector are faring e.g. Royal Dutch Shell. Include a quote on the outlook for the industry and oil prices from Edinburgh-based energy consultancy Wood Mackenzie, Oil and Gas UK or the IEA. For specific company comment, City oil analysts can be quoted with their forecasts for profits and the share price. What are the pros and cons of lower oil prices both domestically and for the global economy? How are emerging economies that rely on oil revenues, such as Nigeria and Russia, coping? How are the financial markets reacting?

Technological progress increases economic growth in two ways: it cuts the average cost of production of a product and it creates new products for the market which consumers want to spend money on. We have seen this with the growth of Apple on the back of its innovative iPhone and iPad products.

Box 3.7 Knowledge-based capital

- Investment and growth in OECD economies is increasingly driven by knowledge-based capital.
- Includes software, patents, design, research and development.
- e.g. physical assets accounted for only 5% of Google's worth in 2009.
- Issues of intellectual property rights, corporate reporting, tax and competition.

Economic growth 67

The government recognises the vital role that science plays in maintaining the UK's competitive edge and boosting economic growth. Even in the depths of the recession the science budget was ring-fenced and protected from the severe spending cuts imposed elsewhere. Graphene, the world's first 2D material, was discovered at Manchester University in 2004.[63]

Box 3.8 Graphene

- World's first 2D material
- 200 times stronger than steel
- World's thinnest and most conductive material
- Ultra light and transparent
- Applications in energy, membranes, sensors, electronics and composites and coatings.

The UK government is keen that Britain should become the European hub for commercial space flight and space technologies with investment in space flight and microgravity research that is estimated to have the potential to boost the UK economy by £11.8bn. In December 2015, the government launched the first UK National Space policy which is forecast to create 100,000 jobs by 2030.[64]

Box 3.9 UK growth industries

- Aerospace
- Media
- Computing
- Animation
- Advanced materials – lasers, liquid crystals
- Synthetic biology-combines science and engineering – GM crops
- Regenerative medicine – stem cell research.

Lower taxes should encourage unemployed people to enter the labour market. In addition, low employment taxes paid by firms, such as national insurance, should encourage firms to take on more staff.

A fast rate of growth is often achieved by economies that are industrialising quickly and starting from a relatively low base.

An emotive issue is that of *migrant labour*. Whatever the political arguments for and against, the reality is that migrant labour is increasingly indispensable for the European economy. Germany has been at the forefront of welcoming migrants which should help it stave off problems associated with the ageing of its native population and the subsequent decline in economic output.[65]

68 *Economic growth*

In the global economy the search for skilled workers crosses national boundaries. Most country studies point to a high degree of complementarity between the native and migrant workforce. The foreign workers fill labour market shortages in sectors where native workers are not willing to work or not qualified to perform the required task.

Increasing the *quality* of the workforce is very important for long-term economic growth. That means investing in an educated skilled workforce.

Box 3.10 Government growth promotion

- Improve the workings of the labour market – promote mobility, employee training.
- Reduce excessive regulation particularly on small businesses.
- Improve access to finance for growing firms.
- Boost infrastructure spending in areas such as transport.
- Attract inward investment.

The economic cycle shows the pattern of economic growth that occurs in economies over time.

Box 3.11 Stages of the economic cycle

- *Boom* – high levels of economic growth.
- Relatively low levels of unemployment.
- Firms have busy order books.
- Prices rising as output cannot match demand.
- Consumption and investment expenditure will be high. Wages will be rising and profits increasing.
- Peak of the cycle – *overheating* economy.

Box 3.12 Stages of the economic cycle

- *Recession*: Two quarters of negative economic growth. Economy at the bottom of the cycle. Increased unemployment, unused capacity, low profits, less investment, business closures, downward price pressure.
- *Recovery*: National income and output rise. Unemployment falls. Consumption, investment and imports begin to rise. Inflationary pressures start to grow, putting upward pressure on wages.

Economic growth 69

In a recession there are less tax revenues for the government because fewer people are earning and less products are being sold. At the same time the government is likely to be paying more in subsidies and benefits which will have a negative effect on government borrowing.

Whilst increasing income is often the aim of government, so is stabilising its growth path. Instability and uncertainty make planning difficult and deter investment.

A branch of economics has emerged in recent years, the *economics of happiness*.[66] The argument goes that economic growth leads to rising living standards and, by implication, greater happiness. However research suggests that the correlation between economic growth and happiness only applies at low income levels.

Research in the UK, US and Japan has shown no increase in happiness in the past 50 years despite strong economic growth. Once basic needs are met in terms of adequate food and shelter, increasing the quantity of goods consumed makes no difference to well-being. Having a new high definition TV or a new car when you already have a perfectly functioning TV or car does not lead to a long-term increase in your well-being.

UK incomes have been squeezed more than in previous recessions. It has taken time for real wages to recover which provided useful political ammunition for the opposition Labour Party which coined the phrase 'squeezed middle', to describe the broad swathe of middle class people feeling financially hard-pressed.

The UK achieves a **Happy Planet Index (HPI)** score of 47.9 and ranks 41 of 151 countries analysed. The index is an efficiency measure, ranking countries on how many long and happy lives they produce per unit of environmental input.

Assignments

Write an 800 word overview of the performance of Chinese economy in the past five years and prospects for the current year.

Write a 300 word new story on the prospects for the UK economy in the coming year.

Glossary of key terms

GDP: a measure of the total sum of all economic activity within a country.

Happy Planet Index (HPI): a global measure of the development of economics based on factors such life expectancy, schooling, adult literacy rate and income.

Organisation for Economic Cooperation and Development (OECD): a group of 34 countries established in 1961. It aims to help governments foster sustainable economic growth policies and fight poverty.

Plenum: a meeting of the Chinese communist party's central committee.

Renminbi: the official name for the Chinese currency, which is also known as the yuan.

Recession: a period of declining GDP. Recessions are distinguished from depressions by the extent of the downturn.

Resource list

The IMF produces regional economic reports that discuss recent developments and prospects for countries in various regions. There is also country specific data and analysis and discussion of the key challenges faced by policy makers: www.inf.org/external/pubs/ft/reo/reorepts.aspx

OECD website: www.oecd.org

Eurostat: www.ec.europa.eu/eurostat

Office for National Statistics (ONS) provides UK data on a number of themes in addition to the economy including business and energy, government, population, travel and transport: www.ons.gov.uk

National Bureau of Statistics of China: www.stats.gov.cn/english

US Bureau of Economic Analysis (BEA) provides a comprehensive, up-to-date picture of the US economy: www.bea.gov

Statistics Bureau of Japan provides data on the Japanese economy: www.stat.go.jp/english

Bank of England website has 'Lessons on a plate. Topics covered relate to the work of the Bank of England and include The Great Productivity Puzzle: www.bankofengland.co.uk/education/Documents/resources/loap/productivitypuzzle.PDF

Notes

1 Kamal Ahmed (24 June 2016). 'Market turmoil as Britain chooses Brexit.' www.bbc.co.uk/news/business-36616430
2 George Parker, Michael Mackenzie and Ben Hall (25 June 2016). 'Britain turns its back on Europe'. www.ft.com/cms/s/0/e4o4c2fc-3913-11e6-9a05-82a9b15a8ee7.html
3 Karishma Vaswani (24 June 2016). 'Brexit: Asian shares fall sharply as UK votes to leave EU.' www.bbc.co.uk/news/business-36613890
4 'Statement by Christine Lagarde on the UK Referendum.' (24 June 2016). www.imf.org/external/np/sec/pr/2016/pr16303.htm
5 'China warns Brexit will "cast shadow" over global economy.' (26 June 2016). www.bbc.co.uk/news/business-36632934
6 Harriet Agnew and Naomi Rovnick (25 June 2016). 'City struggles through nightmarish day and fears for future.' www.ft.com/cms/s/0/5c55483a-3a04-11e6-a780-b48ed7b6126f.html
7 Ping Szu Chan (27 June 2016). 'UK must look beyond Europe after Brexit says CBI boss.' www.telegraph.co.uk/business/2016/06/26/uk-must-look-beyond-europe-after-brexit-says-cbi-boss
8 Arnold Martin and Laura Noonan (27 June 2016). 'Banks begin moving some operations out of Britain.' www.ft.com/s/0/a3a92744-3a52-11e6-9a05-82a9b15a8ee7.html

9 'Brexit briefing: German repurcussions.' (13 July 2016). www.ft.com/cms/s/0/e9499940-48ea-11e6-b387-64ab0a67014c.html
10 Ping Szu Chan and Christopher Williams (28 June 2016). 'UK stripped of final AAA rating and FTSE 350 surrenders £140bn in Brexit aftermath.' www.telegraph.co.uk/business/2016/06/27/george-osborne-to-speak-in-attempt-to-calm-markets-following-brexit
11 Larry Elliott, Katie Allen and Jill Treanor (25 June 2016). 'Brexit wipes $2tn off markets as Moody's lowers UK credit rating outlook.' www.theguardian.com/business/2014/june/24/bank-of-england-markets-pound-shares-plummet-brexit-vote
12 Richard Blackden and Michael Mackenzie (28 June 2016). 'Brexit waves batter global markets.' www.ft.com/cms/s/0/41dec79e3c32-11e6-9f2c-36b487ebd80a.html
13 Mark Vandevelde (24 June 2016). 'Investors flee retail stocks for fear of Brexit backlash.' www.ft.com/cms/s/0/71e81302-39ec-11e6-9a05-82a9b15a8ee7.html
14 Jane Croft (25 June 2016). 'Lawyers prepare for Brexit bonanza.' www.ft.com/cms/s/0/7c08a07a-3a02-11e6-9a05-82a9b15a8ee7.html
15 'For better or worse? The future in store for the pound, your savings, mortgage and investments.' (25 June 2016). *The Daily Telegraph*.
16 Catherine L. Mann (18 February 2016). 'OECD economic outlook, elusive global growth outlook requires urgent policy response'. www.oecd.org/newsroom/elusive-global-growth-outlook-requires-urgent-policy-response.htm
17 Catherine L. Mann (18 February 2016). 'OECD economic outlook, elusive global growth outlook requires urgent policy response'. www.oecd.org/newsroom/elusive-global-growth-outlook-requires-urgent-policy-response.htm
18 Tim Jackson (2009). *Prosperity without Growth, Economics for a Finite Planet*. UK and USA: Earthscan.
19 Professor Jackson was speaking in London at the Intelligence Squared debate, 'Is the party over? When economic stagnation becomes the new normal', on 16 May 2016.
20 Matt Egan (31 January 2016). 'Wild January stock market ends on a high note.' money.cnn.com/2016/01/29/investing/dow-january-2016-worst-month/
21 'Yellen: Brexit significant economic repercussions.' (21 June 2016). www.bbc.co.uk/news/business-36590092
22 'World economic outlook. Too slow for too long.' (12 April 2016). www.imf.org/external/pubs/cat/longres.aspx?sk=43653.0
23 Council on Foreign Relations (October 2013). 'The shale gas and tight oil boom: U.S. states' economic gains and vulnerabilities.' www.cfr.org/united-states/shale-gas-tight-oil-boom-us-states-economic-gains-vulnerabilities/p31568
24 Bloomberg News (2 December 2015). 'China's great economic shift brings little to global rebalancing.' www.bloomberg.com/news/articles/2015-12-02/china-s-great-economic-shift-brings-little-to-global-rebalancing
25 Tom Mitchell (17 January 2016). 'The ugly subtext between China's two track economy tale.' www.ft.com/cms/s/2/bb494388-bb9b-11e5-bf7e-8a339b6f2164.html
26 'China economic growth slowest in 25 years.' (19 January 2016). www.bbc.co.uk/news/business-35349576
27 Phillip Inman (19 October 2015). 'Chinese economic slowdown or a slow rebalancing?' www.theguardian.com/business/economics-blog/2015/oct/19/chinese-economic-slowdown-or-slow-rebalancing
28 Martin Jacques (2012). *When China Rules the World*. London: Penguin (second edition).
29 'Global growth forecast again revised lower to 2.4%.' (7 June 2016). www.worldbank.org/en/news/feature/2016/06/07/global-growth-forecast-again-revised-lower

72   *Economic growth*

30 HM Treasury, Lord O'Neill of Gatley, The Rt Hon George Osborne MP and Regeneration Investment Organisation (24 September 2015). 'Chancellor opens book on more than £24 billion of Northern Powerhouse investment opportunities in China.' www.gov.uk/government/news/chancellor-opens-book-on-more-than-24-billion-of-northern-powerhouse-investment-opportunities-in-china

31 John Detrixhe (20 October 2015). 'London wants to become the Center of Chinese Currency Trading.' www.bloomberg.com/news/articles/2015-10-19/renminbi-dreams-coming-true-as-president-xi-stays-at-buckingham

32 'Chinese to invest abroad in free-trade zone trial.' (29 April 2015). www.scmp.com/topics/shanghai-free-trade-zone

33 Alan Lok (2 June 2015). 'Chinese shadow banking: solution or problem?' blogs.cfainstitute.org?marketintegrity/2015/06/02/Chinese-shadow-banking-solution-or-problem/

34 Chris Papadopoullos (15 March 2016). 'Clock ticks on Argos suitors' mind games.' www.cityam.com/assets/uploads/content/2016/03/cityam-2016-03-15-56e7592fd7ae7.pdf

35 Russell Lynch (23 May 2016). 'Low growth Eurozone disappoints as Draghi's bazooka misfires.' www.standard.co.uk/business/low-growth-eurozone-disappoints-as-draghi-bazooka-misfires-a3254621.html

36 Maria Tadeo (2 December 2015). 'ECB said to present economic outlook with no major revision.' www.bloomberg.com/news/articles/2015-12-02/ecb-said-to-present-economic-forecasts-with-no-major-revisions-ihp50ib3

37 'How Spain fixed its economy.' (4 August 2015). www.bloombergview.com/articles/2015-08-04/how-spain-fixed-its-economy; Mark Deen (13 November 2015). 'French economic rebound suggests best year under Hollande.' www.bloomberg-com/news/articles/2015-11-13/french-economy-rebounds-as-oil-price-drives-consumer-spending

38 Andy Sharman (6 February 2016). 'VW postpones full-year results over emissions scandal.' www.ft.com/cms/s/0/29262182-cc13-11e5-a8ef-ea66e967dd44.html

39 'Bank of England cuts growth forecast.' (4 February 2016). www.bbc.co.uk/news/business-35493474

40 Elaine Moore, Robin Wigglesworth and Leo Lewis (6 February 2016). 'Government bond yields send recession signal.' www.ft.com/cms/s/0/821850f0-cb6c-11e5-a8ef-ea66e967dd44.html

41 Andrew Walker (18 June 2016). 'IMF says EU exit "largest near-term risk" to UK economy.' www.bbc.co.uk/news/business-36561720

42 GOV.UK (18 April 2016). 'EU referendum: HM Treasury analysis key facts.' www.gov.uk/government/news/eu-referendum-treasury-analysis-key-facts

43 GOV.UK (27 June 2016). 'Statement by the Chancellor following the EU referendum.' www.gov.uk/government/speeches/statement-by-the-chancellor-following-the-eu-referendum

44 Larry Elliott and Katie Allen (11 December 2015). 'IMF boss Christine Lagarde says she wants Britain to stay in EU.' www.theguardian.com/business/2015/dec/11/imf-lagarde-wants-britain-stay-in-eu-osborne

45 Andrew Sentence (29 January 2016). 'Britain's world-beating services are a sign of success, not failure.' www.telegraph.co.uk/finance/economics/12130053/Britains-world-beating-services-are-a-sign-of-success-not-failure.html

46 Rashid Razaq (16 May 2016). 'Bridget Jones and Doctor Strange help generate a record £649m for London.' www.standard.co.uk/goingout/film-bridget-jones-and-doctor-strange-help-generate-a-record-649m-for-london-a3249041.html

47 Russell Lynch (4 February 2016). 'Up to Osborne, not Carney, to deliver goods on productivity.' *Evening Standard*, p.51.

48 Chris Papadopoullos (23 September 2015). 'Bank of England's Ben Broadbent: UK productivity is not as bad as it looks.' www.cityam.com/224985/bank-of-englands-ben-broadbent-productivity-is-not-as-bad-as-it-looks
49 Aisha Gani (21 October 2015). 'Xi Jinping signs nuclear deal as UK and China clinch £40bn of contracts.' www.theguardian.com/world/2015/oct/21/xi-jinping-poised-to-sign-nucelar-deal-as-uk-seeks-to-clinch-£30bn-of-contracts
50 Christopher Hope (2 December 2013). 'Chinese premier Li Leqiang wants to help build HS2'. www.telegraph.co.uk/news/politics/david-cameron/10487669/Chinese-premier-Li-Leqiang-wants-to-help-build-HS2.html
51 'George Osborne urges China to pitch for £11.8bn contracts.' (24 September 2015). www.bbc.co.uk/news/uk-34341352
52 Mike Bird (13 March 2015). 'Foreign tourists are flocking to Japan in record numbers.' www.businessinsider.com.au/abenomics-driving-japanese-tourism-2015-3
53 'Forget Greece, Japan is the world's real economic time bomb.' (26 February 2015). Fortune.com/2015/02/26/japan-economic-time-bomb/
54 Friedrich Schneider, with Dominik Enste (March 2002). 'Hiding in the shadows. The growth of the underground economy.' www.imf.org/external/pubs/ft/issues30/
55 Tom Bawden (4 February 2016). 'Shell profits plunge to 13-year low but it's upbeat on BG link.' www.standard.co.uk/business/shell-profits-plunge-to-13year-low-but-it-s-upbeat-on-bg-link-a3173191.htm
56 Kiran Stacey (5 February 2016). 'North Sea oil companies in danger amid debt spillage.' www.ft.com/cms/s/0/e67e4dac-ca76-11e5-a8ef-ea66e967dd44.html
57 Ambrose Evans-Pritchard (8 December 2015). 'Fear grips market as oil leads commodity crash.' www.telegraph.co.uk/finance/economics/12040314/Fear-grips-market-as-oil-leads-commodity-crash.html
58 Matt Egan (15 January 2016). 'Dow plunges 391 points as fear grips markets.' www.money.cnn.com/2016/01/15/investing/stocks-markets-dow-china-oil/
59 'Iran seeks $30bn of new oil contracts.' (29 November 2015). www.bbc.co.uk/news/business-34957575
60 Holly Ellyatt (13 November 2015). 'Record oil stockpiles an "unprecedented buffer":IEA.'www.cnbc.com/2015/11/13/record-oil-stockpiles-an-unprecedented-buffer-iea.html
61 Annabelle Williams (28 January 2016). 'Saudi Arabia under stress: Opec leader is adapting to $30.' www.cityam.com/233315/saudi-arabia-under-stress-opec-leader-is-adapting-to-30-brent-crude-prices-and-its-widening-budget-deficit-by-privatising-state-run-oil-company-aramco-and-will-not-cut-oil-supply
62 'Iran seeks $30bn of new oil contracts.' (29 November 2015). www.bbc.co.uk/news/business-34957575
63 University of Manchester (10 September 2014). 'New £60m Engineering Innovation Centre to be based in Manchester.' www.manchester.ac.uk/discover/news/new-60m-engineering-innovation-centre-to-be-based-in-Manchester
64 UK Space Agency (13 December 2015). 'National space policy.' www.gov.uk/government/publications/national-space-policy
65 David Crossland (25 November 2015). 'Refugees deliver boost to German economy.' www.thetimes.co.uk/tto/business/markets/europe/article4622598.ece
66 Alan Wheatley (December 2015). 'A generous-hearted life.' www.imf.org/external/pubs/ft/fandd/2015/12/people.htm

4 Labour markets

In this chapter you will learn about different types of unemployment, how to measure unemployment and the problem of high youth unemployment around the world and specifically what the UK government is doing to tackle it. It also explains how to produce an informative and newsworthy labour market report when monthly labour market data is released. By the end of this chapter you should be able to discuss some key labour market issues including the minimum wage, migration, flexibility and demographics.

There is a strong correlation between economic activity and employment. That makes sense. If the economy is performing strongly businesses will be optimistic and making money and will want to take on workers to meet demand for their goods and services.

In 2015, the UK was the second fastest growing Western economy, after the US. The independent Office for Budget Responsibility forecasts that one million jobs will be created in the UK in the five years to 2020.

One of the features of the financial crisis was the very high levels of unemployment, particularly youth unemployment, seen in several struggling Eurozone countries such as Greece, Spain and Ireland. Greek youth unemployment is still almost 50% years after the onset of the financial crisis. Even in the countries where unemployment has not risen steeply, such as the UK, real wages have often been squeezed by austerity measures resulting in a marked deterioration in living standards for large sections of the population. This has had a knock-on political effect with discontent rising about the widening inequality gap within society.

Table 4.1 Unemployment rates (%)

Greece	23.2 (July 2016)
Spain	19.3
Germany	4.1
UK	4.9
US	5.0

Source: Eurostat, September 2016

Journalistic practice

Labour markets provide a rich seam of stories from news items about the latest unemployment statistics to features about growth of self-employment, changes in the nature of work with analysis of what are the 'hot' sectors to be in, wages, migration, skills shortages and policy initiatives to tackle specific labour market problems such as long-term or youth unemployment. There is plenty of scope for illustration by way of graphs, interviews with the unemployed or politicians.

There is often a blending of economic and political coverage of labour markets given its importance both socially and economically. This was seen in news reports in September 2015 when 1700 workers were laid off when SSI announced it was halting steel and iron production in Redcar, Teeside. News reports included calls by MPs for government assistance given the region is already an unemployment hotspot.

Publication of the unemployment figures in the UK, US and Europe is always a major news event, particularly in the UK and US where the central banks specifically take the unemployment level into account when determining the future course of interest rates.

A news report should include the latest figures, workforce participation rate, comment on whether the results are in line with market expectations and what they tell us about the state of the economy. What was the employment picture across various industries? What happened to wages? Include a quote from a politician or economist and reaction in the stock market and foreign exchanges.

Example of labour market graphic

The following data could be included:

- Employment total (millions)
- Unemployment total (millions)
- Male (millions)
- Female (millions)
- Youth (millions).

Other graphs can include hours worked and prices versus wages showing how real incomes have been squeezed.

Unemployment is what's known as a lagging indicator. Strong economic growth should help to lower unemployment both by existing businesses taking on new staff and new small businesses starting up.

76 *Labour markets*

Figure 4.1 Job centre in England. Image courtesy of Jim O'Donnell/Alamy.

Measurement of unemployment

There are two ways in which unemployment can be calculated.

The government can undertake a survey of the population to identify the employed and the unemployed. The international standard for this method has been produced by the International Labour Organisation (ILO) and is the basis of the **Labour Force Survey (LFS)**. This survey generates monthly LFS unemployment statistics. The ILO definition of the unemployment rate is the most widely used labour market indicator because of its international comparability and relatively timely availability.

The government can also count all those who register as unemployed. In the UK, claimant count unemployment statistics are produced based on the numbers claiming benefit for being unemployed.

Unemployment can be expressed in two ways. It can be stated as an absolute figure, as millions of workers or it can be stated as a relative measure, as a percentage of the workforce, the *unemployment rate*.

Discussing unemployment as a percentage rate is more useful when comparing against other countries which may have larger populations. The *size of the workforce* is likely to change over time. For example, the changing nature of work in the UK and the growth of the consumer society means there are more female workers than say in the 1950s.

The UK labour market continues to defy the gloom elsewhere. The unemployment rate was 4.9% in the three months to August 2016, the lowest in a decade. The employment rate was at a record high of 74.5% but average wage growth was a subdued 2.3% including bonuses.[1] This was much lower than before the financial crisis and is a major factor in smaller than expected income tax receipts for the government. The average figure masked a mixed picture. Skill shortages in the construction sector led to a generous 7.2% rise in average annual pay in the three months to January 2016.[2]

Unemployment is a globally important issue. The International Monetary Fund (IMF) Articles of Agreement commit the institution to 'the promotion and maintenance of high levels of employment and real income'.[3] Whilst a debate can be had about how successful it has been in this regard, what is less questionable is the link between employment and social cohesion.

The United Nations has acknowledged the seriousness of the problem of world unemployment by including it in its sustainable development goals. Number 8 of the 17 goals is to 'promote inclusive and sustainable economic growth, employment and decent work for all'.[4]

Box 4.1 ILO unemployment outlook

- Global unemployment forecast to rise to more than 212 million by 2019.
- ILO highlights greater inequality resulting in 'sluggish jobs recovery and social instability'.
- European unemployment is expected to decline gradually although it will take longer in southern European countries such as Spain and Greece with very high unemployment rates.
- High unemployment is expected to continue in the Middle East and North Africa.

Youth unemployment

Past IMF reports have described youth unemployment as a 'social and economic time bomb'. Across the OECD, youth unemployment is more than double the unemployment rate affecting the general population. Youth unemployment is particularly high in Greece and Spain.

Although youth unemployment is off its peak, it is still above the levels seen before the financial crisis and the International Labour Organisation (ILO) says the youth unemployment crisis 'is far from over'.

Figures published by the ILO show that the global youth unemployment rate has stabilised at 13%, equivalent to 73.3 million people, compared to 11.7% pre-crisis. However that number masks different stories around the globe.[5]

78 *Labour markets*

Amongst Eurozone countries, youth unemployment is highest in Greece at 42.7% and in Spain at 42.6%. In Italy it is 37.1% and in the UK it is 13.7%.[6] These figures compare with 11.5% youth unemployment in the US in August 2016.[7]

Worryingly, in the European Union (EU) more than one in three of the unemployed youth has been looking for work for more than one year. In February 2013, the EU launched a Euro 6bn Youth Employment Initiative (YEI) to try to get more young people into work, arguably too little, too late. Greece, Spain and Italy are the main beneficiaries of the YEI.[8]

Some commentators suggest that global youth unemployment may be much higher than the ILO's figures due to poor data collection and underemployment in poor countries. Concern about unemployment was cited as one of the factors fuelling the Arab Spring uprisings. The Middle East and North Africa (MENA) have the world's highest youth unemployment rates with even college graduates struggling to get a job. There is a particular problem with training and development of staff in many MENA countries.

Youth unemployment also rose in most of Asia and the Pacific in 2012–2014. This is thought to be largely a reflection of the rapid growth of many of these economies and the associated movement of workers from low paid steady jobs in the countryside to urban areas in search of higher paying jobs.

One of the main reasons cited generally for the high levels of youth unemployment is the mismatch between skills young people have and those which employers want in the workplace. The ILO forecasts that between 2014 and 2019 youth unemployment will rise by up to 8% in parts of Europe, South America and Africa.

Youth unemployment appears to be a structural problem in the UK with the rate staying high even as the economy grows relatively strongly. There are over 800,000 young people who are not in education, employment or training (**NEET**) in the UK, equivalent to around 11% of all 16–24 year olds.

Box 4.2 NEETs (15–29 year olds)

- Amongst the highest in Europe: 27.1% Greece, 23.0% Bulgaria and 20.9% Spain.
- Amongst the lowest in Europe: 8.4% Denmark.
- UK Q2 2016, 11.7% (16–24 year olds).

Source: Eurostat October 2016

Research by the Institute for Public Policy Research (IPPR) suggests that the move away from manufacturing into high skilled service sector jobs may be a contributory factor. Data shows that between 1995 and 2007, the share of youth working in manufacturing halved, while the number of under-25s employed to work in low-skilled jobs – primarily in service industries – rose from 37% to 50% during the same period. In addition, most of these new jobs were temporary ones.[9]

The youth contract

There has been no shortage of policy initiatives proposed to address the problem of youth unemployment, but the government's record in tackling it long term has been disappointing.

In 2012, a *youth contract* was launched that offered businesses up to £2,275 for taking on an under-25 who has been unemployed for a minimum of six months. However the scheme was stopped early in 2014 with only a tiny fraction of the 500,000 it targeted being helped into work.[10]

Criticism of the youth contract

Subsidies were handed to companies that would have employed young people anyway, for example in the retail and hospitality industries.

Local government leaders have consistently called for resources to be focused on locally run schemes that have tended to be more effective. Such schemes would involve partnerships between local businesses and employers, Jobcentres, local councils and specialist youth charities.

More targeted back to work programmes should be created engaging small businesses; these account for almost half of private sector employment.

Schemes should be employer-led and sector based from the outset so that young people are trained in the specific areas that businesses need.

No account was taken of the different regional needs and individual needs of young people, many of whom have issues with drug or alcohol problems, mental illness or lack basic numeracy and literacy skills.

The coalition government's Work Programme, established in 2011, to help the long-term unemployed and the young, has also failed to make a significant impact. The *workfare* programme was devised by former Work and Pensions Minister Iain Duncan Smith. Under the scheme young job seekers with less than six months work history complete 13 weeks of unpaid work in order to retain their entitlement to claim Job Seekers Allowance.[11]

Criticism of workfare

It limits the time available for job search and fails to provide the skills and experience valued by employers.

There are a growing number of workfare schemes that target different groups of people such as trainees rather than the long-term unemployed.

Workfare participants are paid below the minimum wage, averaging £1.78 an hour for their benefits.

The scheme missed every target set by the government in 2014. Only about a quarter of people who have completed workfare placements get a paid job afterwards; 21–24 year olds with more experience tend to get jobs regardless of whether they have done workfare or not.

In trying to make a sustained attack on youth unemployment there could be useful lessons for the government from the successful example of countries such as Germany, Denmark and Sweden where vocational and academic training are more integrated. This approach appears to provide young people with the skills that businesses want. This is reflected in a relatively low youth unemployment rate of 6.8% in Germany.[12]

For many years, British business as a whole has been complaining about the general quality of the youth pool of workers, even in basic areas such as English grammar and personal communication skills.

In his report 'Remember the young ones: improving career opportunities for Britain's young people', Tony Dolphin, IPPR chief economist, outlines five critical policy areas that he says need a focused response to help ensure a successful school-to-work transition.[13]

1. Employers need to be involved in young people's training.
2. Vocational education in England needs to be reformed so that it is held in high esteem by employers and young people alike.
3. There should be more high quality apprenticeships.
4. Specialist careers advisors should be employed in schools to offer careers education and guidance, engaging local employers to provide students with up-to-date information on education and training options and on opportunities in the local labour market.
5. A distinct work, training and benefits system should be established for young people. This would include a youth allowance, replacing all existing benefit payments, a youth job guarantee providing paid work experience for 18–24 year olds who have been seeking work for six months and a personal careers advisor who would help young people to find work or to identify appropriate further education and training opportunities.

Comparative unemployment rates

There is a differing picture of general unemployment across Europe. Prolonged austerity measures in Spain and Greece have decimated the labour market. Unemployment rates are 19.3% (September 2016) and 23.2% (July 2016) respectively. In contrast, Germany has continued to benefit from export growth which has meant that unemployment has remained the lowest in the Euro area at 4.1% in September 2016.[14]

Workers in emerging and developing economies often struggle to find formal, stable employment. Many people work in poverty earning less than $2 per day. The ILO says that millions of young people in low-income countries leave school to take up jobs when they are too young. According to its report, 31% of youth in low-income countries have no educational qualifications at all, compared to 6% in lower middle-income countries and 2% in upper middle-income countries.

As China and India develop their economies, unemployment is expected to rise as people move from low-income agricultural jobs, to middle-income jobs in manufacturing, and then on to higher incomes in the service sector.

The ILO report highlights a persistent gender gap with young women's participation in the labour force being much lower than men in most regions. Women are also more likely to be unemployed than similarly qualified men.

Whilst there are signs of economic recovery in the Eurozone, unemployment is expected to remain significantly above pre-financial crisis levels for some time to come. The employment picture in the US is far rosier than Europe and has been one of the bright spots in the global economy.

Figures published in November 2016 showed the US economy adding 161,000 jobs in October. The unemployment rate remained unchanged at 4.9% – an eight year low. Employment continued to increase in health care, professional and business services, and financial activities.[15]

The US economy grew at an annualised rate of 2.9% in the third quarter of 2016, the strongest quarter of growth in two years. This was attributed to higher inventories and a soybean-related jump in exports but household spending was lower.[16] However, like the UK, good employment growth has not fed through to significant wage growth. In the US, year-on-year growth in average hourly earnings slowed to 2.2% in February from 2.5% in January.[17]

A number of possible causes for the lack of significant earnings growth have been mooted. The number of people looking for work is still higher than before the 2008 financial crisis, more people are working part-time who would prefer to be full time and there still remain a significant number of long-term unemployed.[18]

In March 2014, the Federal Reserve stopped using the unemployment rate as a gauge to the strength of the economy.[19] Similar to the UK, US unemployment fell faster than economists expected and was no longer seen as a reliable indicator of when interest rates should rise. In 2012, the Fed set an unemployment target of 6.5% to signify an era of low interest rates. On domestic grounds the Federal Reserve might wish to raise US interest rates again but may delay the next move up given the stormy world economic climate.

There's concern amongst economists about the falling US labour force participation rate, which is already at its lowest level since 1977.[20]

In June 2016 62.6% of Americans aged 16 and older worked or looked for work compared with 66% in December 2007, the start of the last recession.

Incomes

In the wake of the financial crisis, many employees, particularly in the UK public sector, have had a pay freeze. Given that inflation during the period has not been zero, employees have suffered a cut in real income. As part of its programme of austerity measures the UK government has been reducing the number of people employed in the public sector. In March 2016, there were 5.4 million public sector employees, the lowest number since comparable records began in 1999.[21]

The average earnings figure is watched closely by the Bank of England as it shows wage inflation in the economy. One reason cited by the Bank for keeping UK interest rates at record lows for several years, is that inflation has not been boosted by rising wages. However pay rates are starting to move up in areas where there are skill shortages such as construction and financial services.

In the run-up to the UK general election in May 2015, the gap between wages and the cost of living became a big political issue prompting the opposition Labour Party to talk about a 'cost of living crisis'.

Sluggish economic growth coupled with rising unemployment is expected to lead to a further widening of the income and wealth inequality gap worldwide. The richest 10% of the world will hold 30–40% of total income, while the poorest 10% will earn as little as 2%.

Journalistic practice

How do public sector wages compare with those available in the private sector? UK public sector pay was frozen for many years during the recession.

A rich seam of stories can be mined from executive pay. Voting records of remuneration committees are often stories in their own right along with reports of the huge bonuses awarded to company bosses irrespective of how well the companies have performed under their stewardship, so-called 'rewards for failure'.

Box 4.3 National Minimum Wage

- Introduced in the UK in 1999.
- Minimum amount per hour that most workers in the UK are entitled to be paid. In 2017, the rates for the National Minimum Wage and National Living Wage are:
    - £7.50 for workers aged 25 and over.
    - £7.05 for workers aged 21–24.
    - £5.60 the 18–20 age rate.
    - £4.05 the 16–17 age rate for workers above school leaving age but under 18.
    - £3.50 apprentices under 19 or first year of apprenticeship if 19 or over.

National Minimum Wage (NMW)

In April 1999, the UK government introduced a National Minimum Wage.[22] This set an hourly rate that employers could not go below. The single largest beneficiaries of the National Minimum Wage were female part-time workers. Particular industries are known for their low pay, for example agriculture, hairdressing and social care. In October 2015, the high street retailer Monsoon was 'named and shamed' for not paying around 1400 of its staff the minimum wage.[23]

National Living Wage (NLW)

The minimum wage effectively acts as a floor to wages. The former UK Chancellor George Osborne said he wanted 'an above-inflation increase in the minimum wage'.[24] The Japanese Prime Minister has also called for minimum wage rises.[25]

In his Budget in July 2015, Mr Osborne surprised many by announcing the introduction of a National Living Wage (NLW) to take effect in April 2016. The National Living Wage is higher than that likely recommended by the Low Pay Commission which has historically advised on the level. The minimum wage will still apply for workers aged 24 and under. Minimum wage rates change every October. National Living Wage rates change every April.

In November 2015, prior to his departure as director general of the CBI business lobby group, John Cridland said that the National Living Wage was 'a gamble' and warned that it could 'speed up the replacement of workers with machines'.[26]

A survey carried out by the Manpower recruitment agency in September 2015 of 2,100 employers showed many were scaling back their recruitment plans for the rest of the year. Employers were attempting to avoid paying the new rate by using groups of self-employed workers or employing younger people.[27]

The Office for Budget Responsibility (OBR) estimates there will be:

- 60,000 fewer people employed as a result of the NLW;
- a small fall in economic output;
- a small rise in consumer price inflation as companies raise prices to cover the extra costs.[28]

The imposition of higher wages is a concern in the social care industry which has traditionally suffered from recruitment problems and low wages. Contractors in the long-term care sector said the costs would have to be passed on in higher charges to local authorities and the NHS. The hospitality sector will also face hefty bills falling into line with the NLW.

From April 7, the NLW will rise to £7.50 an hour for people aged over 25. The minimum wage will rise 4% from £7.20 to £7.50 an hour. The NLW is expected to rise so that it reaches 60% of average hourly wages by April 2020, a figure estimated by the OBR at around £9.35 per hour. The NLW will mean a generous 13% increase in the minimum wage by 2020 compared to what would have been expected under the previous system.

Resolution Foundation predictions

- Six million workers, 23% of all UK employees, will be affected by the NLW by 2020.
- £760 added annually to pre-tax wages.
- £4.5bn added to the wage bill of British firms in 2020.
- More women than men will be affected, 29% versus 18% by 2020.
- Workers in the Midlands, Wales and Yorkshire will benefit the most from the introduction of the NLW.[29]

Journalistic practice

Interview bosses in small and large firms in a range of sectors on how they see the NLW affecting their businesses.
Interview workers set to benefit e.g. cleaner, care home worker, bar staff. Illustrate the feature with graphics of wages across a range of different sectors.

In July 2014, the German parliament controversially approved the country's first minimum wage. The wage was set at 8.5 euros per hour, which is higher than the equivalent in the US and UK. It came into effect in January 2014 and will be reviewed annually from 1 January 2018. The minimum wage does not cover minors, interns, trainees or long-term unemployed people for their first six months at work.

Traditionally German employers negotiated with unions. There has been a big increase in non-unionised jobs with low pay which increased political pressure for a minimum wage. The introduction of the minimum wage does not appear to have had a negative impact on the creation of jobs in Germany.[30]

Arguments in favour of a minimum wage

It prevents workers receiving developing world rates of pay. It gives a minimum reward to labour which can be seen as a 'fair' reward.
It should help reduce the inequality between low-income and high-income groups. There are notable benefits to particular groups of low paid workers- care workers in the UK and uneducated and unskilled workers in eastern Germany.

It should mean that less people have to receive benefits.

It forces employers to offer 'regular' jobs that are covered by social security.

Minimum wages in developed countries can help developing countries become more competitive. Low value unskilled jobs will tend to disappear in rich countries that introduce a minimum wage.

Arguments against a minimum wage

It creates unemployment by raising the price of labour. The Low Pay Commission in the UK has warned that it might be deterring firms from taking on young workers.

It generates more bureaucracy, or 'red tape', for individual firms. This is particularly burdensome for small firms. Higher costs will be passed onto consumers in higher prices.

It may reduce firms' profits and therefore funds for investment.

Companies may move production facilities to other countries where labour is cheaper.

It does little to reduce poverty in the UK. This is because most households in the lower income levels are made up of households with no wage earners. These are pensioner households, single parent families and households where all the adults are unemployed.

Costs of unemployment

1. The main problem with unemployment is that it is inefficient. If there are unemployed resources in the economy, then fewer goods and services are being produced than it is possible to produce. There is also a loss of human capital as workers lose skills.
2. High levels of unemployment in an area are likely to lead to lower living standards as there will be less income. There will be less spending on local goods and services which can lead to more unemployment. National retailers have seen a greater slowdown in trade in some of their branches in northern cities as public sector job cuts bite.

    Various government agencies have been deliberately sited in northern cities of the UK to provide employment e.g. the Department for Work and Pensions is based in Newcastle. However public sector employment has dropped by over 300,000 since 2010 as the government seeks to reduce its spending. The Office for Budget Responsibility predicts a total of a million lost jobs over the decade from 2010. These cuts will have a disproportionate effect on areas such as northern England and Northern Ireland. A fifth of workers in north-east England are employed in the public sector, the highest proportion in England.
3. There will be more social problems as people have more free time and lower incomes, which may cause a rise in crime, particularly in domestic burglaries.

4   There will be more spending by the government on benefits. There will be less income for the government from taxation. The government will earn less from direct taxation because people are not earning, and indirect taxation revenue will also fall because people are not spending as much. With less income and higher spending the government's budget position will worsen.
5   There will be increased health costs as the unemployed tend to suffer more illness, such as heart attacks in later life, mental stress and malnutrition.
6   Less investment may occur if firms lose confidence in the economy.

Types of unemployment

Most workers who lose their jobs move quickly into new ones. This is known as **frictional unemployment**.

Seasonal unemployment: this affects demand for some workers, such as construction workers, those working in tourism and agriculture e.g. fruit pickers in East Anglia. This type of unemployment rises in the winter and falls in the summer when these workers are taken on again.

Structural unemployment: in the UK, failure to compete against cheaper overseas producers, principally in Asia, has led to high levels of unemployment in particular geographic regions. For example, we see this in the former mining areas of Yorkshire and Scotland. In December 2015, Kellingley Colliery in North Yorkshire, England's last remaining deep coal mine, closed.[31]

Wales used to have a large steel production industry, north-east England was famous for shipbuilding, steel and chemicals and parts of Lancashire had a large textile industry.

What remains of the UK steel industry was dealt a heavy blow when thousands of job losses were announced within a couple of weeks in the autumn of 2015.[32]

The job losses which occurred in the Teeside area and Scotland were blamed on the Chinese dumping their cheap subsidised steel. Imports of Chinese steel accounted for 11% of UK demand in 2015 up from 2% in 2011. The UK steel industry faces higher costs for business rates and energy. It is estimated that one in six UK steelworkers face losing their jobs if cheaper imports continue to flood the market. In January 2016, Tata Steel announced that it was planning around 1,000 job cuts.[33]

SSI Redcar, one of the UK's biggest steelworks, closed in October 2015 after 98 years with the loss of 2,200 jobs. One labour MP said the closure was 'industrial vandalism'. Recognising the serious blow to the area, the government promised up to £80m to support people who had lost their jobs and lessen the impacts on the local economy.

The unemployment rate in north-east England is the highest in the UK at 6.8% compared to 3.7% in south-east England.[34] In northern cities such as Glasgow, Nottingham and Liverpool, more than three out of every ten households has no one in work.

Without *retraining* and *geographic mobility* these workers become long-term unemployed. High house prices in the south of England where there is more work prevent many potential employees from moving out of areas of high unemployment. As the pace of structural change in the world economy accelerates, this is likely to be a growing problem.

In the UK, there is very much a north/south divide in terms of employment with London and the south-east very dominated by service industries, notably finance in the City of London and telecoms and technology clustered around the so-called M4 corridor, the motorway running through to places like Reading and Newbury. These days technology skills are a key determinant of economic success. In Reading around a quarter of the city's GDP is related to technology. It is one of the fastest growing cities in the UK.

Capital cities always attract a lot of bright individuals and London is no exception. However there is evidence of a major brain drain from the regions of the UK to London.

Analysis by the Centre for Cities, the independent research and policy institute, shows that the UK is effectively a two-tier economy. Its 2015 'Cities Outlook' report found that for every 12 net new jobs created between 2004 and 2013 in cities in the south of England, only one was created in cities throughout the rest of Great Britain. During the period under review London's number of jobs increased by 17.1%.[35]

Northern powerhouse

Former chancellor George Osborne spearheaded a plan to create a 'northern powerhouse' to try to reduce the UK's economic reliance on London and the south-east of England.[36] Greater Manchester is the focus of the programme with Sheffield, Liverpool and Leeds expected to benefit to a lesser degree. The area in question is home to around 15 million people. Greater Manchester is benefiting from growth in professional services and local politicians and business leaders working together for the good of the region.[37]

Regional economic output can be measured by gross value added (GVA), which measures the contribution to the economy of each individual producer, industry or sector in the UK. GVA figures illustrate the scale of the North/South divide. London's total output is 2.3 times that of the North-East, two times the North-West and 2.1 times that of Yorkshire and the Humber.

Local businesses and politicians are calling for serious investment in increasing capacity and connectivity between the North's major cities on the railways. There is criticism that money is not following the rhetoric and some question whether cities with distinct personalities and historic rivalries such as Manchester and Liverpool will work together as one unit. Amongst the attractions for businesses thinking of investing in the area are strong manufacturing capability and expertise in science, technology and the service sectors.[38]

Increasingly the major global cities such as London, New York, Shanghai, Hong Kong and Sydney are competing against each other for jobs and investment. They are major drivers of national prosperity.

Labour market issues

> **Box 4.4** Issues facing the labour market
>
> - European demographic time bomb
> - Flexibility of workforce
> - Skills
> - Productivity.

There are a number of serious labour market issues that need to be addressed. One of the key ones facing European business in the future is the increasing average age of the population, the so-called demographic time bomb. Germany is expected to have 15 million less people by 2050. Fewer workers will have an inevitable negative impact on economic growth.

Angela Merkel has adopted the moral high ground in allowing unfettered numbers of migrants into Germany despite opposition from some of her political colleagues. Mass migration is one way of addressing the demographic issue. In the 1960s, hundreds of thousands of Turkish people moved to Germany for work, the so-called Gastarbeiter, and played a major role in building the German prosperity we see today.[39]

Siemens, the giant German engineering firm, is offering apprenticeships to refugee asylum seekers. It thinks such employees will be more highly motivated than the average applicant. Language tuition is being given to refugees. There is a view taken within Germany that education and integration of the new arrivals will be good for the whole society.

China, the world's most populous nation with 1.3bn people, is going to get even bigger following the surprise decision by the Chinese authorities in 2015 to end its 'one child' policy. It too is facing a problem of an ageing population and with it a loss of competitiveness to other Asian nations.[40]

Total fertility in Europe has fallen dramatically since the 'baby boom' of the 1950s to well below replacement levels. Child and adult mortality rates have also declined while average life expectancies have risen by up to 10 years. The richer countries of northern and western Europe tend to lead their southern and eastern neighbours in these changes.

Firms will need to consider how to recruit older workers and how to retain their younger ones. It also means that many organisations will have to review their pension arrangements. The ageing of the labour force in major economies such as Japan, Germany, the US and UK may adversely affect pay, productivity and mobility thereby reducing the international competitiveness of these nations.

In the UK, anti-discriminatory legislation has been introduced which means that 65 is no longer the default retirement age. Since April 2011, employers have been unable to force someone to retire at 65. Critics argue that it will make it harder for younger people to find jobs and some businesses worry that they will lose their best, younger members of staff, faced with a lack of promotion opportunities.

However, the government needs people to work for longer to keep up income tax receipts and reduce the burden on pension funds as Britain's population ages. Research has shown that over half of people aged 65 cannot afford to give up their jobs, a number unlikely to fall given the high costs of living and cutbacks in social care.

Labour is a vital resource in business and therefore in the economy as a whole. Unemployment levels tend to ebb and flow with the wider economy.

Flexibility

Given the rapid pace of technological innovation and the global nature of many markets, a job for life is no longer what is expected when you enter the labour market. Flexibility is the buzz word these days as you are likely to have several employers during your working life and, depending on the sector you are working in, may have a stint working in a foreign country.

Nowadays, major international companies in both manufacturing and financial services expect promising middle ranking executives in the company to have a few years working in Asia, particularly China, if they want to be promoted eventually to executive positions.

The UK has relatively flexible labour markets compared to the rest of the European Union. In the EU, there is much stricter employment protection legislation so people tend to stay in their jobs for longer relative to workers in the UK. The French labour market is notoriously rigid. The socialist President Francois Hollande recognises that things need to change and is offering tax breaks which should help companies lower labour costs and thereby boost job creation especially for low-skilled workers.[41]

With the rapid rise of *zero hours contracts*, there is concern that the balance of flexibility may have swung too far in favour of UK employers. Under such contracts, employees have no guarantee of regular hours or regular pay. Large numbers of 16–24 year olds are on such contracts, often working in retail.[42] The controversial contracts suit some workers such as students with part-time jobs. Figures from the Office for National Statistics show a record 903,000 or 2.9% of British workers were on zero hours contracts in the three months to June 2016 – up from 747,000 in 2015.[43]

Migration

A flexible and efficient labour force is a key prerequisite for a competitive economy. In the global economy, the search for workers to fill labour and skill shortages often crosses national borders. So for example in the UK, the government is keen to attract highly specialist experts. However, the CBI business lobby group is concerned that some large companies are unable to fill vacant jobs because of a cap on Tier 2 general visas for skilled workers. Firms must demonstrate that they cannot fill a post with a British worker before they can sponsor an application for this visa.

As Britain contemplates its long-term position within the European Union and pressure grows to limit the scale of migration, Standard & Poor's, the ratings agency, has suggested that immigration has been a major factor in the economic success of the UK. 'It is our view that significant net immigration into the UK over the past decade has improved the sovereign's economic and fiscal performance'.[44]

Under EU legislation there is free movement of goods and services including people. This principle is being severely tested by the mass influx of refugees fleeing war in Syria and economic migrants from sub Saharan Africa and eastern European countries such as Rumania.

Journalistic practice

In September 2015, the press was full of stories about the different approaches taken by European nations to deal with the migrant crisis. High prominence was given to Germany's shock decision to unilaterally re-introduce what it said were temporary border controls, as it buckled under the strain of thousands of refugees seeking to settle in the country. There was much debate about whether the migrant crisis would end up breaking the EU.

The negative migrant stories can be balanced with those reflecting the desire of the business community to be able to bring in international talent to maintain London's status as a global hub. Include a quote from organisations such as the London First business group and the employers' organisation, the CBI.

The Migration Advisory Committee (MAC) is a group of experts which advises the government on immigration. After the UK general election in May 2015, Prime Minister David Cameron asked the MAC to look at proposals to cut migration from outside the European Economic Area (EEA), including raising salary thresholds for skilled workers applying for Tier 2 visas. After a preliminary consultation, the MAC said that the government should think carefully before lifting the salary threshold, which currently stands at £20,800 per year for new hires and £41,500 for long-term intra-company transfers.

With much of the Eurozone still showing only tentative signs of recovery from the recession, immigration has become a highly charged political issue. The member nations cannot agree on how best to tackle the global migration crisis. A large migrant workforce has been a feature of the European labour market for many years, e.g. workers from Turkey in Germany, and Polish workers in England. However the scale of the migration in 2015 was on a level not seen since World War II with an estimated one million migrants entering the EU.

At the height of the Eurozone financial crisis, the economic woes of Ireland, Greece, Spain and Poland were reflected in emigrants outnumbering immigrants.

Across Europe, migrants tend to be concentrated in sectors such as agriculture, construction, manufacturing, healthcare, domestic work or hotels and restaurants. Research suggests there is substantial underutilisation of highly skilled foreign labour already residing in the EU due to unemployment and over-qualification. Mark Carney, Governor of the Bank of England, has said that migrant workers are not to blame for lacklustre UK productivity, which has perplexed economists and contributed to low growth in household incomes.[45]

Skill shortages

Skill shortages are a major problem in the UK. Employers are struggling to fill vacancies, particularly in the north-east and north-west which has an impact on growth. Talented staff are proving hard to find in sufficient numbers in information technology, IT, engineering and finance and even for some entry level jobs. This will put upward pressure on wages.

Many large companies are concerned that tighter visa regulations for non-EU skilled workers are hampering their ability to hire talent from around the world, putting the UK at a competitive disadvantage. The pharmaceutical, science and engineering sectors are particularly affected by the clampdown on skilled migration.[46]

There is lots of work to be done to provide people with the skills that potential employers want. There is a widely held view that the education system is failing to deliver the skills needed for long-term global success.[47]

> **Journalistic practice**
>
> Report survey findings of skill shortages in particular sectors. What, if any, pressure is it exerting on wages? Include quotes from one of the researchers and what action is being taken to try to close the skills gap.

The UK's ruling Conservative government is keen to see businesses offering more *apprenticeships*. This is the traditional way of teaching skills to school leavers involving both college and on-the-job training. The think tank IPPR says 'youth unemployment is lower in countries where the vocational route into employment through formal education and training is as clear as the academic route'.[48] Germany has a long established system of apprenticeships.

The UK government's focus is on high value added sectors such as pharmaceuticals, technology, science and the creative industries. The rapid growth of artificial intelligence poses a threat not only to low-skilled jobs but to those which involve administration and the processing of lots of data, such as accountants, radiologists and contract lawyers.

In March 2016, Royal Bank of Scotland announced it was cutting hundreds of face-to-face customer service jobs and replacing them with automated 'robo-advisors'.[49] In contrast, jobs which require high levels of personal interaction such as teaching, nursing and personal training are likely to face less competition from technology.

In the UK, there is still a widespread view that an academic education is more highly valued than vocational training. Research by the Chartered Institute of Personnel and Development showed fewer than a fifth of parents believe an on-the-job training scheme has the same status as a university education.[50]

Non-accelerating Inflation Rate of Unemployment (NAIRU)

> **Box 4.5** NAIRU
>
> - Non-accelerating inflation rate of unemployment (NAIRU).
> - Level of unemployment which is neither so low that wages are likely to move up nor so high that wage settlements are likely to be trending down.
> - Rate determined by time lag in finding a job, structural unemployment, inadequate incentives to work and state of business cycle.

This is the level of unemployment which is neither so low that wages are likely to move up nor so high that wage settlements are likely to be trending down. As its name suggests, the non-accelerating inflation rate of unemployment is the rate that is neutral for inflation, neither boosting it nor restraining it.

The **NAIRU** used to be called the natural rate because some economists argued that the economy would naturally return to this level if left to itself. In the US, NAIRU is thought to be 5.1%. In the Eurozone it is thought to be nearer 8%.[51]

Why is NAIRU not zero and why does it differ from country to country?

In practice, full employment is impossible for a number of reasons. Firstly, there are people who have lost their job and take time to find another one and then there is the structural unemployment where people have the wrong skills or are in the wrong place to find jobs. The third reason for unemployment is inadequate incentives to take work.

If, by taking work, people lose too many benefits and face too much taxation, then the incentives to work are not great. Governments are constantly trying to strike a balance between encouraging people to get back into work and compensating them for losing their jobs.

Hidden economy

In many countries, particularly in Europe, there has been an increase in the number of people who are unemployed and receive benefits but also do casual work in what's known as the 'hidden or informal' economy.[52]

Such people may be disinclined to return to normal taxed work because they would be worse off. High rates of tax and generous benefits make this a particular problem in Europe. It is something that the UK coalition government is trying to tackle with lower taxes for the lowest paid workers.

The final cause of unemployment is lack of demand owing to the state of the business cycle. Weak demand can persist for a prolonged period, taking unemployment well above the natural rate and depressing inflation.

Assignments

Do you agree or disagree with the concept of a minimum wage? Explain your reasoning.

In 800 words, write an article on UK youth unemployment and how it is being tackled.

Glossary of key terms

Claimant count: the number of individuals claiming unemployment benefit at any given time.

Cyclical unemployment: occurs when there is a general low demand for labour within an economy such as seen during a recession.

Frictional unemployment: time taken for workers to move between jobs.

Labour Force Survey: measure of unemployment based on the number of people who want to work but who are not employed.

National Living Wage (NLW): became law on 1 April 2016 for all workers aged 25 and over. The aim was to boost the pay of low wage workers given the record UK employment rate. The current National Minimum Wage for those under 25 still applies.

National Minimum Wage (NMW): this is the minimum pay per hour most workers are entitled to by law. The rate depends on a worker's age and if they are an apprentice.

Non-accelerating Inflation Rate of Unemployment (NAIRU): This is the level of unemployment which is neither too low that wages are likely to move up nor so high that wage settlements are likely to be trending down. As its name suggests, the non-accelerating inflation rate of unemployment is a rate that is neutral for inflation, neither boosting it nor restraining it. The NAIRU used to be called the natural rate because some economists argued that the economy would naturally return to this level if left to itself.

NEET: Young people Not in Education, Employment or Training.

Net migration: immigration minus emigration.

Northern powerhouse: term used to describe the group of northern English cities led by Manchester, including Leeds, Liverpool and Sheffield, that aims to group together to provide an alternative economic growth hotspot to London and south-east England.

Seasonal unemployment: occurs in industries such as farming, tourism and construction. Employees such as fruit pickers and ski guides typically move to a different job when their contact is finished.

Structural unemployment: job loss that occurs when an industry dies out in the face of competition from elsewhere e.g. mining in Wales, shipbuilding in north-east England. Labour supply exceeds demand in a particular sector of the labour market.

Resource list

International Labour Organisation seeks to improve work and employment conditions: www.ilo.org

Low Pay Commission: www.gov.uk/government/organisations/low-pay-commission

Eurostat provides detailed statistics on EU and candidate countries: www.ec.europa.eu/eurostat

Organisation for Economic Cooperation and Development (OECD) is a collection of 34 governments working to promote growth, prosperity and sustainable development: www.oecd.org

Institute for Public Policy Research (IPPR), independent policy research think tank: www.ippr.org.

UK Office for National Statistics (ONS): www.ons.gov.uk

Resolution Foundation is producing a series of papers looking at the opportunities and challenges associated with the National Living Wage: www.resolutionfoundation.org

House of Commons Briefing Paper number 5871, 19 October 2016. Youth unemployment statistics by Marianne O'Neill: researchbriefings.parliament.uk/ResearchBriefing/Summary/SN05871

Notes

1 Office for National Statistics (19 October 2016). 'UK labour market: October 2016.' www.ons.gov.uk/employmentandlabourmarket/peopleinwork/employmentandemployeetypes/bulletins/uklabourmarket/october2016

2 Sarah O'Connor (16 March 2016). 'Jobs data offers ray of sunshine for Chancellor.' www.ft.com/cms/s/0/ba2ae46c-eb6a-11e5-888e-2eadd5fbc4a4.html
3 'IMF Articles of Agreement.' (April 2016). www.imf.org.external/pubs/ft/aa/
4 'United Nations Sustainable Development Goals.' (n.d.). www.sustainabledevelopment.un.org/?menu=1300
5 Global Employment Trends for Youth 2015 (7 October 2015). 'Youth employment crisis easing but far from over.' www.ilo.org/global/about-the-ilo/newsroom/news/WCMS_412014/lang-en/index.htm
6 'Unemployment statistics.' (September 2016). ec.europa.eu/Eurostat/statistics-explained/index.php/Unemployment_statistics
7 Bureau of Labour Statistics (17 August 2016). 'Employment and unemployment among youth.' www.bls.gov/news.release/pdf/youth.pdf
8 Jeevan Vasagar (24 May 2013). 'New deal to tackle Europe's mass unemployment.' www.telegraph.co.uk/news/worldnews/europe/10078892/New-Deal-to-tackle-Europes-mass-youth-unemployment.html
9 IPPR (November 2013). 'States of uncertainty: youth unemployment in Europe'. www.ippr.org/files/images/media/files/publication/2013/11/states-of-uncertainty_nov2013_11453.pdf
10 Press Association (25 July 2014). 'Youth contract "to be ended early".' www.dailymail.co.uk/wires/pa/article-2704971/YOUTH-CONTRACT-to-be-ended-early.html
11 'What is workfare?'(n.d.). www.kvv.org.uk/about-workfare
12 'Unemployment statistics.' (September 2016). ec.europa.eu/eurostat/statistics-explained/index.php/Unemployment_statistics
13 Tony Dolphin (13 August 2014). 'Remember the young ones: improving career opportunities for Britain's young people'. www.ippr.org/publications/remember-the-young-ones-improving-career-opportunities-for-britain's-young-people
14 'Unemployment statistics.' (September 2016). ec.europa.eu/eurostat/statistics-explained/index.php/Unemployment_statistics
15 Bureau of Labor Statistics. (4 November 2016). Employment Situation Summary. www.bls.gov/news-release/empsit.nr0.htm
16 Sho Chandra (28 October 2016). 'US Economic Growth Rebounds on Inventory, Export Boost.' www.bloomberg.com/news/articles/2016-10-28/u-s-economic-growth-rebounds-on-boost-from-exports-inventories
17 Paul Davidson (7 September 2016). 'US lags other countries in wage growth.' www.usatoday.com/story/money/2016/09/06/us-lags-other-countries-wage-growth/89924144
18 Victoria Stilwell (8 January 2016). 'Here's how much slack is left in the US labor market.'www.bloomberg.com/news/articles/2016-01-08/here-s-how-much-slack-is-left-in-the-u-s-labor-market
19 Danny Vinik (24 December 2014). 'How the Fed learned to stop worrying about the unemployment rate and start loving other key economic indicators.' www.newsrepublic.com/article/120611/janet-yellens-fed-inflation-unemployment-rates-not-only-key-stats
20 John Authers (5 February 2016). 'Why nobody is happy with the US economy.' www.ft.com/cms/s/0/f7b8c048-cc10-11e5-be0b-b7ece4e953a0.html
21 Figures from ONS (March 2016). www.ons.gov.uk/employmentandlabourmarket/peopleinwork/publicsectorpersonnel/bulletins/publicsectoremployment/previous/Releases
22 'National Minimum Wage.' (5 February 2016). www.politics.co.uk/reference/national-minimum-wage
23 'Monsoon Accessorize tops minimum wage list of shame.' (23 October 2015). www.bbc.co.uk/news/business-34608028

96 Labour markets

24 'Osborne wants above-inflation minimum wage rise.' (16 January 2014). www.bbc.co.uk/news/uk-politics-25766558
25 Robin Harding and Sarah O'Connor (25 November 2015). 'Japan's Abe joins global trend in calling for minimum wage rises.' www.ft.com/cms/s/0/2fab5872-933f-11e5-94e6-c5413829caa5.html
26 John Cridland (November 2015). 'National Living Wage a gamble.' www.theguardian.com/business/2015/nov/03/national-living-wage-a-gamble-says-cbi-boss
27 Phillip Inman (8 September 2015). 'Living wage fears sending "shockwaves" through UK labour market'. www.theguardian.com/business/2015/sep/08/living-wage-fears-sending-shockwaves-through-uk-labour-market
28 Hazel Sheffield (8 July 2015). 'Budget 2015: Osborne's living wage will leave 60,000 people without jobs, OBR says.' www.independent.co.uk/news/business/news/budget-2015-live-osborne-s-living-wage-will-leave-60,000-job-cuts-says-obr-10375495.html
29 Conor D'Arcy and Gavin Kelly (July 2015). 'Analysing the National Living Wage. Impact and implications for Britain's low pay challenge.' www.resolutionfoundation.org/publications/analysing-the-national-living-wage-and-its-impact-on-britains-low-pay-challenge/
30 Ronald Janssen (9 September 2015). 'The German minimum wage is not a job killer.' www.socialeurope.eu/2015/09/the-german-minimum-wage-is-not-a-job-killer/
31 Terry Macalister (18 December 2015). 'Kellingley colliery closure: "shabby end" for a once mighty industry.' www.theguardian.com/environment/2015/dec/18/kellingley-colliery-shabby-end-for-an-industry
32 'SSI Redcar steelworks to shut.' (12 October 2015). www.bbc.co.uk/news/uk-england-34509329
33 Peggy Hollinger (17 January 2016). 'Tata's Talbot faces 750 job cuts.' www.ft.com/cms/s/0/30af7eba-bd3d-11e5-9fdb-87b8d15baec2.html
34 Figures from ONS (October 2016). www.ons.gov.uk/employmentandlabourmarket/peopleinwork/employmentandemployeetypes/bulletins/regionallabourmarket/october2016
35 Centre for Cities (19 January 2015). 'Cities Outlook 2015.' www.centreforcities.org/publication/cities-outlook-2015/
36 Szu Chan Ping and Peter Spence (10 December 2015). 'Mapped: London driving UK growth as "Northern Powerhouse" falters.' www.telegraph.co.uk/finance/economics/12041461/Mapped-London-driving-uk-growth-as-Northern-Powerhouse-falters.html
37 Deloitte UK (n.d.). 'Northern powerhouse, examining the super north.' www2.deloitte.com/uk/en/pages/regions/articles/northern-powerhouse.html
38 Andrew Bounds and Chris Tighe (25 November 2015). 'Osborne pledges more funds for Northern Powerhouse.' www.ft.com/cms/s/0/e183abb0-9364-11e5-bd82-c1fb87af.html
39 Alison Smale (18 July 2014). 'Needing skilled workers, a booming Germany woos immigrants.' www.nytimes.com/2014/07/19/world/europe/needing-skilled-workers-a-booming-germany-woos-immigrants.html?_r=0
40 'China to end one-child policy and allow two.' (29 October 2015). www.bbc.co.uk/news/world-asia-34665539
41 'Hollande says France in state of economic emergency.' (18 January 2016). www.bbc.co.uk/news/business-353436/1
42 Jim Reed (15 May 2013). 'Record number of 16-24s on zero hours contracts at work.' www.bbc.co.uk/newsbeat/22528914/record-number-of-16-24s-on-zero-hours-contracts-at-work

Labour markets 97

43 Gregory Dixon (9 September 2016). 'Contracts that do not guarantee a minimum number of hours.' www.ons.gov.uk/employmentandlabourmarket/peopleinwork/earningsandworkinghours/articles/contractsthatdonotguaranteeaminimumnumberofhours
44 'A research update: United Kingdom outlook revised to negative AAA/A-1+ ratings affirmed.' (12 June 2015). www.standardandpoors.com/en_US/web/guest/article/-/view/sourceid/20008556
45 Clare Hutchison and Hazel Sheffield (14 May 2015). 'Bank of England governor Mark Carney says UK productivity not harmed by migrant workers.' www.independent.co.uk/news/business/news/carney-speaks-what-the-bofe-governor-has-to-say-on-british-people-interest-rate-10249136.html
46 Clare Hutchison (25 May 2016). 'How Brexit could deepen the city's woes in the hunt to plug Britain's skills gap.' www.standard.co.uk/business/how-brexit-could-deepen-the-city-s-woes-in-the-hunt-to-plug-britains-s-skills-gap
47 'Briefing: schools for skills.' (9 April 2011). *The Week*, p.11; Patrick Howse (27 January 2014). 'Education fails to deliver skills for global success.' www.bbc.co.uk/news/education/25881774
48 'Economic recovery not enough to solve youth unemployment.' (13 August 2014). www.ippr.org/news-and-media/press-releases/economic-recovery-not-enough-to-solve-youth-unemployment
49 Graham Hiscott (14 March 2016). 'Up to 220 staff could be replaced with "robo-advisors" at Royal Bank of Scotland.' www.mirror.co.uk/news/business/up-220-staff-could-replaced-7556013
50 Louisa Peacock (11 March 2013). 'Uphill struggle in bid to raise standing of apprenticeships.' www.telegraph.co.uk/finance/jobs/9920845/National-Apprenticeship-Week-Apprenticeships-not-comparable-to-degree-say-parents.html
51 Carl E. Walsh (18 September 1998). 'The natural rate, NAIRU, and monetary policy.' *FRBSF Economic Letter*. www.frbsf.org/economic-research/publications/economic-letter/1998/september/the-natural-rate-nairu-and-monetary-policy/
52 Friedrich Schneider and Dominik Enste (March 2002). 'Hiding in the shadows. The growth of the underground economy'. www.imf.org/external/pubs/ft/issues/issues30/

5 Fiscal policy

The Greek debt problems are well known but high and rising government debt is a problem in many countries. In this chapter find out why this is the case and what is being done to tackle it. In addition you will learn some of the history of the Eurozone debt crisis and key newsworthy items in a UK Budget.

To cut or not to cut public spending has been the dilemma facing governments around the world, particularly those in Eurozone countries in the aftermath of the financial crisis. According to Catherine Mann, chief economist of the Organisation for Economic Co-operation and Development, (OECD), the global economy is 'stuck in a low growth trap'. The overall global economy is not expected to grow much above 3% in 2017.[1]

There are two serious problems that remain to be tackled, namely low productivity growth and rising inequality. Strong economic growth would improve government finances with increased tax receipts and lower welfare spending.

It is not debt levels per se, although they obviously matter, but how the financial markets view a particular country which determines whether or not it is able to service its debt. It boils down to market sentiment. In 2014, Japan had a *deficit* of 7.7% of GDP, but because of the high level of domestic savings – a high savings ratio – it is not beholden to external capital markets to fund its debt. Government revenues were boosted in 2015 by the 3% hike in **consumption tax** to 8% in April 2014, and higher **corporation tax** receipts from increased profits made at Japanese companies.

However concern remains about the long-term sustainability of such a high deficit, even if interest rates stay at zero forever. Japan's ageing population and low level of immigration limits its real GDP growth potential. Increased government spending is going on pensions and other transfer payments to the old. If interest rates were to rise then the deficit would take off.

> **Box 5.1** Japan
>
> - Japan's debt estimated at 249% of GDP in 2016, higher than Greece and Italy.
> - High domestic savings rate funds the deficit.
> - Prime Minister wants quantitative easing to boost economic growth, increasing inflation to 2% and a weaker yen.

The power of the financial markets to determine a country's fate was amply demonstrated in the aftermath of the financial crisis when a number of Eurozone countries found themselves picked off one by one by the capital markets.[2]

Greece, Ireland, Portugal, Spain and Italy to varying degrees found their bond yields rise as the markets showed their concern about whether said country could pay its debt. This made debt interest payments much higher, unsustainably so in the cases of Greece, Ireland and Portugal who had to go cap in hand to the International Monetary Fund to be bailed out.[3]

> **Journalistic practice**
>
> Coverage of the Eurozone debt crisis was front page news, not just the financial pages. In some ways it was a self-fulfilling prophecy with speculation on which **sovereign debt** market would be next to fall out of favour with the financial markets. As the highly influential debt **ratings agency** such as Moody's and Fitch downgraded sovereign debt, so bond yields would rise, the currency fall and national authorities would publicly intervene with words and deeds with varying degrees of success. If this failed, there was detailed coverage of the political and financial fall-out and subsequent terms of the austerity programme – usually a mixture of large spending cuts and tax rises. Financial markets reports and comment features were done comparing the rising bond yields of countries such as Greece, Ireland and Spain with the low cost of borrowing in safe-haven countries such as Germany and Switzerland.
>
> There was much debate on the power struggle between politicians and financial markets. This was particularly the case with Greece which culminated in the election of the radical left wing Syriza party in January 2015. Its charismatic finance minister Yanis Varoufakis was a skilful media operator although he eventually stood down in July 2015 to pave the way for a new IMF bailout deal.
>
> His colourful personality meant he was often the subject of new stories in his own right, separate from his economic pronouncements. His views on economic and political matters are still widely reported.

100 *Fiscal policy*

Greece was the biggest casualty in the Eurozone crisis and is still making the news, albeit in a less dramatic fashion, as it continues to grapple with its debts and economic reform programme.[4]

In December 2015, against a background of economic recession, the Greek parliament narrowly approved the 2016 Budget that included tax increases and public spending cuts in pensions and defence. Despite this, the budget deficit in 2016 will be larger than that in 2015.[5]

In August 2015, Prime Minister Alexis Tsipras agreed to an economic reform programme in return for a bailout of up to Euro 86bn, its third international bailout in five years.

Journalistic practice

Reports of the bailout should include the sum involved, the terms and conditions attached to the loan and a comment from an economist on the economic prospects ahead. Take into account whether there are differing political views on the policy decisions taken. How do people who will be specifically affected by the budget measures, such as a civil servant, feel about the measures? The economic crisis can be starkly illustrated in a series of graphs such as unemployment, public debt as a share of GDP, nominal interest rates on long-term government bonds and economic growth.

Although saddled with historically large debt, the UK largely managed to retain the confidence of the ratings agencies and financial markets throughout the Eurozone debt crisis. However former UK Chancellor of the Exchequer, George Osborne, was dealt a blow when the UK lost its top AAA credit rating for the first time since 1978.

In February 2013, Britain was downgraded by one notch from AAA to AA1 by Moody's and Fitch credit rating agencies. Mr Osborne had staked his economic and political credibility on retaining the premium rating.

The financial crisis, subsequent recession and financial bailouts of a number of banks, including RBS and Lloyds, took its toll on government finances. These have deteriorated sharply since 2009. This despite the fact that the UK economy was quicker to recover from the financial crisis than its main European partners and topped the Eurozone economic growth chart in 2015 at 2.2%.

George Osborne talked tough on debt reduction and made some high profile announcements on spending cuts but in reality there is still a huge debt mountain to conquer.

In the period 2010–2015, the UK ran a very tight fiscal ship but the level of net debt continued to rise. The UK has one of the largest **structural, or underlying, deficits** in Europe.

Figure 5.1 The Rt Hon George Osborne MP Former Chancellor of The Exchequer speaks to conservative candidates and supporters at Saunton Sands Hotel, Devon. Image courtesy of NDPhotos/Alamy.

Public sector net debt (excluding public sector banks) is historically high. It was £1.6 trillion in September 2016, equivalent to 83.3% of GDP.[6]

This is a sharp reversal of past fortunes. In the period 1947–1974, the government ran a budget surplus every year.

Box 5.2 December 2015 debt to GDP ratios (%)

- Japan 229.2
- US 104.17
- UK 89.2
- Greece 176.9
- China 43.9
- Brazil 66.23
- Italy 132.70.

Source: www.tradingeconomics.com

The IMF flagged up the UK's high debt level in its otherwise positive economic assessment of the UK published in December 2015. 'While the UK continues to benefit from record low interest rates, maintaining deficits and debts at these levels would constrain the space to respond proactively to future large negative growth shocks'. This translates roughly as 'the cupboard is pretty bare'.[7]

Mr Osborne made front page newspaper headlines with reports of his desire for a budget surplus to be seen as the new normal as far as UK **fiscal policy** is concerned. 'George Osborne moves to peg public finances to Victorian values' said the left-leaning *Guardian* newspaper.[8] It referred to Micawber, a character in Charles Dickens's 1850 novel *David Copperfield*, who espoused fiscal rectitude.

In more measured tones the *Financial Times* front page story headline was 'Osborne seeks to secure legacy with a budget surplus law'.[9]

Journalistic practice

In reporting a major fiscal policy announcement, the following guidelines will be useful. The opening sentence should describe what the new policy is and why it is being done. (In the case of the Osborne policy announcement above, the aim being to turn up the pressure on the opposition Labour Party to follow suit). Include a quote from the Chancellor. What is the historical context? Has such a policy been tried before and if so how successful was it?

A feature can be done on the scale of the government debt, illustrated by a graph showing the rise over time. Included can be the view of the financial markets in terms of the ease of servicing that debt. Greece has been the subject of many news stories since the financial crisis. These included features on the effects on the ground of the austerity measures, the wrangling between various Eurozone finance ministers on how tough to be on Greece, the amount of capital flight out of the country as investors voted with their feet, the likely impact on the rest of the Eurozone of any Greek exit, so-called 'GREXIT'. Included with such stories should always be the response of the financial markets, specifically the bond and currency markets.

Headline writers have had a field day with titles including the phrase 'Greek tragedy'.

There were also stories on the Greek government entering talks with Russia to try to arrange alternative finance. These stories crossed into political territory with comment on the myriad ways by which Russia under President Vladimir Putin is seeking to try to increase its sphere of influence in the world.

In recent years there has tended to be flurry of reports in January about stalemates in US Budget negotiations reflecting battles between the Democrat and Republican parties. Such reports highlight the volatility in the financial markets – with both the Dow Jones and US dollar marked down – that accompanies the effective shutdown of parts of the US government whilst the wrangling continues.

Other fiscal stories that can be done include analysis of the tax take of various nations. For example, the high level of tax avoidance in some southern European nations such as Greece and Italy has been cited as a factor in their poor fiscal position.

The ideological battleground between US Republicans and Democrats has been visibly demonstrated in recent years in debt negotiations.[10] Most Republicans are opposed to raising the US debt ceiling in principle, believing it encourages government profligacy.

In agreeing to any higher debt ceiling, Republicans would like concessions such as spending cuts in healthcare and other benefit programmes. The Democrats want a no-strings attached agreement. In the past President Obama has called for tax increases for wealthy Americans. Only Congress can raise or suspend the debt ceiling.

You might hear the term **fiscal cliff**, which was coined by former Federal Reserve Board chair Ben Bernanke to describe the combination of tax rises and across-the-board spending cuts that accompany a stalemate in US deficit reduction talks. There are fears that going over such a cliff might put a serious brake on growth in the US economy.[11]

In 2014, there was a partial shutdown of the US government for a short period when no agreement on the borrowing cap was reached. The spectre of the US defaulting on its debts unsettled the financial markets and attracted the attention of the International Monetary Fund, which is not surprising given America's leading role in the world economy.

Economic uncertainty is not welcomed by financial markets particularly given the myriad economic and geopolitical problems elsewhere. More uncertainty translates into weaker confidence, less investment, fewer jobs created and ultimately lower economic growth. This in turn would undermine confidence in the dollar as a safe haven for investors.

In 2011, Republicans demanded deep spending cuts in return for raising the debt ceiling. This prompted the first ever downgrade in US debt with ratings agency Standard & Poor's moving from AAA to an AA+ rating. In reality, it is not thought likely that the US would default on its debt as it can prioritise payments to international bondholders and delay domestic payments on pensions and other benefits. Given the relative strength of the US economy it should have no problems servicing its debt.

Office for Budget Responsibility

The **Office for Budget Responsibility (OBR)** was formed in May 2010 to provide independent authoritative analysis of the UK's public finances.[12]

There are a growing number of official independent watchdogs around the world. Box 5.3 shows its five main roles.

Box 5.3 Office for Budget Responsibility

- Formed in May 2010 to:
  - Make an independent assessment of the public finances and the economy.
  - Judge progress towards the government's fiscal targets.
  - Assess the long term sustainability of the public finances.
  - Look at the Treasury's costing of Budget measures.

Journalistic practice

The OBR is highly respected and so its pronouncements around the time of the Budget and Autumn Statement are widely reported. Coverage is not always favourable when OBR forecasts turn out to be erroneous. It produces five-year forecasts for the economy and public finances twice a year.

The OBR produces economic and fiscal forecasts for the government. In March 2016, it forecast that the public sector would borrow £72.2bn during the financial year ending March 2016.

In the event borrowing in 2015 is estimated to have been £74.9bn. This is above the OBR forecast and reflected lower bonuses paid in the financial sector than were originally expected.

George Osborne wanted to have a £10bn surplus on the public finances by 2020. At the time of the March 2016 Budget the OBR said that continued weak productivity growth meant that the UK will only manage 2.1% growth a year.[13]

This level of growth would make it difficult for the Chancellor to achieve his budget surplus on time unless he raised taxes or made further spending cuts. Borrowing forecasts were revised up but public finances are still projected to achieve a £10.4bn surplus in 2019–2020. The deficit as a share of GDP is projected to fall to 2.9% in 2016–2017, 1.9% in 2017–2018 and 1% in 2018–2019.

The OBR has a difficult job deciding what constitutes 'normal' times in terms of government spending. In post-war times, the accepted wisdom has been that government spending during a recession is good.

UK Budget

Historically, once a year, usually in March, the UK Chancellor of the Exchequer sets out the government's plans for the economy based on the latest forecasts from the Office for Budget Responsibility, as well as any proposals from the government for changes to taxation.

On 16 March, 2016, George Osborne delivered his third Budget in 12 months.[14]

Box 5.4 Budget

- UK Chancellor updates Parliament on the state of the economy, public finances and on progress towards the government's economic objectives.
- Chancellor forecasts government spending and taxation in the coming year.
- Changes in taxation announced.

Within a Budget there are specific measures for business and consumers.[15] In 2016, some of the newsworthy Budget announcements were:

- A further reduction in corporation tax from 20% to 17% by 2020, despite the fact that the UK already had the lowest rate in the G20, including the US.
- Capital gains tax to be cut from 28% to 20% and from 18% to 10% for basic-rate taxpayers.[16]
- A new sugar tax to be introduced on the soft drinks industry in two years' time, raising £520m to be spent on increased funding for primary school sport in England. This measure is aimed at cutting childhood obesity. This measure garnered lots of press coverage with a number of angles taken. Views on the measure were sought from doctors and health charities and there was speculation about whether a legal challenge to the tax would be mounted by the drinks industry.[17]
- Fuel **duty** frozen at 57.95p for the sixth year in a row.[18]
- Beer, cider and spirits duties frozen but wine and cigarettes going up.
- Confirmation of the Crossrail 2 commission in London and the HS3 link between Manchester and Leeds.[19]
- Increase in flood defences.
- Introduction of new 'lifetime' ISAs for the under 40s with the government putting in £1 for every £4 saved.[20]

The Treasury produced a short explanatory video on the Budget available at: www.youtube.com/user/hmtreasuryuk.

Spending review and Autumn Statement

This was the second most important economic statement that the Chancellor made every year. It included updates on the state of the economy and the government's taxation and spending plans based on projections provided by the OBR.

In November 2016, Chancellor Philip Hammond announced in the Autumn Statement that it was being abolished. The spring Budget of 2017 will also be the last. Starting in autumn 2017, the UK will have an autumn Budget announcing tax changes and from 2018, a Spring Statement will be made solely responding to the OBR's forecast with no fiscal measures announced.

The **spending review** and Autumn Statement used to be a major news story and was covered by the press in a similar way to the Budget.[21]

The broadsheet newspapers often have a separate supplement full of comment and analysis of the statement.

The IMF thought the 2015 Autumn Statement 'appropriately targets steady declines in the deficit and the achievement of a small surplus by 2019/20'. However it suggested that the government may need to 'show flexibility in finding alternative fiscal measures' if it fails to achieve the large spending cuts and efficiency gains envisaged in the Autumn Statement.[22]

Journalistic practice

In the UK, ahead of a formal Budget statement there is typically a week or so of speculation in the press about what measures might be included in the Budget. This might be on the back of surreptitious leaks by the authorities of a particular measure aimed at generating positive headlines ahead of the formal Budget statement or sounding out opinion ahead of a potentially controversial measure. This was graphically illustrated by the appearance of stories suggesting the Chancellor was going to abolish the tax free lump sum on retirement incomes in a bid to raise £4bn.[23] Following a public furore and discontent amongst fellow Tory MPs, the Chancellor abandoned the plans.[24]

Media coverage may be a reflection of the intensive lobbying by various vested interests that takes place ahead of the Budget. For example, stories may appear about the high numbers of pubs closing with the associated loss of a community hub in the case of rural areas. Such stories would hope to influence the Chancellor to not raise alcohol duties which may deter people from visiting their local pub.

There is usually a pre-Budget report on the UK bank levy. There will be speculation on the scale of any rise coupled with comments from the British Banker's Association on the detrimental impact it will have on the image of London as a place for banks to do business. In recent years, as the size of the levy has risen so has comment about whether certain banks might decide to relocate their headquarters overseas to avoid having to pay the charge.

The annual bank levy, effectively a profit surcharge, was introduced after the financial crisis and is based on a bank's global balance sheet. British banks complain that it puts them at a competitive disadvantage. In the five years to 2015 it raised £8bn.

In the 2015 Budget, the Treasury said the bank levy would be cut from 0.21% to 0.1% in 2021. From that date the levy will only be payable on British balance sheets.[25]

George Osborne justified previous increases in the levy on the back of the financial support provided by the taxpayer to bail out the industry in the financial crisis. The opposition Labour Party would like to see the introduction of a windfall tax on banks.

HSBC is the world's third biggest bank, with a large proportion of the company based in Hong Kong. It pays a large chunk of the UK's Bank Levy, around 40% of the total receipts equivalent to around £750m in 2014. The scale of its bank levy has been cited as one of the reasons it might relocate its headquarters out of Britain.

> **Box 5.5** Reporting on the Budget
>
> - Economic growth forecasts for current and next year
> - Borrowing forecast and debt to GDP ratio
> - Public sector pay and pensions
> - Benefit changes – state pension
> - Any specific businesses measures – carbon tax
> - Infrastructure spending
> - Housing market measures.

The election of the radical left wing politician Jeremy Corbyn as leader of the opposition Labour Party in the UK prompted fresh appraisal of his alternative anti-austerity economic agenda.[26]

Journalistic practice

The press drew comparisons with the rise of the anti-austerity Syriza party in Greece and Podemos in Spain. Questions for Mr Corbyn are what are the key elements of his economic policy? Has it been tried before and if so what is its record? What do economists/investment managers think of the proposals?

The tortuous process of trying to sort out the Greek financial mess with severe austerity measures has depressed not only the Greek people but has spawned a growing movement of people who want to follow an alternative path to deficit reduction. Post financial crisis there is a big trust deficit with the establishment in many countries whether that is the financial or political establishment.

The UK Labour Party wants to run down the deficit by promoting economic growth and cracking down on tax avoidance. In September 2015, it set up an economic advisory committee made up of well-respected global economists.[27]

These included Thomas Piketty, best known for his book *Capital in the Twenty-First Century*,[28] which proposed a radical system of progressive wealth taxes to combat inequality and prevent wealth being concentrated in a small elite.[29] He resigned in June 2016 due to work commitments.

It also includes Joseph Stiglitz, a Nobel prize-winning economist and former chief economist at the World Bank. He has argued against what he sees as the tide of unnecessary, destructive austerity that has swept across Europe.[30] They are to report to the Shadow Chancellor and Business Secretary four times during the year.

Institute for Fiscal Studies

The **Institute for Fiscal Studies (IFS)** is a widely respected microeconomic research institute. It covers a number of public policy areas including tax and benefits.

Box 5.6 Institute for Fiscal Studies

- Leading independent research institute into public finances, tax and welfare policy and pensions.
- In response to the March 2016 Budget, and bleaker forecasts for economic growth, IFS Director Paul Johnson said the Chancellor was 'running out of wriggle room'. His chances of having a surplus in 2019–2020 are 'only just the right side of 50/50'.

The IFS publishes its influential Green Budget every year in the run-up to the Chancellor's Budget statement.[31]

It is a thick document that, in addition to providing an outlook for the UK economy, assesses some of the issues the Chancellor will have to address. These include options for reducing spending on social security, the scope for departmental spending cuts and options for increasing tax.

Journalistic practice

The IFS Green Budget is always referred to by journalists when assessing the Chancellor's Budget statement. The director of the IFS is often quoted and interviewed live.

The media always sounds out the IFS on the Budget announcements. The IFS' assessment of the 2016 Budget can be viewed at www.ifs.org.uk/tools_and_resources/budget/512.

The IFS' warning of a slowdown in wage growth and that George Osborne 'has only 50:50 chance' of hitting his £10bn budget surplus target for the public finances by 2020 were picked up by the press.[32]

Since 2008, national debt has risen sharply due to the recession which particularly hit stamp duty receipts because of falling house prices, government bank bail-outs and lower income tax and corporation tax receipts.

Former UK Chancellor George Osborne thought that for economic security, debt needs to be reduced so that a surplus can form in good times. Lower debt also means lower debt interest payments.

Box 5.7 Some key fiscal terms

- Budget deficit: the gap between what the government brings in annually in revenues such as taxes and what it spends.
- Structural deficit: persistent budget deficit that will not disappear when the economy recovers.
- National debt: the total amount of money that a government owes.

There are certain features that are routinely included in a Budget. These include measures to help and support the growth of small and medium enterprises. For many years small firms have complained that they cannot get access to bank funds. In contrast, many large companies are sitting on big cash piles but are reluctant to spend.

Other measures that might be taken to help SMEs include: a *cut in business rates*. These are non-domestic property taxes collected by local authorities. Retailers both large and small have been campaigning for reform of business rates for some time. They say it puts them at a disadvantage to internet retailers who do not have premises.[33]

There could be an increase in the *annual investment allowance*. Investment allowance is a tax incentive offered to business to encourage capital investment. They can deduct a percentage of capital costs including depreciation from taxable income.

There are usually some housing-related measures, either proposals for new housebuilding or schemes launched to help boost home ownership, particularly for first time buyers.

Any announcement of childcare measures will be widely reported not least because UK families pay the most for childcare in Europe which means that it is not cost effective for many women to go out to work.

Carbon tax, also known as the carbon price floor, is designed to encourage investment in green energy and reduce greenhouse gas emissions. It is a tax levied on the carbon content of fossil fuels. There is opposition to the tax. The Engineering Employers Federation (EEF) says it accounts for 10% of the electricity bill of big industrial firms and puts British companies at a disadvantage relative to their European competitors.

Box 5.8 Types of taxes

- *Direct taxes*: placed on households' income and firms' profits. Income tax, corporation tax, capital gains tax, national insurance and inheritance tax.
- *Indirect taxes*: incurred when items are purchased. These include value added tax, excise duties and customs duties.

The Chancellor may want to do something to make people feel better about their own personal financial position, and thereby increase consumer confidence. After the financial crisis of 2008/9, real incomes in the UK were depressed for several years due to static wages and high inflation.

The parlous state of the government finances has ruled out a headline-grabbing cut in the basic rate of income tax. Such a measure always goes down well with the Tory Party faithful and the wider public.

There are usually calls to raise the threshold for the 40p tax rate which many more people now pay. In the March 2016 Budget, it was announced that the threshold at which people pay 40% income tax will rise from £42,385 to £45,000 in April 2017.

The British Government is keen for pension funds to invest in UK infrastructure in areas such as road improvements, power stations, flood defences and the roll out of high speed broadband to rural areas. Investment by UK pension funds is less than 1% in the UK compared to 8–15% in Australia and Canada[34].

In the current low interest rate environment, there is the attraction to funds of long-term, stable financial returns. However there is some reluc-tance to invest in the more risky early stages of infrastructure schemes.

The opposition Labour Party wants the Bank of England to take advantage of low interest rates to offer cheap loans for infrastructure investment that will eventually boost productivity. The money would be spent on building houses, schools and hospitals. This policy has been dubbed 'People's QE'.

There are perennial calls to remove universal benefits for wealthier pensioners such as the winter fuel allowance and free bus passes. This would be in line with moves made to restrict child benefit.

The government coffers could be boosted quite substantially by reducing the tax relief on pension contributions from 40% to 20%. This would save the Treasury more than £7bn. At the moment for every 60p saved in a pension by a higher rate taxpayer, the government contributes 40p in tax relief to make it up to £1.

Property taxation changes will always make it onto the editor's list. In the 2015 Autumn Statement the Chancellor further tightened the screw on wealthy homeowners with the announcement of an extra 3% stamp duty to be paid on second properties, such as holiday homes and buy-to-let properties.[35]

Fuel pricing is always an emotive issue with a very vocal motoring lobby in the UK. A large proportion of the cost of petrol at the pump, almost 80%, goes to the Treasury in the form of fuel duty and VAT.[36]

In September 2000, there was a week of protests and blockades of oil refineries and distribution depots in response to soaring fuel prices. Rationing was introduced in some petrol stations.

112 *Fiscal policy*

Other newsworthy topics include **Air Passenger Duty (APD)**. APD is the government's tax on all passengers departing from a UK airport. Originally introduced in 1994, as is the way with most taxes, it has steadily risen under successive governments. The opposition Labour Party intends to increase APD.

Critics argue that APD sends the wrong signal to potential business investors. The UK has some of the highest air ticket taxes and charges in the world. Airlines and travel organisations dislike the tax which is said to distort the market for long-haul flights.[37]

The government has championed the scientific base in the UK and views science and research as an area where the UK could have a competitive advantage. Particular focus is on supporting areas such as **synthetic biology**, energy storage and advanced materials. The science budget is one of the few ring-fenced areas of government spending along with overseas aid, health and education.[38]

Duty on alcohol and tobacco is usually raised in the Budget. It is an easy way to raise money and the government can justify it on health grounds.

Journalistic practice

There is always comprehensive coverage of the Budget with detailed analysis and comment on the economic backdrop combined with illustrations of how the measures will impact certain groups such as pensioners, families, welfare recipients, etc.

Among the features that should be included in any report are the OBR's economic growth, borrowing and debt to GDP ratio forecasts for the current financial year and the following year.

Other newsworthy items are any announcements on public sector pay and pensions, benefit changes, specific high profile measures for business such as the introduction of the apprenticeship levy, cuts in business rates, large infrastructure projects such as HS2 and housing market measures.

What is the reaction of the financial markets to the Budget statement? Stock markets usually like tight fiscal policy combined with looser monetary policy provided it is not risking recession. Tighter fiscal policy is also good for bonds.

UK Government borrowing figures are published monthly by the **Office for National Statistics (ONS)**. Attention is focused on how well the Chancellor is meeting his objectives despite the fact that overall, annual government spending is more than its income. There is usually a spike in tax receipts in January with money coming in from people who submit self-assessment tax forms.

> **Journalistic practice**
>
> What was the trend in public sector net borrowing (excluding public sector banks rescued at the time of the financial crisis) and how does this compare with the same period a year earlier? What were the figures for government spending and tax receipts? How does the borrowing figure compare with forecasts from the OBR? Include reaction to the data from a City economist.

Concerns about debt, both government and private individual, is not confined to the industrialised nations of the UK, US and Europe.

There is widespread unease about the rapid growth in recent years of credit in China, much of it unregulated in the so-called **shadow banking sector**. It has allowed small firms to get access to credit and helped to maintain strong growth in the Chinese economy.[39]

Demand for shadow loans remains high as it is difficult for private firms to borrow from official banks. Borrowing from a shadow bank is efficient and quick even though interest rates are higher, as much as 30%.

There is concern that if there are a series of major defaults in the shadow banking sector the ensuing government rescue could derail China's economic growth. As the world's second largest economy, that would adversely impact growth elsewhere.

The change in Japanese leadership with the election of Shinzo Abe in December 2012 turned the spotlight on world's third biggest economy. Japan's annual budget deficit is higher than that of Greece and Italy. A high rate of domestic and corporate saving has allowed Japan to fund its budget deficit domestically.[40]

Prime Minister Shinzo Abe wants to boost Japanese economic growth by quantitative easing that will raise inflation to 2–3% and weaken the yen. However his plans have been thrown off course by volatile financial markets. The yen is seen as a safe ship in stormy waters. A cheaper currency will boost Japanese exports of cars and electronic goods.

Despite negative borrowing costs, Japanese government debt exceeds 230% of GDP. The population and labour force are shrinking suggesting even higher debt ratios in the future. However Prime Minister Abe is confident that rising tax revenues coupled with a rise in the consumption tax to 10% in 2019, will enable the government to eliminate the deficit by 2020. This seems optimistic given the IMF is forecasting Japanese GDP growth of 0.1% in 2017 and only slightly higher growth in the medium term.

Assignments

Write a 300 word news story on the increase in Japanese consumption tax and its impact on the economy.

114 *Fiscal policy*

Glossary of key terms

Air Passenger Duty (APD): an excise duty charged on passengers flying from a UK airport. The duty is not payable on inbound passengers flying to the UK en route to somewhere else.

Autumn Statement: the UK Chancellor updates Members of Parliament on the state of the economy and the government's future plans in his/her Autumn Statement.

Austerity: term applied to the combination of public spending cuts and tax increases aimed at balancing the government's books in the aftermath of the financial crisis.

Bank levy: an annual tax on the value of all the debts in large UK banks and overseas banking groups carrying out business in the UK. It was introduced by the Chancellor in 2011 as punishment for the banks' role in the financial crisis.

Borrowing requirement: the net total of government spending less revenues is the amount that has to be financed by borrowing or which allows debt to be repaid in the case of a negative borrowing requirement.

Budget: an economic report presented by the Treasury to the UK parliament. In this report the Chancellor can review taxes and spending plans. Many of the measures announced in the Budget are implemented in a Finance Bill.

Budget surplus: amount by which a government's income exceeds its spending over a particular period of time.

Business rates: a local authority tax on business property.

Capital gains tax: a tax on capital gains – the difference between the price something was purchased for and its selling price e.g. a house.

Consumption tax: sales tax in Japan equivalent to VAT in the European Union and UK.

Corporation tax: a tax on company profits. Companies can claim various allowances, including investment allowances, which can be set against their profits. This reduces their taxable profits in any one year.

Debt Management Office (DMO): part of the UK Treasury, established in 1998, with responsibility for minimising financing costs for the government over the long term, taking account of risk.

Debt service: amount of money required to make payments on the principal and interest on outstanding loans, the interest on bonds or the principal of maturing bonds.

Deficit (or Budget deficit): the amount by which government spending exceeds government income during a specified period of time (usually a year).

Duty: a tax levied by a government. There are customs duties which are linked to imported goods and excise duties. The latter are levied on a narrow range of goods including fuel, alcohol, tobacco and betting. It is sometimes known as the 'sin tax'.

Fiscal policy 115

Finance Bill: the UK's Finance Bill puts into law the tax measures announced for the year in the Budget.

Fiscal cliff: combination of expiring tax cuts and across-the-board government spending cuts in the US that could hit economic growth.

Fiscal policy: the use of government spending and tax policy to effect changes in the economy.

Inheritance tax: a tax on the value of assets left on death by an individual.

Institute for Fiscal Studies (IFS): an independent research institute that looks at public finances, tax, welfare policies and pensions.

Office for Budget Responsibility (OBR): the UK office that produces an independent assessment of the public finances and the economy for each Budget.

Office for National Statistics (ONS): the UK's national statistical institute. It is the largest independent producer of official statistics.

Ratings agencies: these assign credit ratings which rate a debtors' ability to pay back debt. In financial markets there are three main agencies: Standard & Poor's (S & P), Moody's and Fitch.

Shadow banking: unregulated non-bank providers of credit. This includes a range of organisations including hedge funds, private equity firms and investment banks.

Sovereign debt: bonds issued by a national government denominated in a foreign currency. The economic and political stability of the issuing country determines the level of risk associated with the debt.

Spending review: sets out how the government intends to spend taxpayers' money through each government department.

Structural deficit: persistent budget deficit that will not disappear when the economy recovers.

Synthetic biology: design and fabrication of biological components and systems that don't already exist in nature. Interdisciplinary branch of biology and engineering. It includes the likes of genetic engineering, biotechnology and molecular biology.

Value Added Tax (VAT): a tax on expenditure e.g. fuel. Some items deemed essential such as food, water and children's clothes, books and public transport are tax exempt, i.e. zero rated.

Resource list

UK Treasury: www.gov.uk/government/organisations/hm-treasury
Office for Budget Responsibility (OBR): www.budgetresponsibility.org.uk
Institute for Fiscal Studies (IFS): www.ifs.org.uk
Oxford Economics offers macroeconomic forecasts and data: www.oxfordeconomics.com
Office for National Statistics (ONS): www.ons.gov.uk
Smith & Williamson, the accountancy and investment management firm, provides detailed analysis and commentary on the Budget. Pensions,

investments and taxes are the focus of its attention: www.smith.williamson.co.uk

Recommended reading

IFS Green Budget 2016 (2016). www.ifs.org.uk/publications/8129
Piketty, Thomas (2014). *Capital in the Twenty-First Century*. Trans. Arthur Goldhammer. Cambridge, MA and London, UK: Belknap Press of Harvard University Press.
Wheatcroft, Martin (2015). *Simply UK: A Summary Guide to UK Government Finances 2015–16*. Oxford: Pendan.

Notes

1. 'OECD economic outlook. Policymakers: act now to keep promises.' (1 June 2016). www.oecd.org/eco/economicoutlook.htm
2. David Oakley and Hugh Carnegy (10 November 2011). 'France furious over S & P downgrade error.' www.ft.com/cms/s/0/6ccfa48c-0bbd-11e1-9310-00144feabdc0.html
3. David Oakley and Richard Milne (30 November 2010). 'Eurozone bail-out plan fails to lift bond market.' *Financial Times*.
4. Matt Phillips (2015). 'The complete history of the Greek debt drama in charts.' www.qz.com/440058/the-complete-history-of-the-greek-debt-drama-in-charts
5. Karolina Tagaris (5 December 2015). 'Greek parliament approves austere budget for 2016.' www.reuters.com/article/us-eurozone-greece-budget-idUSKBN0TO0SF20151206
6. Office for National Statistics (September 2016). 'Public sector finances, September 2016.' www.ons.gov.uk/economy/governmentpublicsectorandtaxes/publicsectorfinance/bulletins/publicsectorfinances/September2016
7. International Monetary Fund (11 December 2015). *United Kingdom – 2015 Article 1V Consultation Concluding Statement of the Mission*. www.imf.org/external/np/ms/2015/121115.htm
8. Larry Elliott and Frances Perraudin (10 June 2015). 'George Osborne moves to peg public finances to Victorian values.' www.theguardian.com/politics/2015/jun/10/george-osborne-public-finances-victorian-values
9. Chris Giles and George Parker (10 June 2015). 'Osborne seeks to secure legacy with a budget surplus law.' *Financial Times*.
10. Brian Knowlton (29 September 2013). 'The battle in Congress on spending and debt.' www.nytimes.com/2013/09/30/us/politics/questions-and-ansers-on-a-possible-government-shutdown.html?_r=0
11. Suzy Khimm, Ezra Klein, Dylan Matthews and Brad Plummer (27 November 2012). 'The fiscal cliff: absolutely everything you could possibly need to know, in one FAQ.' www.washingtonpost.com/news/wonk/wp/2012/11/27/absolutely-everything-you-need-to-know-about-the-fiscal-cliff-in-one-faq/
12. Office for Budget Responsibility (2016). 'What we do.' budgetresponsibility.org.uk/about-the-obr-what-we-do/
13. Emily Cadman (16 March 2016). 'Budget 2016: bleak outlook for economy as productivity downgraded.' www.ft.com.cms/s/0/a882921c-eb94-11e5-888e-2eadd5fbc4a4.html
14. George Osborne (16 March 2016). 'Budget 2016: George Osborne's speech.' www.gov.uk/government/speeches/budget-2016-george-osbornes-speech

15 'Budget 2016 Summary: key points at-a-glance.' (16 March 2016). www.bbc.co.uk/news/uk-politics-35819797
16 Rowena Mason (27 March 2016). 'Capital gains tax cut gives £3,000 to rich 0.3%, says Labour.' www.theguardian.com/uk-news/2016/mar/27/john-mcdonnell-osborne-capital-gains-tax-cut-gives-richest-population
17 Denis Campbell, Rebecca Smithers and Sarah Butler (17 March 2016). 'Sugar tax: Osborne's two-tier levy brings mixed response.' www.theguardian.com/uk-news/2016/mar/16/budget-2016-george-osborne-sugar-tax-mixed-response; Luke Graham (21 March 2016). 'Will soft drinks companies sue the UK government over the sugar tax?' www.cnbc.com/2016/03/21/will-soft-drink-companies-sue-the-uk-government-over-the-sugar-tax.html
18 'Budget 2016: fuel duty frozen for sixth year in a row.' (16 March 2016). www.bbc.co.uk/news/business-35822029
19 Jack Doyle (17 March 2016). 'Rail projects galore – but when will they ever be completed? High Speed 3 and Crossrail 2 get backing in the Budget.' www.dailymail.co.uk/news/article-3496161/Rail-projects-galore-completed-High-Speed-3-Crossrail-2-backing-Budget.html
20 Brian Milligan (16 March 2016). 'Budget 2016: new lifetime Isa for homebuyers and retirement.' www.bbc.co.uk/news/business-35820757
21 Francis Elliot and Jill Sherman (25 November 2015). 'Osborne finds billions to help workers onto housing ladder.' www.thetimes.co.uk/tto/news/politics/article4622924-ece; Richard Evans (5 December 2014). 'Six important personal finance changes this week.' www.telegraph.co.uk/finance/personalfinance/11274836/Six-important-personal-finance-changes-this-week.html
22 'United Kingdom-2015 Article 1V Consultation Concluding Statement of the Mission.' (11 December 2015). www.imf.org/en/News/Articles/2015/09/28/04/52/mcs121115
23 Tim Shipman (21 February 2016). 'Osborne to abolish pension perk.' www.thesundaytimes.co.uk/sto/news/article1670490.ece
24 Heather Stewart and Nadia Khomami (5 March 2016). 'George Osborne backs down on radical pension reform.' www.theguardian.com/money/2016/mar/04/george-osborne-backs-down-on-radical-pension-reform
25 'Budget 2015: bank levy to be reduced.' (8 July 2015). www.bbc.co.uk/news/business-33444127
26 'Jeremy Corbyn wins Labour leadership contest and vows "fightback".' (12 September 2015). www.bbc.co.uk/news/uk-politics-34223157
27 'Labour announces new Economic Advisory Committee.' (27 September 2015). www.press.labour.org.uk/post/129975218774/labour-announces-new-economc-advisory-committee
28 Thomas Piketty (2014). *Capital in the Twenty-First Century.* Trans. Arthur Goldhammer. Cambridge, MA and London, UK: Belknap Press of Harvard University Press.
29 Thomas Piketty (June 2014). 'New thoughts on capital in the twenty-first century.' www.ted.com/talks/thomas_piketty_new_thoughts_on_capital_in_the_twenty_first_century?language=en
30 Terry Macalister (26 July 2015). 'Joseph Stiglitz: unsurprising Jeremy Corbyn is a Labour leadership contender.' www.theguardian.com/politics/2015/jul/26/joseph-stiglitz-jeremy-corbyn-labour-leadership-contender-anti-austerity
31 Carl Emmerson, Paul Johnson and Robert Joyce (8 February 2016). 'IFS Green Budget 2016.' www.ifs.org/publications/8129
32 'Budget 2016: "Wage growth to slow down" warns IFS.' (17 March 2016). www.bbc.co.uk/news/business-35830754; Heather Stewart and Larry Elliott (17 March 2016). 'Budget 2016: Osborne "has only 50:50 chance" of hitting surplus

target.' www.theguardian.com/uk-news/2016/mar/17/budget-2016-osborne-chances-of-delivering-surplus-50-50-ifs
33. Ashley Armstrong (7 December, 2015). 'Business rates revaluation adds to pressure on Britain's struggling high street retailers.' www.telegraph.co.uk/finance/newsbysector/constructionandproperty/12034280/Business-Rates-Winners-and-Losers.html
34. Geoffrey Spence (14 May 2015). 'Infrastructure investment: the case of the UK.' www.imf.org/external/pubs/ft/surveys/so/SinglePodcastHighlight.aspx?podcastid=352
35. Kathryn Cooper (13 December 2015). 'Osborne in new blitz on buy-to-let-lending.' *The Sunday Times*, p.2.
36. Rozina Sabur (25 November 2015). 'Autumn statement: will George Osborne cut fuel duty?' www.telegraph.co.uk/finance/autumn-statement/12013672/Autumn-Statement-Will-George-Osborne-cut-fuel-duty.html
37. Tom Newcombe (4 January 2016). 'Willie Walsh urges end to "rip-off" APD.' www.buyingbusinesstravel.com/news/0425132-willie-walsh-urges-government-end-'rip-off'-apd
38. 'UK must increase science funding to keep up with competitors.' (9 November 2015). www.parliament.uk/business/committees/committees-a-z/commons-select/science-and-technology-committee/news-parliament
39. Stephen Grenville (31 March 2015). 'Are China's shadow banks going to bring the economy down?' www.businessspectator.com.au/article/2015/3/31/china/are-chinas-shadow-banks-going-bring-economy-down
40. Noah Smith (24 June 2015). 'The two sides of Japan's deficit trap.' www.bloombergview.com/articles/2015-06-24/abe-s-deficit-plans-will-face-two-immovable-forces

6 Trade

By the end of this chapter you should be able to discuss the pros and cons of globalisation, be familiar with what trade agreements and regional alliances exist and understand how to produce a report on monthly trade figures, including key facts. Additionally, this chapter examines the reasons behind the success of the UK car industry and the strengths and weaknesses of the fair trade business model.

Trade between nations has existed for centuries but the mixture of enhanced technological and transport networks in the past century has accelerated the growth of trade. Whilst that has undoubtedly been a good thing it has created political and environmental tensions in several areas that show few signs of abating despite the efforts of organisations such as the **World Trade Organisation (WTO)**.

Journalistic practice

Monthly trade statistics from major economic nations such as the US, China and UK are routinely reported on in the news with attention focused on the size of deficit or surplus and causes. You should summarise the trade position with a descriptive comment. For example, UK trade deficit narrows but manufacturing weakens.

Trade statistics can be erratic so it is important not to read too much into one month's figures when discussing long-term trends. It is recommended to compare the latest three months against the preceding three months and the same three months of the previous year.

What are the implications of the figures for overall economic growth? Good trade figures can be expected to boost overall economic growth and improve employment prospects as domestic firms look to increase production to meet demand.

Compare the data with the previous month/quarter. Were the figures better or worse than expected? What were the causes of any surprises? For example, heavy snow may disrupt traffic from factories to ports.

(Continued)

Add comment from a City economist and give a trend forecast for the months ahead if possible. Give financial market reaction. A disappointing figure will tend to cause the currency to weaken due to concerns about inflation.

The nature of trade and the relationship between trading nations provides ample scope for features and analysis. For example, in the UK, many reports have focused on how the UK economy has moved from being a largely manufacturing to service economy. Such reports often start with examples of historic manufacturing strength in areas such as shipbuilding, steelmaking and coal production. They then focus on what the growth sectors are now which are wholly in the service sector.

Reports can be done on a specific industry in terms of how much revenue it generates for the UK economy, how many people are employed in the sector, what are its key competitive advantages, profile key players in the industry and discuss future prospects.

The formation of inter-country trade alliances, the machinations of the World Trade Organisation in seeking to promote free trade in specific sectors such as agriculture, and social stories around fair and sustainable trade, all provide plenty of material for features and analysis. Illustration can be done via graphs, photography and interviews with politicians, company representatives, small traders and trade associations.

Debate on the winners and losers from **globalisation** is continuing. It has become more heated following the prolonged negative effects of the 2008 financial crisis. The press has given lots of space to the growing number of influential thinkers questioning whether there should be a new world economic order which benefits the majority rather than the few members of the global elite. Even political leaders such as President Barack Obama have expressed their disquiet about income inequality.

TEST YOUR KNOWLEDGE

Name two of the UK's main trading partners.
Answer: US, Germany, Netherlands, France, Ireland, Belgium/Luxemburg, China, Spain, Italy, United Arab Emirates (also Norway for imports instead of UAE).

Is the UK a net exporter of cars?
Answer: Yes. Large investment by the likes of Honda, Nissan and Tata of India has transformed the UK car industry.

What is the name of the organisation promoting global free trade?
Answer: World Trade Organisation, WTO.

Attractions for the UK as a place to do business

- Relatively flexible labour market
- Good labour relations
- Financial support from the UK government
- The English language
- Laws observed
- Relatively low level of corruption
- Multinational workforce
- Relatively low corporation tax.

A very good news story as far as Britain is concerned has been the performance of the UK car industry in recent years. The UK car industry employs around 800,000 people and makes an annual contribution to the UK economy of around £15bn. In February 2016, sales of new vehicles accelerated 8.4% compared to the same period of 2015, with a total of 83,395 new registrations. These were the best February sales in a decade, in what is usually a quiet month for new car sales.[1]

Substantial inward investment from the likes of Nissan and Tata, owner of Jaguar Land Rover, have revitalised the industry. Tata acquired Jaguar and Land Rover from Ford for just over £1bn in 2008.[2] Other carmakers with significant UK businesses include Toyota, General Motors, Mini and Aston Martin.

Concern about the long-term investment plans of these companies was triggered by the surprise vote leave result in the UK's referendum on membership of the European Union (EU). Analysts believe that car companies will be wary of making substantial investments until it became clear whether trade **tariffs** would be imposed on UK exports.[3]

Paradoxically, car manufacturers employ thousands of workers in parts of England and Wales that voted strongly in favour of leaving the EU. Ford employs 14,000 people at its sites in Bridgend in South Wales and Dagenham in east London. Nissan runs the UK's largest car plant in Sunderland, northeast England, employing almost 7,000 people.

Box 6.1 UK car industry

- UK car industry continued to drive forward in 2016 with January new car registrations at an 11 year high at just over 167,000 units.
- Four out of five cars built in UK sold abroad.
- By 2020 manufacturing forecast to be more than 2 million cars/year.

Source: Society of Motor Manufacturers and Traders (SMMT)

The Society of Motor Manufacturers and Traders (SMMT) campaigned strongly for Britain to remain within the EU. Following the UK vote to

Figure 6.1 Jaguar Landrover assembly line in Halewood, Merseyside. Image courtesy of Howard Barlow/Alamy.

leave the EU, Mike Hawes, chief executive of SMMT said 'Government must now maintain economic stability and secure a deal with the EU which safeguards UK automotive interests. This includes securing tariff-free access to European and other global markets, ensuring we can recruit talent from the EU and the rest of the world and making the UK the most competitive place in Europe for automotive investment'.[4]

The UK car industry is expected to take a leading role in the development of driverless cars. The UK Department of Transport is helping to fund test centres.[5]

As a globally important market and a major employer, stories about the motor industry are common. The admission in September 2015 by Volkswagen – Germany's leading motor manufacturer and an iconic global brand – that it had cheated in testing diesel emissions in its cars was a major news story around the world.[6]

Journalistic practice

Reporting on the Volkswagen scandal threw up lots of questions. How did it happen, who knew what when in terms of senior management?

The collapse in the share price was noted with analysts interviewed on what they thought were the prospects for the shares in both the short and long term. Sales figures were analysed around the world with commentators suggesting options that VW management might take to regain consumer confidence in the brand.

Was the scandal confined to just one market or given its global reach was the problem likely to exist throughout its worldwide markets?

There was speculation on scale of fines from the various national and international regulatory bodies and civil actions by individual car owners.

Analogies were drawn with the long-term damage done to BP following the fatal 2010 Gulf of Mexico oil spill. There was also the question of whether the incident would lead to wider reputational damage to Germany PLC which has always prided itself, and indeed centred a lot of its marketing, on the quality and integrity of its engineering.

The balance of payments is one of the most important economic statistics and is a guide to whether a country is paying its way in the international economy.

The *balance of payments account* shows all the inflows of money to and outflows of money from a country. Inflows must equal outflows overall and therefore the balance of payments must always balance.

Box 6.2 Balance of payments account

- A record of all financial dealings over a period of time between one country and all other countries.
- UK is the world's fifth largest trading nation.
- UK imports about a third of its food, all almost all its iron, lead, zinc, rubber and raw cotton.
- UK exports pharmaceuticals, telecoms, cars and aircraft.
- Split into two components: current account where payments for the purchase and sale of goods and services are recorded.
- Capital and financial account which is the difference between money flows into the country e.g. overseas savings in UK banks and money flows out of the country.

The *current account* of the balance of payments is itself split into several components.

Trade in goods: this is often called **visibles**. This is trade in *raw materials* such as copper and oil, *semi-manufactured goods* such as car components and finished manufactured goods such as cars and televisions.

Trade in services: a wide variety of services is traded internationally including *financial services* such as banking and insurance, *transport services* such as shipping and air travel, and other items such as advertising, royalties, education and tourism. Trade in services is an example of trade in **invisibles**. These are *intangible* services.

> **Box 6.3** Current account
>
> - Income: comes in from interest profits and dividends on assets owned abroad. Remittances – repatriation of earnings from national workers in foreign countries. Turkey, Mexico and Philippines have many foreign workers.
> - Current transfers: range of mainly government transfers to and from overseas organisations – EU and payments of foreign aid.

Income and current transfers: not all flows of money result from trade in goods and services. For example, income comes in from interest profits and dividends on assets owned abroad. For some countries, their main income comes from the repatriation of earnings from national workers in foreign countries. Curbs on migrant workers in host countries can have a big impact on earnings of people working abroad.

These *remittances* are a particularly important source of foreign currency for poor countries with workers in the rich oil-exporting Gulf States. *Turkey* is one country whose citizens work as guest workers abroad. This explains its positive transfers balance, as is the case for *Mexico* where remittances in 2015 were at a three-year high in August as many people rushed to take advantage of the dollar's surge against the peso.[7] *Sweden* is the opposite situation: many foreign workers live there and remit their money to their home countries. This is also the case of the EU and USA.

Income and current transfers are examples of invisibles along with trade in services.

When countries specialise in producing goods or services in which they have lower opportunity costs than competitors, it is known as **comparative advantage**. For example, India has a comparative advantage in cotton goods relative to the USA, because of lower wages and the availability of raw cotton at cheap prices.

For developing countries, the difference between exports and imports of goods and services is often referred to as the *resource gap*. That is the extent to which the country is dependent on the outside world. Many developing countries have resource gaps equivalent to 25–50% of GDP.

> **Box 6.4** Balance of trade
>
> - The relationship between a country's imports and its exports.
> - If a country is exporting more by value than it imports, it is said to have a *trade surplus*.
> - If it imports more than it exports, it has a *trade deficit*.

The balance of payments account is a record of all financial dealings over a period of time between one country and all other countries. The UK is the world's fifth largest trading nation. It imports about a third of its food, almost all of its iron, lead, zinc, rubber and raw cotton. Strong export earners include pharmaceuticals, telecoms, cars and aircraft.

Since World War II there have been a number of consistent trends on the UK current account:

- The balance of trade in goods has been *negative*. Visible exports have tended to be *less* than visible imports. Britain's current account deficit hit a peacetime record of 7% in 2015. Why? It is a reflection of the decline of the UK as a manufacturing base.
- The overall balance on trade in services, income and current transfers has been *positive*. Invisible credits have been greater than invisible debits. The UK has one of the world's largest surpluses on invisibles.
- Breaking down invisibles, the balance of trade in services has nearly always been positive – more services have been sold abroad than have been bought from abroad. These services include items such as insurance, software plus spending by foreign visitors. The UK is a very popular tourist destination and visitor numbers were boosted in recent years by hosting multinational sporting events, the Paralympics and Olympics in 2012 and the Rugby World Cup in 2015.
- London is one of the world's largest centres for *financial services*. More than *two million people* work in financial services throughout the UK, in Edinburgh, Manchester, Birmingham and Glasgow in addition to London. Financial services contribute over 10% of the government's taxes each year. The UK banking sector has had a torrid time in recent years and is not totally out of the woods yet. However, financial services will continue to be a major contributor to government funds in the future not least because of the growth of the UK FinTech sector.[8]
- The use of technology within the financial services sector is not new but what is exciting is the large focused investment being made in new and growing FinTech businesses. In 2014, around £500m was invested in such firms with digital banking a major beneficiary.[9]
- The balance on income has usually been positive too. Income brought into the country by UK people living abroad and income earned from investments abroad have been greater than income leaving the country.
- Current transfers since the 1960s have always been negative. Since joining the European Union in 1973, most of the negative balance is due to the UK paying more into the EU than it receives in grants.

There is often a time lag between business sentiment and what is actually happening on the ground in terms of hard trade data. The UK government is keen for the economy to move away from domestic consumption – which in recent times has been the main driver of economic growth – in favour of higher exports, the opposite to China.

Survey data, which is discussed in more detail in its own chapter, is very closely followed for an insight into the trading environment and how that might impact on actual performance in the months ahead.

UK/China trade

Despite the slowdown in its economic growth rate, China still represents a huge growth opportunity for British business. China accounts for about a quarter of global economic growth, enough to add an economy the size of the UK's over five years.

Box 6.5 UK/China trade

- Government keen to boost trade between UK and China. George Osborne wanted China to be UK's second biggest trading partner by 2025.
- UK attracts more than double the investment of any other European nation.
- China overtook the US to become the world's largest trading nation in 2013.

Multi-billion pound deals across a range of sectors were announced in October 2015, during the state visit to the UK by the Chinese President Xi Jinping. Amongst the major deals was the controversial £6bn 33.5% stake made by Chinese investors in the Hinkley Point nuclear power station in a joint venture with EDF of France.[10]

Other deals included a £2.6bn joint venture between Carnival and the China State Ship Building Company to own and operate a fleet of cruise ships to serve the domestic Chinese market.[11]

China Construction Bank, through its subsidiary CCBI, is to spend £6bn funding research into regenerative medicine and tissue engineering at Oxford University.

The UK has beaten a regular path to China in recent years, keen to strengthen ties and increase business. In December 2013, Prime Minister David Cameron led a three-day trade mission to China, the biggest ever, taking 100 business leaders with him from both large and small companies.[12] The visit prompted some criticism from human rights activists.

Businesses, particularly small ones, worry that they do not know how to go about doing business in China. A government agency, the Department for International Trade (formerly **UK Trade & Investment, UKTI**), provides help to firms wanting to export to China.[13] UK exports of goods to China have more than doubled since 2010. Jaguar Land Rover is the UK's biggest exporter to China. In 2014, China was the UK's 7th largest export market.

Top UK Exports to China in 2013

- Vehicles
- Medicinal and pharmaceutical products
- Power generating machinery/equipment
- Metalliferous ores and scrap metal
- General industrial machinery, equipment and parts.

The importance of China to the UK economy has grown consistently since 2004. In 2014, Britain exported £18.7bn of goods to China, a quadrupling since 2004. The slowdown in the Chinese economy is making it harder for UK firms to make headway. Profits from luxury goods companies such as Burberry are down and the UK's trade deficit with China is growing.[14]

Chinese imports to the UK were £38.3bn in 2014, up from £11.4bn in 2004. As Chinese imports exceed exports, the UK's goods trade deficit with China, at £19.6bn, has grown to be the second largest after Germany. China is now the UK's third largest import-partner. In comparison, the UK ran a trade surplus with China in services of £2.2bn in 2014.

There is thought to be scope to do more business with China across a range of industries in both the manufacturing and service sectors. In December 2015, Powa Technologies, a British e-commerce tech firm announced that it was forming a strategic alliance with China's biggest payments processor, state-owned China UnionPay.[15]

Powa's technology enables shoppers to pay for goods quickly in store and online using their smartphones. Around two-thirds of the Chinese population has a smartphone. China UnionPay has about 4.5 billion credit and debit card users worldwide. Dan Wagner, Powa's chairman and chief executive, thinks the joint venture could generate £3.3bn in revenues over three years.

Prime Minister Theresa May is keen to follow the example of former Chancellor George Osborne in championing closer trading relations with China.[16] However, the prospect of Chinese involvement in the UK's nuclear power industry raised eyebrows amongst some of its Western allies, notably the US. Senior security and defence staff also expressed their misgivings with the UK accused of being craven at best and dangerously naive at worst.

After meeting the Chinese Premier in 2013, Mr Cameron said 'Some in Europe and elsewhere see the world changing and want to shut China off behind a bamboo curtain of trade barriers. Britain wants to tear those trade barriers down'.[17] Mr Cameron believes that closer trading ties between the two countries are mutually beneficial.[18]

UK Trade and investment has identified a myriad of opportunities for UK businesses in China: finance, professional and business services.

Liberalisation and more transparent regulation of China's insurance market are expected to create significant opportunities. China's rapidly growing middle-class and ageing population is creating a demand for life and on-life insurance products.

Oil and gas

China is the world's largest energy consumer using over 20% of world energy. Demand is expected to grow by 72% by 2030. Opportunities are thought to exist in China's oil and gas production and supply in areas such as safety, subsea engineering and deep water oil and gas developments.

Renewable energy

China leads the world in renewable energy. It installed 20.7 gigawatts of wind power in 2014, nearly half the world's total. In September 2013, the UK signed a Memorandum of Understanding with China on offshore wind cooperation. UK companies could get involved in environmental assessment and risk management, consultancy and design, feasibility studies and modelling and marine cabling supply and installation.

Aerospace

Airbus forecasts that China will need more than 5,300 new passenger aircraft and freighters from 2014 to 2033, worth $820bn. This represents 17% of world total demand in the next 20 years. There are also more airports being planned and built than anywhere else in the world. There is also a growing Chinese space programme.

There are thought to be opportunities for UK companies with products or technologies in automation, avionics, composite materials and structures, upstream and downstream satellite signal processing and airport security.

Marine

China is the world's leading ship building nation with 45% of all orders by gross tonnage. There could be opportunities for small and medium sized UK companies to supply equipment and services to some of the higher margin, complex vessels. UK businesses might also get involved in design, and the operation of ship yards.

Life sciences and healthcare

Large-scale investment has improved access to healthcare in China but there are some issues still to be resolved against a background of an ageing population. There is a widening gap between what is available in urban and rural areas and some technologies are outdated. Many wealthy Chinese travel to Hong Kong or Singapore for medical care.

The Chinese admire the UK's National Health Service. Opportunities for UK companies are available in the prevention and control of chronic diseases such as diabetes, cancer and asthma. There is also scope to upgrade or replace many of China's 22,000 hospitals and to facilitate the spread of digital health technology to provide instant access to health services and information.

Culture

There is strong Chinese government backing for culture and sport. A group of Chinese companies led by China Media Capital (CMC) wants to invest around $1.5bn in Formula One motor racing.

The UK has much to offer in terms of cultural industries, for example, TV and animation programme licensing and co-production, mobile gaming, film, visual effects and post-production, theme park and leisure attractions, museums and other cultural venues, advertising and marketing, and the promotion of elite sports such as equestrian, sailing and golf.

Visit www.youtube.com/user/uktiweb for information on the scope for creative collaborations between the UK and China.

With economic growth anaemic in much of the mature Western economies, many countries are looking to China for trade and investment. Scotland's first minister Nicola Sturgeon visited China in 2015 to help foster closer trading links with China.[19] Chinese visitors make a valuable contribution to the Scottish economy and exports to China were at record levels of almost £580m in 2013. Attention is focused on promoting innovation in the low carbon energy, education, food and drink, technology and textile sectors.

Countries with large manufacturing sectors, such as Germany and Japan, have tended to run visible-trade surpluses and invisibles deficits.

Germany

The German economy proved to be resilient throughout the financial crisis on the back of its strong manufacturing performance. It is Europe's largest economy and in 2014 benefited from a weaker euro. Since 1952, Germany has run a regular trade surplus due to its strong exports of cars – models include Mercedes, Audi and Volkswagen.

Representatives of German companies were quick to say they wanted to maintain trading relationships with the UK after the referendum vote. German Chancellor Angela Merkel said there was 'no need to be nasty' in negotiations with the UK. 'It's important we work together to get the right outcome'.[20]

> **Box 6.6** German trade
>
> - 2016 trade surplus expected to overtake China to be the world's largest (www.tradingeconomics.com).
> - Strong manufacturing base.
> - Exports of cars, machinery, pharmaceuticals, electronic equipment and metals.
> - World's third largest exporter and importer.

German exports have been boosted by the weak euro. The European Commission and IMF have warned of the dangers of Germany's trade surplus hampering recovery in the eurozone's crisis-hit economies. They would like to see Germany increase public investment.[21]

Germany has established strong trading links with China and other emerging markets. In February 2016, Beijing Enterprises paid Euro1.44bn for the German EEW Energy from Waste business, the largest Chinese acquisition of a German business.[22]

In 2014, Germany exported $99bn worth of goods to China. Germany's other key trading partners include the USA, France, Italy and the Netherlands. Aside from cars, other German exports include machinery, pharmaceuticals, electronic equipment and metals.[23]

Japan

Japan's decision to shut all its nuclear reactors in the aftermath of the tsunami and earthquake in 2011 meant it had to import gas which pushed its trade balance into deficit.[24]

In April, 2015, Japan recorded its first surplus since 2012 helped by lower global oil prices and a weaker yen which boosted the value of exports. These trends continued through the year and Japan ended 2015 with a narrower annual trade deficit of 2.8 trillion yen.[25]

> **Box 6.7** Japanese trade
>
> - Made Y496.2bn trade surplus in October 2016, 373% higher than a year earlier.
> - Benefited from lower commodity prices and import costs. Japan has high energy imports after all nuclear reactors were shut after the tsunami and earthquake in 2011.
> - Value of yen dropped more than 20% against the dollar.

Fallout from the UK's decision to leave the European Union in June 2016 prompted a surge in the value of the Japanese yen as investors sought safe havens for their money. The Japanese Prime Minister Shinzo Abe held an emergency meeting, concerned at the impact of the strong yen on Japanese exports and his efforts to boost Japanese economic growth after years in the doldrums.

There are also concerns that a stronger yen could reduce Japanese investors' appetites for investment in Asian emerging markets.

Currency effect

Japan has been following an aggressive economic growth strategy known as Abenomics, after the Prime Minister. This has led to a sharp decline in the value of the yen.[26]

A weaker currency is good for Japan's exports as it makes them cheaper for foreign buyers. A weak yen also boosts profits of exporters when they repatriate their overseas earnings back home.

However the weak currency has made imports more expensive and exports are not rising fast enough to offset this increased cost and so the trade balance has been adversely affected.

The IMF estimates that a 10% real effective **depreciation** in an economy's currency is associated with a rise in real net exports of, on average, 1.5% of GDP, with substantial cross-country variation around this average. Although these effects fully materialise over a number of years, much of the adjustment occurs in the first year. The boost to exports associated with currency depreciation is found to be largest in countries with initial economic slack and with domestic financial systems that are operating normally.[27]

There are fears that a new currency war could flare up after back door moves by the Chinese authorities to devalue the renminbi. In December 2015, the People's Bank of China announced that it would measure the level of the renminbi against a basket of currencies rather than just the dollar.[28]

Such a change in policy would enable the Bank to guide the renminbi lower versus the dollar. Some market watchers think it will help smooth the path to a flexible exchange rate and that there is less of a case for tying the value of the renminbi to just the dollar given the divergence between the economies and monetary policies of the US and the rest of the world.

However, the policy could lead to a bout of turmoil in the financial markets such as that which accompanied the unexpected devaluation of the currency in August 2015 when the currency dropped 3.3% in three days. The sell-off is widely thought to have been instrumental in the decision by the US Federal Reserve to delay its much anticipated rise in US interest rates.

Despite its economic might, China acknowledges that it is not immune from the secondary effects of the Brexit vote. Analysts are concerned that a prolonged phase of dollar strength (it being one of the main beneficiaries of the flight to safe investments) could force the Chinese authorities to pursue currency depreciation, triggering a chain reaction among China's Asian suppliers.[29]

Box 6.8 US trade

- Goods and services deficit $36.4bn in September 2016.
- Surpluses with the UK, OPEC, South and Central America.
- Deficits with China, EU, Mexico, Germany, Japan and Saudi Arabia.

Globalisation

Globalisation has led to a greater movement of money, products and people across the globe. Increasingly, economies depend on each other for success. More and more firms are operating globally and developing global brands such as Nike, Apple and Marlboro.

If you visit countries all over the world then you are likely to see a brand you know, for example Starbucks, Ford, Coca Cola and of course McDonald's. The latter two brands are available in all five continents.

Various factors have enabled globalisation to take hold.

Higher incomes and standards of living in some economies have led consumers and firms to search abroad for a wider range of products.

Better communication systems and information technology have made it easier for firms and consumers to know and buy what is available abroad.

Better transport links and lower transport costs have made trade more economically viable.

The financial crash of 2008 has prompted many people to question how the world economy operates. In his interesting book *The Collapse of Globalism*, John Ralston Saul suggests that globalisation was effectively over by around year 2000.

A combination of technology, capitalism and regulation has produced a permanent glut in trade goods. The direct result has been an ever-growing drive to manage the surplus by cutting back on competition, consumers have been turned into speculators and prices have been driven down beyond the production costs of middle-class, educated citizens.

'We have been following a global economic theory flying the flag of wealth creation, but ending up pushing cheaper goods as an excuse for lower wages, which means wealth reduction'.[30]

Concern about the effects of globalisation and rising income inequality were some of the reasons cited for the surprising majority vote by Britain to leave the European Union.

World Trade Organisation (WTO)

> **Box 6.9** World Trade Organisation
>
> - The WTO is an international body which aims to liberalise trade between its members.
> - Established in 1995, it encourages countries to lower protectionist barriers, increasing trade flows between countries. Polices trade agreements made.

Some people think trade not aid is the best way to help less developed countries. However many developing countries face **protectionism**. This takes the form of high trade barriers to their exports for example in agricultural commodities to the USA and the EU. This limits exports and therefore GDP growth.

Proponents of free trade face a more difficult battle when the world economy is in recession.

A major stumbling block continues to be the **Common Agricultural Policy (CAP)** which rewards large industrial-scale farmers, promotes the overproduction of food and prevents the import of many foodstuffs from developing nations into Europe.[31]

Protectionist forces are unlikely to reduce significantly against a backdrop of declining commodity prices due to weaker economic growth in emerging markets and abundant supply.[32]

However in December 2015 in what was described as an 'historic' farming subsidy deal, countries in the World Trade Organisation (WTO) agreed to abolish $15bn of subsidies on farming exports. The deal, agreed in Kenya, is intended to help farmers in poorer countries to compete more fairly.[33]

The great economic Depression of the 1930s led countries to adopt very protectionist policies. These proved to be self-defeating and so in 1947, 23 countries signed the **General Agreement on Tariffs and Trade (GATT)**.

Under GATT rules, member countries were not allowed to increase the degree of protection given to their domestic producers. However, it did nothing to reduce protectionism. For this reason GATT and its successor organisation, the WTO, World Trade Organisation, have over the years organised a series of negotiations (called rounds) aimed at reducing tariffs and **quotas**.

Since the end of World War II, trade has increased rapidly and has been the main agent of economic growth. Developing countries in general have a comparative advantage in agriculture and low technology, labour intensive manufactured goods. However many goods exported from developing nations find themselves in direct competition with goods made in long established industries in the mature industrialised countries.

Not surprisingly, these industries press their governments for protection against these cheaper imports. Those protectionist voices are growing louder around the world. Agriculture is heavily protected in Europe and North America. The European Union even exports farm products to the developing world at hugely subsidised prices. Textiles is another industry that until 2004 was heavily protected in the industrialised world. However as part of the Uruguay Round of trade talks, tariffs and quotas were removed in 2004.

The result was a sudden leap in world exports of textiles, particularly from China, to mature industrialised countries in Western Europe, US, Canada and Australia. Textile producers in the developing world gained market share whilst consumers gained cheaper products.[34]

Doha Round of trade talks

The Doha Round of trade talks was launched in November 2001 and is the ninth round of talks. The trade negotiations cover a variety of areas, including increased duty-free access for developing countries, lower tariffs on agricultural products, textiles and clothing, foreign companies bidding for government contracts and intellectual property rights.[35] The talks are expected to lead to further reductions in trade barriers which should boost world trade. The International Chamber of Commerce (ICC) forecasts that streamlining customs procedures could add $1 trillion and 21 million jobs to the world economy.

However, the talks stalled in 2008 over disagreements about agriculture imports. Agriculture is particularly important for developing countries because three-quarters of the population live in rural areas and the vast majority are dependent on agriculture for their livelihoods.

The lack of progress has led some countries to seek agreements among smaller groups, undermining the legitimacy of the WTO.

Box 6.10 Types of government trade restriction

- *Tariffs*: government taxes on imports or exports. For example the EU imposes dumping tariffs on cheap Chinese steel.
- *Quotas*: restrictions on the quantity of imports allowed.
- *Subsidies*: payments made by governments to companies in order to assist the manufacture or export of particular goods (not a restriction but anti-competitive).

Banana deal

In 2011, banana wars finally ended after 15 years, one of the world's longest international trade disputes. Eight separate cases were dealt with by the

WTO. The agreement to reduce EU tariffs on South American imports means fewer bananas from the Caribbean and Africa.[36]

Bananas are the world's most traded fruit and make up about 10% of the exports of Ecuador, Costa Rica and Panama.

Tech tariffs

Some long overdue progress in trade liberalisation was announced in December 2015 with the elimination of restrictions on the $1.3tn trade of 201 information technology (IT) products. It was the biggest tariff reduction deal in almost two decades.[37]

IT goods account for about 7% of trade and have overtaken the likes of textiles, automotive goods and iron and steel. The 53 countries signed up to the deal include China and account for 90% of the trade in IT products.

Tech experts predict the expansion of the 1996 Information Technology Agreement will boost global growth by at least $190bn a year as the costs are cut in trading a range of goods. These include GPS devices, video game consoles and next-generation semiconductors but not LED displays.

It is hoped the tariff reduction deal will also help to re-energise the WTO.

Britain may turn to the WTO to regulate its trading relationship with the European Union following the Brexit vote. This would mean the introduction of tariffs, also known as import duty or customs duty. These are taxes on imported goods which have the effect of raising the domestic price of imports and therefore inevitably reducing demand for them. Economists think this would be the least attractive outcome for Britain.

There are concerns that after over 40 years of EU membership, Britain lacks sufficient numbers of experienced trade negotiators within the Civil Service. The gap in expertise is likely to have to be filled by commercial law firms and management consultancies.

Fair trade

In recent years there has been considerable growth in sales of **fair trade products**.[38]

Fair trade aims to give farmers in the developing world a better deal by guaranteeing them a minimum price for their produce. Over 1.3 million farmers and workers in 70 countries are part of the 1,145 Fairtrade producer organisations.

In 1964, the charity Oxfam created the first fair trade organisation and shop. However, the first Fairtrade-labelled product, coffee, was available in 1988. Since then it has grown enormously with more than 30,000 certified products on sale in more than 125 countries. Popular Fairtrade products are coffee, tea, bananas, chocolate and sugar.

Critics argue that its impact on the developing world is insignificant and that it is a distraction from the real issue of development.

It leads to overproduction of certain crops because of the financial stability that the scheme offers.

Farmers become dependent on the Western world and too focused on the narrow fair trade market rather than developing modern agricultural methods.

There is a move away from smaller farms in favour of large-scale operations.

For supermarkets it is good marketing because it makes them appear ethical.

Advantaging some producers can leave other producers worse off.

In his book *Doing Good Better*, William Macaskill says there is little altruistic reason to buy Fairtrade products.

> When you buy Fairtrade you usually aren't giving money to the poorest people in the world.
>
> Of the additional money that is spent on Fairtrade, only a very small portion ends up in the hands of the farmers who earn that money. Middlemen take the rest.
>
> Even the small fraction that ultimately reaches the producers does not necessarily translate into higher wages.[39]

Supporters argue that for millions of people, fair trade makes a difference.

It allows producers to invest, improve their agricultural processes, move up the value chain, diversify and grow a business.

Fair trade is growing fast and doing something, however small, is better than doing nothing. However they acknowledge that the scheme can be improved to address problems of oversupply and product quality.

Sovereign nations are increasingly joining together in *regional economic groupings* which may or may not turn out to be a good thing for overall free world trade. Some economists think these regional agreements are inherently inefficient and discriminatory. Arguably the growth of globalisation alongside digital technology invalidates the need for trade blocs and protected regions.

Box 6.11 Regional trade groups

Advantages

- Economies of scale reduce costs and should lower prices for consumers.
- Job creation from increased trade.
- Market access should boost trade between members.

Disadvantages

- Distorts world trade and encourages more blocs.
- Protects inefficient producers in the bloc.

The *European Union (EU)* is a single market of over 500 million people. The EU was originally called the Common Market after its formation following the treaty of Rome in 1957. The original six members were Germany, France, Italy, Belgium, Netherlands and Luxembourg. The UK joined in 1973. Following continuous enlargement the EU has 28 members, until Britain formally leaves. The EU is by far the UK's biggest trading partner, accounting for around 44% of British exports.

The members of the *European Economic Area (EEA)* include all those in the European Union plus Norway, Iceland and Liechtenstein. Members have full access to the single market in goods and services, but not in agriculture, in what is known collectively as an internal market. EEA members have to contribute to the European Union budget and accept freedom of movement of goods, services, persons and capital. EEA members co-operate in important areas such as research and development, education, social policy, the environment, consumer protection, tourism and culture.

UK industry and the EU

Industry jobs share of exports going to the EU:

- Aerospace 110,000 47%
- Chemicals and pharmaceuticals 136,000 54%
- Financial services 1,069,000 41%
- Food manufacturing 373,000 53%
- IT and telecoms 1,364,000 46%
- Transport 1,065,000 44%.

Source: HM Government EU referendum booklet[40]

It is thought that the UK would like to have a version of EEA membership but with the ability to control immigration, a major factor in the campaign to leave the EU. The fact that Britain imports far more from the EU than it exports to it should give it some leverage in trade negotiations. German car makers and French wine producers are just two groups who would like to continue to trade as easily as possible with one of their biggest trading partners.

After around 5 years of negotiation, the **Trans-Pacific Partnership (TPP)** was finally agreed in October 2015. It is a *free trade area* covering the US, Canada and ten countries in the Asia Pacific region.[41]

Membership of the TPP

Members are the US, Japan, Malaysia, Vietnam, Singapore, Brunei, Canada, Australia, New Zealand, Mexico, Chile and Peru.

The countries involved account for 40% of the world's trade and with a collective population of 800 million people are almost double the size of the European Union's single market. Japan is expected to be the major beneficiary of the pact. Critics of the agreement are wide ranging including US former Secretary of State Hilary Clinton and president-elect Donald Trump and consumer groups who fear the negotiated deal favours large corporations.

Following the US election the TPP will not be approved by Congress. Some analysts think inflation, especially in consumer goods, could become an issue in the years ahead as a result of rising protectionism in the US and Europe.[42]

The glaring omission in the TPP group is *China*. Indeed critics see the Partnership as an attempt by the US to lessen the economic impact of China in the region. Added impetus for the US to reach agreement undoubtedly came from the formation of the Asian Infrastructure Investment Bank, (AIIB) in June 2015. It is moving quickly to widen its sphere of influence with plans to expand its lending activities beyond Asia to Africa and Latin America. Brazil was the only Latin American founding member of the Bank.[43]

The Chinese authorities hope that the TPP and other free trade agreements in the region would contribute to investment and economic growth.[44]

As part of the deal, 98% of tariffs will be eliminated on a wide range of products including dairy, beef, sugar, wine, rice, seafood and energy. In addition to trade agreements the Partnership is expected to cover a broad range of regulatory and legal issues in areas such as intellectual property and employment practices. The US lobbied hard for stronger copyright protections for music and film, as well as broader and longer-lasting patents.

Closer trading ties between the EU and the US, known as the **Transatlantic Trade and Investment Partnership** (TTIP) are also expected to be a casualty of the Trump presidency. Talks started in 2013. Even before the election tension was high due to European tax demands against American multinationals such as Apple, and the large fines levied on European banks by US regulators.

In October 2016, the EU and Canada signed a free trade deal, Ceta.[45]

Under Donald Trump, Britain could get its first trade deal before Article 50 is triggered setting in train Britain's withdrawl from the European Union.

The withdrawal of Britain from the EU is thought likely to make it harder to secure agreement from the remaining EU nations for TTIP. Several countries including Germany and Austria already had misgivings about the benefits of the alliance.[46]

In Asia, regional leaders hope to create a trade area to rival China and India. The ten-member **Association of South-East Nations** (ASEAN) is an economically disparate group including Singapore, Malaysia, Cambodia and the Philippines. According to World Bank figures, in 2015, Cambodia's GDP per head was $1158.7 compared to Singapore's $56,284.8.[47]

Potentially, ASEAN could be a major economic force as a single market and a single production base, with more than 600 million people and a GDP of over $2.5 trillion. For a decade, the region has achieved average annual economic growth of 6–7%.

Almost all categories of goods traded within the bloc are tariff-free. The ASEAN population is younger than that of China which suggests that rapid growth is sustainable for many years as the workforce grows and consumer spending increases.[48]

Mercosur is South America's leading trade bloc. It has been likened to the European Union but with an area of 12 million square kilometres, it is four times as big. The bloc's combined market encompasses more than 250 million people. It was set up in March 1991 by Argentina, Brazil, Paraguay and Uruguay. Bolivia, Chile, Columbia, Ecuador and Peru are associate members.

Critics have accused Mercosur of becoming politicised and moving away from its free trade origins. However, the EU is currently negotiating a trade agreement with Mercosur covering a range of issues including trade in industrial and agricultural goods, services, intellectual property and customs.[49]

In July 2015, African leaders agreed to create a Continent-wide free trade zone, the **Tripartite Free Trade Area (TFTA)** covering 26 countries in an area from Cape Town to Cairo. It is an opportune moment given the Continent's healthy economic growth rates of 5% in recent years. It is hoped that by 2017 the agreement will have been endorsed by the parliaments of all member nations.[50]

The aim of the pact is to give Africa a louder voice on the world stage when it comes to negotiating international deals, help intra-regional trade and boost growth across the region of more than 600 million people. The poor state of roads, railways and airlines has hindered intra-African trade in the past. The agreement is expected to lead to greater cooperation in infrastructure and energy projects in the region. The bloc includes South Africa, Zimbabwe, Kenya, Botswana, Egypt and Libya.[51]

A question increasingly asked is whether multinational organisations like the World Trade Organisation or the International Monetary Fund, which support or promote trade liberalisation are controlled by the rich countries of the world and do they act against the interests of poorer countries.

Recommended reading

Some see globalisation as evidence of the benefits of trade. Others think it is destroying local producers and local identities, and that the power of some of the huge multinational corporations is too great.

This latter view is certainly the case put in Naomi Klein's international best-selling book *No Logo*. As an example, she cites the fact that in 1992 Michael Jordan's salary for endorsing Nike trainers was more than that of the entire 30,000 strong Indonesian workforce employed in making them.

In his book *Future Files*, a brief history of the next 50 years, futurologist Richard Watson predicts that everything from countries to computers to gadgets and global banking will be hyperlinked together. This trend is expected to accelerate even faster with the loss of privacy. Transparency and risk may increase, the latter due to risks being networked and traded globally.

Globalisation is not just an economic phenomenon. It is a political, social, technological and cultural phenomenon too. In his best-selling book *Globalisation and Its Discontents*, economist Joseph Stiglitz argues that the developed world needs to reform the international institutions that govern globalisation.

He says that development is not about helping a few people get rich or creating a handful of pointless protected industries that only benefit the country's elite, nor is it about bringing in Prada and Benetton, Ralph Lauren or Louis Vuitton, for the urban rich and leaving the rural poor in their misery. He says development is about transforming societies, improving the lives of the poor, enabling everyone to have a chance at success and access to healthcare and education.

Box 6.12 Book recommendations

O'Brien, Robert and Williams, Marc (2010) *Global Political Economy Evolution and Dynamics*. London: Palgrave Macmillan.

Peet, Richard (2009) *Unholy Trinity: The IMF, World Bank and WTO*. www.zedbooks.co.uk

Roubini, Nouriel and Mihm, Stephen (2011) *Crisis Economics: A Crash Course in the Future of Finance*. London: Penguin.

Stiglitz, Joseph (2002) *Globalisation and Its Discontents*. London: Penguin.

Tourism

One manifestation of globalisation is that more people are experiencing is tourism. As people become more affluent they tend to want to travel. Travel and tourism is thought to be the largest industry in the world, sustaining more than one in eleven jobs. It has been a major driver of global economic growth and is the main source of income for many developing countries.

Box 6.13 World tourism

- 10% GDP
- 1 in 11 jobs
- $1.5 trillion in export earnings in 2015
- 7% of world exports
- 30% of services exports
- 4.6% rise in international tourist arrivals in 2015 to £1.184 billion.

Source: World Tourism Organization (UNWTO)

However, the scale of the global tourism industry has put huge pressure on local people, environments and natural resources such as water. Many high-end hotels have golf courses. These require large amounts of water to maintain their appearance. Other negative factors are: the loss of locally owned land to large foreign corporations, prostitution, drug abuse, crime and the abandonment of traditional values and practices.[52]

Assignments

Write 300 words on Chinese investment in the UK.
Globalisation is a force for good in the world, discuss in 800 words.

Glossary of key terms

Association of Southeast Asian Nations (ASEAN): Singapore, Malaysia, Brunei, Thailand, Indonesia, Philippines, Vietnam, Laos, Cambodia and Burma.

Balance of payments account: this records all transactions between one country and the rest of the world. It is made up of the current account and the capital account. The current account records the value of imports and exports of goods and services. The capital account records the inflow and outflow of investments and other financial flows.

Common Agricultural Policy (CAP): European Union (EU) policy aimed at providing stable food supplies for the 500 million people of the European Union whilst providing a good standard of living for the EU's 22 million farmers and agricultural workers.

Comparative advantage: when a country has lower costs associated with providing a particular good or service relative to other countries.

Depreciation: decline in value.

Dumping: the sale of goods at less than cost price by foreign producers in the domestic market e.g. Chinese steel in Europe.

Fair trade: international movement aimed at providing producers in developing countries with a 'fair' price for their goods e.g. coffee and bananas.

General Agreement on Tariffs and Trade (GATT): replaced by the World Trade Organisation (WTO) in 1995.

Globalisation: the increasing integration of national economies into a single world market for goods, services and the free movement of labour between countries.

Gross Domestic Product (GDP): the measure of the total sum of all economic activity within a country, both goods and services.

Invisibles: trade in services such as banking, insurance and tourism.

Mercosur: the South American trade bloc set up in 1991 by Argentina, Brazil, Paraguay and Uruguay.

Protectionism: when governments try to protect their domestic firms from foreign competition. This can take several forms including quotas and tariffs.

Quotas: limits placed on the number of products from a particular country.
Remittances: repatriation of earnings from national workers in foreign countries.
Tariffs: taxes placed on specific goods and services from overseas. In April 2016, China imposed 46% import duty on imports of a type of high tech steel from the EU.
Trans-Pacific Partnership (TPP): a trade deal between 12 Pacific Rim countries including the US and Japan aimed at lowering the cost of trade and setting common standards. Member countries account for about 40% of the global economy.
Transatlantic Trade and Investment Partnership (TTIP): a trade partnership between the European Union (EU) and the US.
Tripartite Free Trade Area: an African free trade zone of 26 countries.
UK Trade and Investment (UKTI): the government body focused on increasing the number of exporters and inward investors to the UK.
Visibles: trade in goods such as raw materials and manufactured goods such as cars.
World Trade Organisation (WTO): the international body whose role is to promote free trade by persuading countries to abolish import tariffs and other trade restrictions.

Resource list

ONS provides the UK official trade statistics: www.ons.gov.uk
The UK Trade & Investment website has guides on doing business in various countries including China: www.gov.uk/government/organisations/uk-trade-investment
World Trade Organisation: www.wto.org
ASEAN: www.asean.org
Make Poverty History: www.makepovertyhistory.org
Fairtrade International: www.fairtrade.net
IMF World Economic Outlook (WEO) October 2015: www.imf.org
World Tourism Organization (UNWTO): www.unwto.org.
World Travel & Tourism Council, Economic Impact Analysis: www.wttc.org/research/economic-research/economic-impat-analysis/

Recommended reading

Goldin, Ian and Reinert, Kenneth (2012). *Globalisation for Development. Meeting New Challenges*. Oxford: Oxford University Press.
Guinness, Paul (2003). *Globalisation*. London: Hodder Education.
Klein, Naomi (2010). *No Logo*. London: Fourth Estate (10th edn).
Lamb, Harriet (2009). *Fighting the Banana Wars and Other Fairtrade Battles. How We Took on the Corporate Giants to Change the World*. London: Rider (2nd edn).
Porritt, Jonathon (2008). *Globalism and Regionalism*. London: Black Dog Publishing.
Stiglitz, Joseph (2002). *Globalisation and Its Discontents*. London: Penguin.

Stiglitz, Joseph and Charlton, Andrew (2005). *Fair Trade for All. How Trade Can Promote Development.* Oxford: Oxford University Press.
Watson, Richard (2010). *Future Files. A Brief History of the Next 50 Years.* London: Nicholas Brealey Publishing (2nd edn).

Notes

1. Alan Tovey (5 March 2016). 'Car sales buck trend with strongest rise in more than a decade.' www.telegraph.co.uk/business/2016/03/04/car-sales-buck-trend-with-strongest-rise-in-more-than-a-decade/
2. 'Tata buys Jaguar in £1.15bn deal.' (26 March 2008). news.bbc.co.uk/1/hi/business/7313380.stm
3. Peter Campbell (25 June 2016). 'Ford considers job cuts on currency concerns.' www.ft.com/topics/people-peterc_ampbell
4. 'SMMT statement in reaction to EU referendum result.' (24 June 2016). www.smmt.co.uk/2016/06/smmt-statement-in-reaction-to-eu-referendum-result/
5. GOV.UK (19 July 2015). 'UK to lead the way in testing driverless cars.' www.gov.uk/government/news/uk-to-lead-the-way-in-testing-driverless-cars; Matthew Lynn (10 August 2015). 'Driverless cars could turn the UK into Europe's leader in autos – but only if we de-regulate first.' www.telegraph.co.uk/finance/comment/matthew-lynn/11794415/Driverless-cars-could-turn-the-UK-into-Europes-leader-in-autos-but-only-if-we-de-regulate-first.html
6. Damien McGuinness (22 September 2015). 'VW scandal threatens "Made in Germany" brand.' www.bbc.co.uk/news/world-europe-34328689
7. 'Remittances to Mexico rise more than 6% in first 8 months of 2015.' (2 October 2015).latino.foxnews.com/latino/politics/2015/10/02/remittances-to-mexico-rise-more-than-6-pct-in-first-8-months-2015/
8. 'London Fintech Boom: the UK has a world leading Fintech footprint.' (15 October 2015). www.crowdfundinsider.com/2015/10/75801-london-fintech-boom-the-uk-has-a-world-leading-fintech-footprint/
9. 'Within Fin Tech, investors turn from "neobanks" to "digital challenger" banks'. (16 December 2015). www.cbinsights.com/blog/challenger-banks-fin-tech/
10. Damian Carrington (20 October 2015). 'China to take one-third stake in £24bn Hinkley nuclear power station.' www.theguardian.com/environment/2015/oct/20/china-to-take-one-third-stake-in-24bn-hinkley-nuclear-power-station
11. Gene Sloan (28 October 2015). 'Carnival cruise line to transfer two ships to China.' www.usatoday.com/story/travel/cruises/2015/10/28/carnival-cruise-china-ships/74729596/
12. Sean Farrell (2 December 2013). 'Business chiefs join David Cameron in China to drum up trade.' www.theguardian.com/business/2013/dec/02/business-chiefs-david-cameron-china
13. Gov.uk. (21 December 2015). 'Doing business in China: China trade and export guide.' www.gov.uk/government/publications/exporting-to-china/exporting-to-china
14. (18 May 2016). 'Burberry profits fall in challenging market.' www.bbc.co.uk/news/business-36319567
15. Matthew Wall (16 December 2015). 'Shopping tech firm Powa in major Chinese joint venture.' www.bbc.co.uk/news/business-35112364
16. Joe Watts and Jon Stone (3 September 2016). 'Theresa May promises a golden era of relations between Britain and China after Brexit.' www.independent.co.uk/news/uk/politics/theresa-may-promises-a-golden-era-of-relations-between-britain-and-china-after-brexit-a7223961.html

17 'David Cameron defends China trade mission.' (3 December 2013). www.bbc.co.uk/news/uk-politics-25198517
18 'My visit can begin a relationship to benefit China, Britain and the world.' (2 December 2013). www.theguardian.com/commentisfree/2013/dec/02/david-cameron-my-visit-to-china
19 'First Minister Nicola Sturgeon leads China trade mission.' (25 July 2015). www.bbc.co.uk/news/uk-scotland-scotland-business-33663593
20 Liam Halligan (27 June 2016). 'This courageous vote is our best chance to reshape Europe's future.' www.telegraph.co.uk.business/2016/06/26/this-courageous-vote-is-our-best-chance-to-reshape-europes-future/
21 Nicholas Hirst (24 July 2014). 'IMF warns of dangers of Germany's trade surplus.' www.politico.eu/article/imf-warns-of-dangers-of-germanys-trade-surplus
22 Guy Chazan (5 February 2016). 'Beijing buys German waste-to-energy group.' *Financial Times*, p.20.
23 Andrew Moody (21 October 2015). 'Will the UK or Germany be China's main trading partner?' www.telegraph.co.uk/sponsored/china-watch/business/11938977/will-uk-or-germany-be-china-main-trading-partner.html/
24 David Batty and agencies (5 May 2012). 'Japan shuts down last working nuclear reactor.' www.theguardian.com/world/2012/may/05/japan-shuts-down-last-nuclear-reactor
25 Yoshiaki Nohara (25 January 2016). 'Japan's annual trade deficit narrows as energy import costs fall.' www.bloomberg.com/news/articles/2016-01-25/japan-s-annual-trade-deficit-narrows-as-energy-import-costs-fall
26 Wes Goodman and Sandy Hendry (31 March 2015). 'Japan bulls rest hopes for Abenomics on yen weakening beyond 130.' www.bloomberg.com/news/articles/2015-03-31/japan-bulls-rest-hopes-for-abenomics-on-yen-weakening-beyond-130
27 International Monetary Fund (28 September 2015). 'Transcript of the press conference on the release of the analytical chapters of the October 2015 World Economic Outlook.' www.imf.org/external/np/tr/2015/tr092815.htm; Phillip Inman (28 September 2015). 'IMF currency study shows power of devaluation.' www.theguardian.com/business/2015/sep/28/imf-currency-study-shows-power-of-devaluation
28 Sophia Yan (11 December 2015). 'China's currency has fallen to 4-year lows.' www.money.cnn.com/2015/12/11/investing/china-yuan-depreciation/
29 James Kynge (25 June 2016). 'Markets pass their first Brexit stress test-FT.com.' www.ft.com/cms/s/0/88e2bc9e-3ad5-11e6-92fc-36b487ebd80a.html
30 John Ralston Saul (2009). *The Collapse of Globalism*. London: Atlantic Books, p.293.
31 Trinity College Dublin (25 August 2010). 'The development critique of the CAP.' www.tcd.ie/iiis/policycoherence/eu-agricultural-policy/development-critique-cap.php
32 International Monetary Fund (April 2016). Commodity Special Feature from World Economic Outlook. www.imf.org/external/pubs/ft/weo/2016/01/pdf/SF_Commod.pdf
33 WTO (19 December 2015). '2 WTO members secure "historic" Nairobi Package for Africa and the world.' www.wto.org/english/news_e/news15_e/mc10_19dec15_e.htm
34 WTO (n.d.). 'Textiles: back in the mainstream.' www.wto.org/english/thewto_e/whatis_e/tif_e/agrm5_e.htm; Gambrell Smith and LLP Russell (Winter 2016). 'preferential treatment: how textile trade agreements limit or benefit free trade.' www.sgrlaw.com/resources/trust_the_leaders/leaders_issues/tt18/903/
35 WTO (n.d.). 'The Doha Round.' www.wto.org/english/tratop_e/dda_e/dda_e.htm

36 Tom Lamont (6 February 2011). 'Banana wars over as trade truce agreed between Latin America and EU'. www.theguardian.com/lifeandstyle/2011/feb/06/banana-trade-latin-america-europe; Rick Peters (4 February 2011). 'Banana wars: who are the real winners?' www.theguardian.com/lifeandstyle/wordofmouth/2011/feb/04/banana-wars-winners-losers
37 John Aglionby (December 16 2015). 'IT tariffs slashed in biggest WTO deal since 1990.' www.ft.com/fastft/2015/12/16/ic-tariffs-slashed-in-biggest-deal-since-1996/
38 Rebecca Smithers (3 September 2014). 'Global Fairtrade sales reach £4.4bn following 15% growth during 2013.' www.theguardian.com/global-development/2014/sep/03/global-fairtrade-sales-reach-4-billion-following-15-per-cent-growth-2
39 William Macaskill (2015). *Doing Good Better. A Radical New Way to Make a Difference.* London: Guardian Books and Faber & Faber, pp.164–166.
40 The 14-page pro-EU membership document was sent to every household in the UK 27 million homes, ahead of the UK's EU referendum on 23 June: www.eureferendum.gov.uk/why-the-government-believes-we-should-remain/eu-referendum-leaflet/
41 United States Trade Representative (n.d.) 'TPP full text.' ustr.gov/trade-agreements/free-trade-agreements/trans-pacific-partnership/tpp-full-text
42 Matt Dabrowski (27 June 2016). 'Free trade will not have an ally in the White House next year.' www.ft.com/cms/s/0/6e3451d6-37a7-11e6-9a05-82a9b15a8ee7.html
43 Tom Mitchell (26 June 2016). 'AIIB expansion plans underscore China's global ambitions.' www.ft.com/cms/s/0/1e53b6fe-3b74-11e6-8716-a4a71e8140b0.html
44 South China Morning Post TV (19 January 2016). 'China's AIIB to rival World Bank?' www.scmp.com/video/china/1902803/chinas-aiib-rival-world-bank
45 James Moore (9 November 2016). 'What President Trump's victory means for the most important trade deal in the world.' http://www.independent.co.uk/news/world/americas/us-elections/donald-trump-president-wins-live-results-us-election-ttip-trade-deal-hillary-clinton-loses-a7394611.html
46 (12 November 2016) 'Donald Trump election win could spark UK trade deal before Article 50 is triggered.' www.express.co.uk/news/politics/730594/US-president-Donald-trump-election-anticipate-UK-trade-deal-brexit-article
47 The World Bank (2016) 'GDP per capita.' data.worldbank.org/indicator/NY.GDP.PCAP.CD
48 ASEAN (n.d.). 'History – the founding of ASEAN.' www.asean.org/asean/about-asean/history/; Royal Thai Embassy, Singapore (n.d.). 'ASEAN economic community: aspirations vs preparations.' www.thaiembassy.sg/press_media/news-highlights/asean-economic-community-aspirations-vs-preparations
49 'Profile: Mercosur – common market of the south.' (15 February 2012). news.bbc.co.uk/1/hi/world/americas/5195834.stm
50 Lerato Mbele (10 June 2015). 'Africa creates TFTA-Cape to Cairo free-trade zone.' www.bbc.co.uk/news/world-africa-33076917
51 Chloe Hogg (23 June 2015). 'Africa's new free trade area: what will it mean for development?' impakter.com/africas-new-free-trade-area/
52 United Nations Environment Programme (n.d.). 'Impacts of tourism.' wwwunep.org/resourceefficiency/Business/SectoralActivities/Tourism/FactsandFiguresaboutTourism/ImpactsofTourism/tabid/78774/Default.aspx

7 Emerging markets

In this chapter you will learn some characteristics of the key economies of Brazil, Russia, India and China collectively known as the BRICs. You will be able to discuss the importance of China in the world economy and understand some of the areas of concern in emerging markets and what the newsworthy topics for each of the BRICs are.

The shift of global economic power eastwards away from the mature Western industrialised countries towards China and India has been well documented and will continue to generate column inches in the years ahead. Irrespective of the ups and downs of specific **emerging markets**, the fact remains that in the long run the growth prospects for these markets are much better than for the mature industrialised markets in the West.

Box 7.1 Emerging markets

- Nations in the process of rapid growth and industrialisation.
- In 2006, there were 28 emerging markets but now there are more than 40.
- Major developing markets of Brazil, Russia, India and China universally known as BRICs.
- Term invented in 2001 by Jim O'Neill of Goldman Sachs.

Table 7.1 IMF GDP growth forecasts (%)

	2016	2017
China	6.6	6.2
India	7.6	7.6
Russia	−0.8	1.1
Brazil	−3.3	0.5
South Africa	0.1	0.8

Source: World Economic Outlook, October 2016

Journalistic practice

The importance of China as the world's second largest economy means that its economic data releases are closely followed by the financial markets and regularly top the financial news. In addition to reporting the news item, comment should be included on the implications for the global economy or Western economic policy. This was demonstrated in August 2015 when the Chinese authorities devalued their currency, the **renminbi** also known as **yuan**, in the wake of disappointing export figures in July. There was press speculation as to whether this would delay the timing of interest rate rises in the UK and US.

Another aspect of emerging markets that can be explored is the make-up of the economy in question. The scene can be set with some historical background charting the progress of the economy. In any overview outline what are the major industries? What are their growth opportunities? What is the extent of foreign direct investment and how easy is it to do business in the country? Trade missions by the UK government are always extensively reported with typically one or more large trade deals announced at the same time providing a useful photo opportunity.

Emerging markets are often reported on collectively such as when there are large movements in the financial markets or when discussing the impact of fluctuating commodity prices. Strong Chinese demand for metals and minerals such as iron ore and coal during its period of rapid economic growth pushed up prices of these commodities and boosted the economies of the likes of Australia and Brazil.

Regular coverage is given in the financial press of the impact on emerging markets of quantitative easing in the US, UK and Europe. The scaling back, so-called tapering, of the US programme of quantitative easing led to a sharp drop in demand for emerging markets assets. Investors appeared to prefer higher yielding, less risky US assets.

Market reports can be done on the volatility of emerging market currencies including comparisons with safe havens such as US and German government bonds and gold. Include a quote from a market analyst and graphs showing currency movements against the dollar. Other indices that can be included are the CBOE Vix volatility index, which gauges the cost of US equity portfolio protection and the MSCI emerging markets equity index.

There are several topics within emerging markets that can provide personal finance stories. These include the opportunities for investing in particular countries, the pros and cons of such investment and the launch and performance of emerging market funds. In the case of fund launch stories, content should include the investment strategy of the manager, a quote from the manager on their hopes for the fund, how

(Continued)

much money the fund is hoping to attract and an opinion of an independent financial advisor such as Bestinvest or Hargreaves Lansdown, the investment supermarket, on the track record of the manager, the attractiveness of the fund to potential investors, with a mention of rival funds in the sector.

Emerging markets is obviously a huge topic which cannot be covered entirely here but there are some common issues to bear in mind when assessing the prospects for these economies.

Causes for concern

Events in the Ukraine underlined the political risks associated with investing in Russia. *Political risk* is often greater in emerging markets than in mature developed markets, although this is country and region specific.

The Russian currency, the rouble, initially dropped to a five-year low and the Russian stock market suffered in the immediate aftermath of the Russian military move into the Ukraine.[1]

Shares in companies with Russian and Ukrainian exposure also fell. Carlsberg is one of the biggest brewers in Russia and the Ukraine, which are responsible for almost 40% of its earnings. Carlsberg shares dropped more than 5%.

Looking elsewhere, politics can often loom particularly large in emerging economies markets, often casting a shadow over the financial attributes of such markets. Political instability, relative to mature Western economies, is a feature of many emerging markets. Politics is an issue in Russia, India, Indonesia, Brazil and Turkey. In China it is hard to know the extent of any behind the scenes manoeuvrings but obviously any open wide-scale political dissent would disturb the financial markets.

Box 7.2 Transparency international corruption index (2015)

- Denmark 91
- UK 78
- US 76
- France 70
- Turkey 42
- Brazil 38
- Italy 44
- China 37
- India 38
- Mexico 35
- Indonesia 36
- Russia 29
- Nigeria 26.

Various factors have the potential to impact negatively on emerging markets. The tapering of the US quantitative easing programme from

$85–$65bn a month had a knock-on effect on emerging markets, widely referred to as a 'taper tantrum', with investors preferring to put their money in higher yielding US entities. Emerging markets are particularly exposed to flows of foreign capital.

During the recession, investors seeking higher yields indiscriminately put large amounts of money into emerging markets. Subsequently they became more discerning so those countries with underlying economic problems such as current account deficits, in the case of Turkey and South Africa, are losing out. They both had to raise their interest rates to protect their currencies.[2]

Box 7.3 Market indices

- S & P 500 – US equity benchmark
- FTSE 100 index of leading UK shares
- Pan-European FTSE Eurofirst 300
- Hang Seng – Hong Kong equities
- Micex – Russian stock market index
- Shanghai Composite – Chinese stock market index.

Emerging economies tend to be more energy intensive than mature Western economies. Some economies such as Russia, Nigeria and Angola are heavily dependent on *oil revenues* for their foreign earnings and so the precipitous drop in crude oil prices during 2015 was very bad news.[3]

Even Saudi Arabia had to tighten its belt at home due to the drop in its oil revenues.[4] A concern for all of us is that the sharp drop in oil revenues will impact on the ability of countries such as Iraq, Algeria and Libya to fend off Islamic militants.

Currency valuations are an issue. By keeping its real exchange rate down China is subsidising production of its exports. Since China is the world's biggest exporter, this must have a significant negative effect on world trade.[5]

Emerging market currencies can be very volatile on the foreign exchanges. There have been dramatic revaluations of currencies such as the Indian rupee and Argentine peso. The Brazilian authorities have complained in the past that their currency has been the victim of a currency war with the real pushed to unsustainably high levels. The surge in commodity prices during the boom years put upward pressure on the real, which jumped by 10% in 2012 alone, clobbering Brazilian manufacturing which lost ground in both global and domestic markets.

In the aftermath of the UK's decision in June 2016 to leave the European Union, emerging market currencies were dumped in the stampede for safe havens. Much of the impact was seen in central and eastern European currencies that have strong commercial links to Britain. The Polish zloty and Hungarian forint dropped in value against the dollar.

Pollution is a major concern given the economic growth rates of China and India. In the past, China's environment minister has warned that pollution threatens to imperil growth. China is the world's largest greenhouse gas emitter accounting for almost 30%. (The US, with a population more than four times less than China is number two in the polluter list.) The problem of smog is particularly bad in Beijing. Research suggests air pollution from coal burning has cut more than five years from the life expectancies of those living in northern China.

China is the world's biggest polluter but it is also the biggest investor in solar, wind and nuclear power. China is the world's largest solar manufacturing economy. There is a problem of oversupply and falling prices in the market. There have been trade problems with the US so Chinese manufacturers are investing in Africa and South America.

It is probably inappropriate to refer to China and India as emerging markets when they are already major players on the world economic stage. Even before the earthquake and tsunami in Japan in March 2011, China had overtaken it to become the world's second biggest economy. There are almost 600 dollar billionaires in China, more than in the US. In 2003 there were none.

The emerging markets are creating disruption on a massive scale, arguably bigger than the UK industrial revolution. Tianjin in China currently has the same GDP as Stockholm, the capital of Sweden. Its economy is forecast to be as big as the whole of Sweden in the not too distant future. Indeed in his book *When China Rules the World*, Martin Jacques sees a scenario 'in which China becomes the world's leading power, enjoying global hegemony in the manner of the United States, and before that Britain'.

A lot of attention is focused on the **BRIC** economies of Brazil, Russia, India and China and to a lesser extent South Africa, but there are a host of other nations, the so-called **MINT** countries of Mexico, Indonesia, Nigeria and Turkey, who are quietly moving up the economic league table.

Box 7.4 Other growth markets

- Mexico
- South Korea
- Turkey
- Indonesia
- Nigeria
- Philippines
- Vietnam.

These economies are thought likely to experience rising productivity coupled with favourable demographics and therefore a faster growth rate than the world average going forward. These countries along with the BRICs are expected to be the largest contributors to global GDP increases in the years ahead.

There is an interesting growth story coming out of the African continent generally. We are more used to hearing about war and famine. These still exist in certain areas but more encouragingly in recent years an increasing number of countries have been growing faster than mature Western economies and they managed to largely avoid the fall-out from the global financial crisis.

In Ethiopia, there is Chinese investment in a new light railway. China is providing the trains and training drivers and maintenance workers. Better education and family planning has helped halve the numbers of deaths amongst children under five years of age.

In the past decade, only the bloc of developing Asian countries lead by China has grown faster than Africa. The IMF's forecast for sub-Saharan African GDP in 2016 is 1.4%, rising to 2.9% in 2017. Nigeria's GDP in the same period is predicted to be −1.7% and 0.6% respectively, with growth adversely impacted by lower commodity prices, particularly oil. Increased trade with China, the Continent's main export market, has helped boost African economic growth. China's manufacturing boom required plentiful supplies of commodities such as iron ore and copper, which are abundant in Africa.

Even with the slowdown in the Chinese economy, growth is expected to continue on the continent with many countries such as Ethiopia, Kenya and Uganda less reliant on commodities and instead focused on exports of services, agriculture and manufactured goods. There are some countries such as Ghana where growth is being held back by failure to invest in infrastructure − electricity generation capacity in the case of Ghana.[6]

Demographic trends are positive in Africa with the number of people reaching working age in sub-Saharan Africa expected to exceed that of the rest of the world combined by 2030. Two hundred million people in Africa are aged 15–24 which is the youngest population in the world and this figure is forecast to double by 2045.

There is still a way to go for the vast majority of Africans to see the benefits of economic growth. There is a huge variation in GDP per capita as measured at purchasing power parity, the exchange rate that would equalise the price of goods and services across countries. Figures from the World Bank showed Equatorial Guinea topping the African league table.

African countries 2015 GDP per capita ($)

- Equatorial Guinea 11,120.9
- South Africa 5691.7
- Nigeria 2640.3
- Mozambique 525.

Source: The World Bank[7]

These figures compare with GDP per capita of $7,590.0 in China during the same period.

Nigeria, which accounts for around 20% of Africa's population, has enormous economic growth potential but it also has serious ethnic and political tensions. The problem of Boko Haram's Islamic extremism in the north of the country is well documented.

Nigeria has overtaken South Africa to be sub-Saharan Africa's largest economy. It has oil reserves but is diversifying its economic base, an even more pressing imperative given the collapse in the oil price since 2014. One of the country's major weaknesses is its poor infrastructure. It suffers from severe shortages of power, which adversely impacts growth.

China

> **Box 7.5** China milestones
>
> - 680 million people lifted out of extreme poverty in 30 years.
> - Largest owner of US Treasury Securities.
> - World's largest trading nation.
> - World's largest e-commerce market.
> - World's largest economy in purchasing power parity terms.

The global might of the Chinese economy was demonstrated in the financial markets during the summer of 2015 when the Chinese stock market suffered heavy double digit falls in volatile trading.[8] However it had risen more than 140% in the previous 12 months.

Whilst the Chinese stock market is not as intrinsic to growth as the UK's, the drop did unnerve markets around the world which were already fretting about whether China will continue to be the engine of global economic growth. A surprise move by the Chinese authorities to cut interest rates and ease reserve requirements for some banks revived market fears that the Chinese economy may be heading for a hard rather than soft landing.

Such worries may be misplaced. Although the Chinese economy is undoubtedly slowing down, particularly the manufacturing and property sectors, other areas such as financial services and the technology sector continue to do well. Given the lack of transparency in financial reporting in China it is difficult to get an exact reading of the state of its economy. The IMF is forecasting a continued slowdown in the Chinese economy with GDP of 6.2% in 2017. That compares to 6.9% as recently as 2015.[9]

China has the largest population in the world at about 1.37 billion. The population size of a country has a direct impact on the potential size of its economy. A large population capacity can drive economic growth and development. The mass migration of people from rural areas to Chinese cities in recent years means that cities such as Shanghai, Beijing and Shenzhen are expected to feature in future amongst the world's top performing cities in terms of contribution to global GDP.

Within the BRIC group, China has made the greatest progress in terms of human development with a transformation in the living standards of millions of Chinese people.

Investment

The British government is very keen to open the doors wide to the UK economy for Chinese investment. Both countries think it is a golden time in Sino-British relations. The Chinese President Xi Jinping made a four-day visit to Britain in October 2015 – the first by a Chinese leader in 10 years.

When he was chancellor, George Osborne wanted China to become the UK's second biggest export market after the European Union by 2025. The UK hopes to be able to increase its exports of educational, legal and financial services to China's growing number of middle class people. These sectors have historically been dwarfed by China's colossal manufacturing industry.

In 2015, the British law firm Baker & McKenzie became the first foreign law firm to establish a joint operation with a Chinese counterpart, FenXun Partners, in the Shanghai free-trade zone. There are hopes that further liberalisation of the Chinese legal market will enable law firms to service multinational companies operating in the world's second largest economy more efficiently.[10]

Perhaps not surprisingly, the Chinese authorities liked Mr Osborne's pragmatic approach. 'Let us embrace the golden era' said Liu Xiaoming, Chinese ambassador to the UK, on the eve of the President's state visit.[11]

Key facts

- China's outward direct investment (ODI) has tripled since 2005. On current trends China will triple its stock of ODI by 2020 making it the world's second largest (well behind the US) outward investor.
- The UK's foreign direct investment (FDI) inflow of $11.8bn in 2013 was the largest in Europe, more than France and Germany combined.

Source: HM Treasury[12]

In the rush to promote trade and business with China the UK authorities pragmatically draw a veil over certain issues that would each on their own set alarm bells ringing. Journalists can have a freer rein to shine a light in some of the corners.

Newsworthy issues that the authorities would like to downplay

- There are longstanding and widespread concerns about the lack of human rights for large numbers of Chinese citizens whether that's defence lawyers or members of the Uigher minority Muslim population.

- Disregard for intellectual property rights.
- The publication of questionable official economic statistics.
- Creative accounting by some stock market listed companies.[13]
- Cyber attacks against rival international companies and government organisations.[14]
- The difficulties multinational companies face in treading a fine line not to upset the Chinese authorities in the course of doing business. Google pulled out of the Chinese market in 2010 after disputes with the authorities over censorship. The story was widely covered by the media alongside speculation about Google's negotiations to return to the Chinese mainland.[15]

Periodically the Chinese authorities like to make an example of a foreign company to show it is cracking down in a certain area, e.g. corruption. Given the huge growth potential in the Chinese market companies feel they cannot afford to be out of the market despite the difficulties encountered in doing business.

There has been huge growth of the largely unregulated shadow banking sector which is storing up problems for a future financial crisis.[16] Debt-laden local authorities are likely to be badly hit.

Britain is not putting all its eggs in the Chinese trading basket which is just as well as there are sizeable growth opportunities elsewhere in the world, not least in India.

India

> **Box 7.6** India
>
> - Business opportunities have expanded from traditional bases of Mumbai, Delhi and Bangalore to cities such as Jaipur.
> - Life sciences, manufacturing, energy and infrastructure are attractive sectors for British investors.
> - Infrastructure problems illustrated by two-day power cut in July 2012 affecting more than 600 million people.

India is the third largest country in Asia and the seventh largest in the world. The Indian economy has vast untapped potential but has failed to meet growth expectations in recent years. It has been weighed down by a number of issues not least its poor infrastructure, particularly transport, inadequate power supply, excess regulation and corruption.

In addition, it is having difficulty coping with the huge growth in population in some of its cities. According to the 2011 census, the number of Indians living in urban areas jumped to 400 million, just under a third of the population. The country has 54 cities with more than 1 million people.

The census showed almost 65.5 million people living in urban slums, as well as 13.7% of the urban population living below the national poverty line. A World Bank report suggests that Indian cities can take more advantage of urbanisation for economic growth. To do this the governance and financing of cities needs to be improved. In addition, 'policies are also required to improve the ways in which cities are connected and planned, the working of land and housing markets, and cities' resilience to natural disasters and the effects of climate change'.[17]

The IMF has identified energy infrastructure as an area in need of urgent investment. More than 600 million people in 20 out of India's 28 states were affected by the largest power cut in history when three electricity grids collapsed in July 2012. Transport and water supplies were severely disrupted. Electricity shortages are also a feature of many low income and emerging market economies in sub-Saharan Africa.

Infrastructure investment is one of the mechanisms to increase income, employment, productivity and consequently the competitiveness of an economy.

The Indian government under pro-business Prime Minister Narendra Modi is trying to boost the economy by encouraging companies to manufacture in India. It is also allowing more investment from abroad in areas such as retail, insurance and aviation. However this latter policy has attracted protests from Indian unions.

In June 2016, the government announced a radical overhaul of its foreign ownership rules to attract more overseas investment. For the first time, Indian airlines can be controlled by non-Indian companies. Retailers such as Ikea and Apple are keen to move into the Indian market.[18]

Figures from the UK business lobby group, the CBI, suggest that between 2000 and 2015, the UK accounted for about 9% of India's foreign direct investment equivalent to $22bn. India is the third biggest source of foreign investment in the UK. In 2014, investment from India into the UK increased by 64% with 122 projects funded. The government body, UKTI estimates that this investment created 7,730 new UK jobs in 2014 and safeguarded a further 1,620.

Financial services, technology and engineering are identified as sectors where bilateral trade could increase markedly. UK companies already well established on the ground in India include Unilever, the consumer products company whose brands include Flora, Jif, Magnum and Dove, the banks HSBC and Standard Chartered, and British American Tobacco.

However, it is not the easiest place to do business, ranking 130 out of 189 in the World Bank's Ease of Doing Business Index. Some companies such as Nokia and Cairn Energy have been the subject of arbitrary treatment by the Indian tax authorities. Such disputes damage the reputation of the country as a good place for foreign companies to invest.

There are several positives for the Indian economy, which prompt some to talk about it becoming the new engine of world economic growth, replacing China. Its GDP in 2016 and 2017 is forecast by the IMF to be ahead of China's at 7.6%.[19]

The Indian Central Statistics Office reported growth accelerated to 7.9% in the first quarter of 2016. However there are some doubts about the reliability of Indian growth data with some economists and business leaders highlighting lacklustre bank credit and business confidence indicators.[20]

Indian advantages over China

- A more diversified economy with world-class software and business services companies.
- It has 1.2 billion people including a larger number of young people entering the workforce. It has the fastest population growth and within the next 20 years is expected to overtake China as the most populous country, partly due to China's historic one child policy.
- For all its faults, India has a democratically elected government.

Like former Prime Minister David Cameron, Theresa May sees huge opportunities to increase trade and investment between Britain and India. Speaking in the House of Commons in September 2016, after returning from her first G20 summit, she said India was 'keen to remove trade barriers'.[21] Amazingly, Belgium exports more to India than the UK. The Indian car manufacturer Tata is one of the largest private sector employers in the UK.

India/UK business score card

- 110,000 Indian businesses in the UK.
- 13 Indian companies each employ more than 1,000 people in the UK.
- 65,000 people work for Tata Group, which owns 5 of the 13 companies, including Tetley Tea producer; Tata Global Beverages and Tata Steel, which is still a significant employer despite job losses associated with falling demand due to cheap Chinese imports.
- 28,000 of those people work for Tata Motors, which owns Jaguar Land Rover.

Source: Grant Thornton India Tracker 2015[22]

Mr Cameron led a trade mission to India in February 2014, the largest trade mission ever made by a British Prime Minister to any nation. It was Mr Cameron's third visit to India since he came to power. The Indian Prime Minister Narendra Modi, made a three-day visit to Britain in November 2015, at the invitation of David Cameron. Surprisingly, given the historic and cultural ties between the two countries, this was the first trip to Britain in a decade for an Indian Prime Minister. There were around 800,000 visitors from the UK to India in 2014.

Given its position as one of the world's leading financial markets, Britain is well placed to assist India in developing its capital markets. The growing numbers of India's middle class provide a large consumer market for British retailers.

Indian companies see Britain as a gateway to Europe. Other positives in Britain's favour include ease of doing business, English language, access to raising capital and familiarity with UK institutions.

Russia

> **Box 7.7** Russia
>
> - Amongst world's top ten retail markets.
> - Over-reliance on oil and natural gas.
> - Aside from domestic political tensions, major demographic problem of very high mortality due to alcohol abuse.
> - Corruption is a major problem in Russia.

Russia is the biggest country by land area followed by China and then Brazil. The Russian economy has a problem of over reliance on oil and gas. The 2015 slump in the oil price was very bad news for Russia with the economy sliding into recession. GDP sank around 4%, living standards dropped sharply and the rouble halved in value against the dollar in the 18 months to December 2015. The recessionary effects rippled outwards with leading auction houses seeing significantly fewer buyers and sellers in the Russian art market. This has been largely based in London since the end of the Soviet Union. The economic outlook is not good with the IMF expecting a move from recession to subdued growth in 2017.

Germany is Russia's second biggest trade partner after China, with companies such as Siemens and Volkswagen investing in the country. This is one reason for the cautious stance taken by the EU over sanctions on Russia because of the concern of the knock-on effects to the recovery in the Eurozone if gas supplies to Europe are disrupted in retaliation by Russia.

Russia supplies 30% of EU gas needs. A number of European politicians including Donald Tusk, President of the European Council, have expressed their disapproval of plans for a new pipeline bringing Russian gas to Germany. The $11bn Nord Stream 2 project appears to undermine the EU's goal of reducing energy dependence on Moscow.

Even before events in the Ukraine, Russia faced a problem of capital flight due to political and economic uncertainty. The Russian Central Bank said the net outflow was $56.9bn in 2015. That was down from $153bn in the same period of 2014 but still represents a massive loss of tax revenue.

One home for Russian money is the prime central London property market. Roman Abromovich, owner of Chelsea football club, is the most high profile member of the large Russian community in London. His London property portfolio includes a £90m house on Kensington Palace Gardens where neighbours include the future King of England, Prince William. The number of Russian millionaires moving to London rose from 117 in 2013 to 184 in 2014.

The World Bank ease of doing business index in 2015 ranked Russia 51 out of 189. China is grouped with Hong Kong at 5, from its individual reading the previous year of 84. The UK's rank is 6 with the US at 7.

Brazil

> **Box 7.8** Brazil
>
> - World's fifth largest country with 185 million people.
> - GDP per head much greater than India or China, at around $11,384.
> - Possible economic boost from hosting 2016 Olympics.
> - Shortage of experienced workers in areas such as finance and engineering.

Brazil is widely thought to have squandered the opportunity it had in recent years to move decisively up the economic ladder, particularly as it managed to avoid the worst effects of the 2008 global financial crisis.

A number of factors are blamed including political instability, corruption and inefficiency. Reforms are still needed across a range of sectors including education, health care and infrastructure. Public spending on research and development has lagged behind that of its emerging market rivals China, Russia and South Korea. There is a lack of skilled labour leading to low productivity.

Brazil is expected to remain mired in recession in 2016 with the IMF forecasting a contraction of 3.3%. Brazil has been particularly badly affected by the collapse in commodity prices and the slowdown in the Chinese economy. China is a major importer of Brazilian commodities, notably iron, soy and oil.

There is scope to increase foreign investment in the country but it is hard to do business as demonstrated by Brazil's ranking in 2015 of 116 out of 189 in the World Bank's Ease of Doing Business Index. The country is widely thought to be over reliant on commodity exports. The US ratings agency Fitch gave its verdict on the country in October 2015, downgrading Brazilian debt to 'BBB' – almost junk status – with a negative outlook, implying that a further downgrade is possible. (BBB is the lowest investment grade level).

The Brazilian currency, the **real**, subsequently dropped in value against the US dollar. The agency cited the rising government debt burden, increased challenges to financial cutbacks and a worsening economic environment, as reasons for the downgrade. The government's general debt burden is forecast

Emerging markets 159

Figure 7.1 Real, Brazilian currency. Image courtesy of Bruce McIntosh/iStock.

to rise above 70% of GDP in 2017. Political scandals are adding to the negative atmosphere with growth and investment suffering.[23]

The government that replaced that of Dilma Rousseff in 2016 promised to bear down on government spending. Central government spending jumped from 14% of GDP in 1997 to 18.6% in 2015.[24]

Brazil's rise as an economic power is largely due to the big increase in the value of the real against the US dollar and many other currencies. It has a growing middle class within its population of around 180 million. It has the fifth largest population in the world with a high percentage of young people. The growth of Brazil has had a big impact on its neighbours, Chile, Argentina and Mexico. Argentina is a key destination for Brazil's manufacturing exports.

South Africa

Faith in the South African economy has been sorely tested by the unexpected sacking by President Jacob Zuma in December 2015 of his well-respected finance minister, Nhlanhla Nene. Two replacements followed in quick succession. The financial markets were unimpressed with seeing three different finance ministers in five days and showed their disapproval. The South African rand slumped against the dollar and there was a sell-off in equities and government bonds.

Journalistic practice

Several angles can be taken with such political/financial stories. Give timeline of events leading up to the news story, profile the key players involved, speculate on what may follow and the reaction of the financial markets.

Opinion is divided on whether South Africa should have been admitted to the BRIC club in April 2011, with Nigeria mentioned as a better candidate. The latter has a larger population and has also enjoyed on average a faster economic growth rate.

In favour of South Africa

- Viewed as a gateway to Africa by many international companies.
- High per capita spending.
- Leader in finance, retailing and automotive industries.
- The overall quality of infrastructure is better than many of the other members, possibly because of its smaller geographic area which makes it easier to maintain.

Against South Africa

Its economy is too small to be compared to those of the BRIC countries. Its GDP has consistently been the lowest of all the BRICs members. The South African currency dropped to a record low of 24 rand to the pound – almost half its value three years ago – after President Jacob Zuma dismissed his finance minister Nhlanhla Nene, in December 2015. The departure fuelled concerns about the country's weak economy and political governance.

A combination of historically low commodity prices and higher borrowing costs will act as a major drag on South Africa in 2016. The IMF is expecting very modest growth of just 0.1% with some recovery in 2017 GDP to 0.8%.

On balance, political considerations undoubtedly helped South Africa's case, and it would have had an important advocate in China. China is South Africa's largest trading partner. China sees South Africa as an attractive place to do business given its large number of consumers, many of them relatively wealthy. China has large investments in the country, mainly in banking, infrastructure, mining, transport and renewable energy.

Like many countries in Africa it has a number of serious issues to deal with including income inequality, poverty, unemployment and corruption.[25]

Since the early 1990s the main driver for economic growth in South Africa has been retail trade, tourism and communications. It is particularly strong in mobile software and electronic banking services.

South Africa has traditionally been known for its mining. Its companies are market leaders in the global industry. However in December 2015, in the face of the collapse in commodity prices, the South African government had to rescue London-listed Lonmin, the world's third largest platinum producer. The government, through the Public Investment Corporation, (PIC), which manages the pensions of state workers, became the single biggest shareholder with a 25% stake in the miner, after an emergency rights issue.

The automotive industry is one of South Africa's most important sectors. Many multinationals such as BMW and Ford use South Africa to source components and assemble vehicles for both the local and international markets.

The IMF has identified electricity shortages as a major constraint on growth. Real GDP growth hit a post-crisis low of 1.5% in 2014 due to protracted strike action and electricity shortages. Over the medium term growth is expected to improve to around 2.8% as energy availability increases but unemployment is expected to remain above 25%.[26]

South Africa is the world's biggest producer of gold and platinum and one of the leading producers of base metals and coal. However it is also one of the most unequal countries in the world in terms of income distribution. The top 10% of households earn almost half of income. This has implications for the size of the overall consumer market not to mention social cohesion.

Growth of BRIC consumer markets

Together Brazil, Russia, India and China account for 40% of the world's population and more than a quarter of its land mass. By 2025, the BRIC consumer is expected to become as large as the US consumer reflecting increased urbanisation and rising wages.

> **Box 7.9** Chinese consumer
>
> - Increasingly important in global markets for property, consumer goods and luxury items.
> - Buyers from mainland China are big spenders in prime central London property market.
> - China has overtaken London as world's second largest art and antiques auction market.
> - China is world's biggest car market by sales.

As incomes rise, an increasing number of people start travelling in their country of residence as well as outside. Countries are keen to attract Chinese tourists as they spend a lot. In the case of the UK, they spend much more than any other nationality at around £2600 per head. The number of Chinese visitors more than doubled in the five years to 2015, contributing £500m per year to tourism revenues.

162 *Emerging markets*

However, figures published by the UK's Office for National Statistics showed the numbers of Chinese visitors dropped by 7.6% in 2014 compared to the previous year. Spending was also lower, down 1% on the year before.

In October 2015, the British government bowed to pressure from UK airport operators and retailers who had lobbied hard for simplification of the visa system, which they say puts off tourists from coming here. They say billions of pounds a year extra could flow into the economy.[27]

From 2016, a pilot scheme will allow Chinese tourists to get a two-year tourist visa for £85, a large reduction on the previous cost of £324. In the past few years, Paris has attracted eight times more Chinese tourists then the UK.

Despite political tensions between the two countries, China accounted for the largest number of visitors to Japan, 731,000 out of 2.29million visitors in July 2016.[28] Hong Kong and Thailand are the most popular destinations for Chinese tourists.

The slowdown in the Chinese economy has reduced demand for art and antiques. It is the second largest market after the US. Chinese artists such as Qi Baishi are now amongst the world's best-selling artists. Sotheby's has a joint venture in China and Christie's runs a standalone business. In addition, there are many local galleries and museums. Much of the demand is driven by local demand for Chinese antiquities.

The global markets for consumer durables, luxury goods, travel and tourism are expected to grow strongly. These include spirits, champagne, cosmetics, jewellery, watches, leather goods and upmarket fashion brands such as Gucci and Prada.

Anaemic growth in mature Western markets in the US and Europe is prompting retailers to look for untapped consumer markets around the world.

China is now the world's largest market for groceries, luxury goods and e-commerce. There are thought to be opportunities for UK companies in food and drink and luxury fashion. In April 2016, Burberry disappointed investors with a profits warning. The company, famous for its check trench coats and scarves, saw fewer wealthy Chinese tourists in Europe on the back of security concerns. China and the Asia Pacific region account for about 40% of Burberry's revenues.[29] China's stock market turmoil in August 2015 is also thought to have reduced general demand for luxury products.

Journalistic practice

To cover the Burberry news story, report the retail sales figures with comment from the chief executive or finance director. Did the results meet City expectations? Include a quote from a retail analyst such as

> Nick Bubb; retail consultant to Zeus Capital and a longstanding retailer watcher, on the results plus trading prospects in the months ahead. Give some of the history of Burberry's trading performance in China. Include the share price and movement on the day. Were other shares in the luxury goods sector e.g. LVMH affected?

Aside from the BRICs, consultants AT Kearney have identified a number of smaller markets with good growth potential such as Oman and Georgia.[30]

Global food retailers such as Wal-Mart, Tesco and Carrefour are seeing faster revenue growth in developing markets than in their home markets.

Other sectors such as financial services and insurance are also likely to benefit significantly from rising demand driven by higher wealth.

Luxury car makers such as Mercedes are increasingly taking into account the important Chinese market when designing their models. China is already the largest car market by sales with more than 21 million cars sold in 2015. However, the deceleration in the Chinese economy was reflected in a slowdown in vehicle sales growth, up 7.3% compared to 10% in 2014. China has the most brands and models – 130 car brands in May 2016. Sport utility vehicles and electric vehicles are popular, the latter helped by a 5% sales tax break.

China could also become the world's largest aviation market. It is home to the fastest growing aviation sector with its growing numbers of middle class citizens keen to venture further afield. A new $11.2bn airport terminal for Beijing is scheduled for completion in 2018. Terminal 1 will span 700,000 square metres and 45 million passengers a year are expected to pass through the terminal. Beijing International Airport is the busiest airport in China and the second busiest in the world.

BRIC investment funds

Whilst there is undoubtedly enormous growth potential in emerging markets, there are a number of uncertainties and that is something financial markets tend to dislike.[31] However, in recent years many BRIC funds have been launched for those investors willing to take a long-term view. However it is not for faint hearted investors or those seeking a quick return.

Volatility will always be an issue. Indeed the average fund fell by 12% over the five years to 2015 and 10% in the three year period 2012–2015. The main catalyst was the slowdown in the Chinese economy and the sharp drop in commodity prices. Brave investors may decide to take advantage of an opportunity to buy when US interest rates rise. This is because typically a large number of investors will panic and sell, because higher interest rates make emerging market debt more expensive to service.

Countries that treat investors with respect and have business friendly politics tend to be the most attractive, so that favours many of the South East Asian economies and possibly Mexico over the BRICs.

The difficulties of investing profitably in China were very publicly demonstrated by the initial poor performance of the high profile Fidelity China Special Situations Investment Trust. One of the most highly regarded UK fund managers Anthony Bolton, who ran a similar UK fund, came out of retirement in 2010 to launch a China Special Situations Investment Trust. Initially, its shares traded at a discount to their underlying investments' value.

Mr Bolton blamed the poor performance on a number of factors including fraud and the fund's large exposure to small and medium firms rather than larger state-owned enterprises.

He retired in 2014 and the trust has performed well since helped by the surge in Chinese shares.[32] Holdings in the overvalued IT sector and Hong Kong focused banks have been cut in favour of insurance companies and railways. In China there is a low penetration of traditional protection-type products. Moves towards more market-based pricing are expected to boost valuations and returns in freight and passenger railways.

Not all fund managers are bullish on China because of concerns about the high level of Chinese debt, much of it associated with the property boom and the lack of corporate transparency. Chinese companies listed in New York have performed particularly poorly after dozens were accused of fraud or accounting discrepancies and suspended from trading on the US stock exchange.

Assignments

Write a 300 word news story on British trade and investment with China or India.

Write an 800 word economic profile of one of the BRIC or MINT countries.

Glossary of key terms

BRIC: acronym for the economies of Brazil, Russia, India and China.
Emerging markets: markets in newly industrialised countries.
MINT: acronym for Mexico, Indonesia, Nigeria and Turkey.
Real: Brazilian currency.
Renminbi or yuan: the Chinese currency.

Resource list

Jim O'Neill (now Lord O'Neill of Gatley) was a highly regarded economist and inventor of the term BRICs. Listen to his four-part series on BBC Radio Four, *MINT: The Next Economic Giants*: www.bbc.co.uk/programmes/b03pn2h6

Recommended reading

Jacques, Martin (2012). *When China Rules the World.* London: Penguin.
Jim O'Neill has also published two books on emerging markets:
O'Neill, Jim (2011). *The Growth Map – Economic Opportunity in the BRICs and Beyond.* London: Penguin (1st edn).
O'Neill, Jim (2013). *The BRIC Road to Growth.* London: Publishing Partnership. This book looks at the MINT economies.

Notes

1 Natalie Kitroeff and Joe Weisenthal (16 December2014). 'Here's why the Russian ruble is collapsing.' www.bloomberg.com/news/articles/2014-12-16/no-caviar-is-not-getting-cheaper-everything-you-need-to-know-about-the-russian-ruble-collapse
2 James Kynge (4 February 2014). 'Oil price fall takes fizz out of traders' bash.' www.ft.com/cms/0/c2de31ea-cb67-11e5-be0b-b7ece4e953a0-html
3 Anjli Raval, David Sheppard and Neil Hume (24 February 2014). 'Frontier market havens come under threat as frailties appear.' www.ft.com/cms/s/0/6074e0aa-9d5e-11e3-a599-00144feab7de.html
4 The New Arab and agencies (29 December 2015). 'Stung by low oil prices, Saudi makes unprecedented cuts.' www.alaraby.co.uk/english/indepth/2015/12/29/stung-by-low-oil-prices-saudi-makes-unprecedented-cuts
5 David Dollar (6 January 2016). 'Anchor aweigh? China's currency devaluation and the global economy.' www.brookings.edu/blogs/order-from-chaos/posts/2016/01/06-chinese-currency-devaluation-global-economy-dollar
6 Maggie Fick (8 July 2015). 'Power shortages cut growth prospects in Ghana.' www.ft.com/cms/s/0/fa56bb02-2481-11e5-bd83-71cb60e8f08c.html
7 World Bank (n.d.). 'GDP per capita.' Data.worldbank.org/indicator/NY.GDP.PCAP.CD
8 John Authers (13 February 2016). 'Many suspects behind murderous markets.' www.ft.com/cms/s/2/fcca701c-d0fd-11e5-831d-09f7778e7377.html
9 'IMF cuts global forecasts on Brexit, warns of risks to outlook.' (19 July 2016). www.imf.org/en/News/Articles/2016/07/18/18/11/NA07192016-imf-Cuts-Global-Growth-Forecasts-on-Brexit-Warns-of-Risks-to-Outlook
10 Tom Mitchell (31 May 2016). 'Law firms benefit from China's liberalization.' www.ft.com/cms/s/0/6e7d100a-2641-11e6-8ba3-cdd781d02d89.html
11 Carrie Gracie (19 October 2015). 'China and 'the Osborne Doctrine.' www.bbc.co.uk/news/world-asia-china-34539507
12 'Chancellor kicks off week-long China tour.' (18 September 2015). www.gov.uk/government/news/chancellor-to-kick-off-week-long-china-tour
13 Gina Chon (23 January 2014). 'SEC auditor ban could hit US companies in China.' www.ft.com/cms/s/0/f28f1fd2-8454-11e3-b72e-00144feab7de.html; Simon Rabinovitch and Paul J. Davies (4 December 2012). 'Chinese companies caught in SEC crossfire.' www.ft.com/cms/s/0/0b08be98-3dce-11e2-b8b2-00144feabdc0.html
14 Ken Dilanian (19 October 2015). 'Chinese cyberattacks on US companies continue, report says.' www.news.yahoo.com/chinese-cyberattacks-us-companies-continue-report-says-084407426--finance.html
15 Dan Levin (2 June 2014). 'China escalating attack on Google.' www.nytimes.com/2014/06/03/business/chinas-battle-against-google-heats-up.html?_r=0
16 Simon Rabinovitch (10 March 2014). 'China shadow lending slows sharply.' www.ft.com/cms/s/0/729b8510-a856-11e3-8ce-1-00144feab7de.html

17 The World Bank (24 September 2015). 'Indian cities can take more advantage of urbanization for economic growth.' www.worldbank.org/en/news/press-release/2015/09/24/indian-cities-can-take-more-advantage-urbanization-for-economic-growth
18 Simon Atkinson (20 June 2016). 'India overhauls foreign ownership rules.' www.bbc.co.uk/news/business-36575755
19 World Economic Outlook (October 2016). 'Subdued Demand: Symptoms and Remedies.' www.imf.org/external/pubs/ft/weo/2016/02
20 Victor Mallet (31 May 2016). 'Faster growing India confirmed as most dynamic emerging market.' www.ft.com/cms/s/0/06b63142-2748-11e6-8ba3-cdd781do2d89.html
21 Theresa May: UK will lead world in free trade.' (7 September 2016). 'www.bbc.co.uk/news/uk-politics-37291832
22 Grant Thornton (20 April 2015). 'Tracking the UK's top Indian companies in 2015.' www.grantthornton.co.uk/en/insights/india-meets-britain-tracking-the-uks-top-indian-companies/
23 Jonathan Watts (9 March 2016). 'Brazil corruption scandal claims scalp as top industrialist jailed for 19 years.' www.theguardian.com/world/2016/mar/08/brazil-corruption-scandal-marcelo-odebrecht-jailed
24 Joe Leahy (1 June 2016). 'Brazil moves to shrink the state.' www.ft.com/cms/s/0/e8327b28-2bd8-11e6-83e4-abc22d5d5d108c.html
25 Aislinn Laing (30 September 2015). 'South Africans march to call time on mass government corruption.' www.telegraph.co.uk/news/worldnews/africaandindianocean/southafrica/11902575/South-Africans-march-to-call-time-on-mass-government-corruption.html
26 IMF (22 May 2008). 'Africa's power supply crisis: unraveling the paradoxes.' www.imf.org/external/pubs/ft/survey/so/2008/CAR052208C.htm
27 William James (21 October 2015). 'Britain changes China visa rules to woo big-spending tourists.' uk.reuters.com/article/uk-china-britain-visas-idUKKCN0SE2Z120151021
28 Japan Macro Advisors (2016). 'Number of visitors to Japan'. www.japanmacroadvisitors.com/page/category/economic-indicators/gdp-and-business-activity/numt
29 Angela Monaghan (14 April 2016). 'Fewer wealthy Chinese tourists hits Burberry sales in Europe.' www.theguardian.com/business/2016/apr/14/fewer-wealthy-chinese-tourists-hits-burberry-sales-europe
30 Helen Rhim and Fabiola Salman, AT Kearney (June 2012). '2012 global retail development index'. www.atkearney.com/consumer-products-retail/global-retail-development-index/2012
31 Olivia Goldhill (31 January 2014). 'Emerging market stocks suffer worst sell-off since 2011.' www.telegraph.co.uk/finance/markets/10610517/Emerging-market-stocks-suffer-worst-sell-off-since-2011.html
32 Darren Boey and Alexis Xydias (17 June 2013). 'Fidelity's Anthony Bolton to stop managing China fund.' www.bloomberg.com/news/articles/2013-06-17/fidelity-s-anthony-bolton-to-retire-from-china-fund-next-year

8 The International Monetary Fund and World Bank

You will almost certainly have heard of at least one of the large multinational organisations, the IMF, World Bank and World Trade Organisation. In this chapter you will learn about the make-up and roles of these organisations. By the end of this chapter you should be able to discuss criticisms of some of their actions and you will be able to produce a news story based on forecasts from the IMF's influential World Economic Outlook.

The **International Monetary Fund (IMF)** has been regularly topping the financial news for a number of years given its central role in trying to deal with the economic fall-out from the financial crash of 2007–2008.

Box 8.1 IMF and World Bank

- Created in 1944 to monitor and promote the stability of the international financial system.
- Assist with post war reconstruction and development.

Box 8.2 IMF's regulatory and financial role

- To promote international monetary cooperation.
- To promote exchange stability, to maintain orderly exchange arrangements among members and to avoid competitive exchange depreciation.
- To foster economic growth and high levels of employment.
- To provide temporary assistance to countries to help ease balance of payments adjustment.
- Christine Lagarde is managing director of the IMF.

IMF funds were used to help bail out nations including Ireland, Portugal and Greece after they were effectively priced out of the credit markets by high yields i.e. banks were only willing to lend them money at very high interest rates reflecting what they saw as the inherent risks in lending to these countries. The IMF also provided financing to Iceland when its banking system collapsed in 2008.[1]

The IMF works independently and in European countries, in cooperation with European institutions such as the European Commission and the European Central Bank. This cooperation between the IMF, EC and ECB has become known as the **Troika**.[2]

The most high profile casualty of the Eurozone crisis was Greece which agreed to a series of painful economic reforms and spending cuts in return for a Euro 240bn international bailout.[3] The austerity programme prompted widespread social unrest and political turmoil.

The twists and turns of the Greek saga provided and continues to provide lots of material for financial reporters.[4]

The format of news coverage discussed below refers to Greece but could be equally applied to another country faced with a similar situation.

Journalistic practice

News articles focusing on the latest negotiations between Greece and its creditors, setting out each side's case and commenting on the likelihood of agreement with a quote from an economist. Radical Greek government saying emphasis should be on growth with social justice, creditors say should focus on debt repayment otherwise says to other countries you don't have to pay your debts. Such an article should also include the reaction of the bond markets to the news, with German bond yields given as an example. Mention can also be made of the amount of capital leaving the country which illustrates loss of investor confidence.

Longer comment and analysis reports can take a number of angles. One example being speculation about the possible consequences of a Greek exit from the Eurozone, the so-called 'Grexit'. A system of fixed exchange rates rather than EMU would be the new scenario, under which one could anticipate seeing a round of competitive currency devaluations and destabilisation in Eurozone.

News stories focused on the debate switching from technocrats and finance ministers to politicians. The differing views between Angela Merkel, the German Chancellor, and her party colleagues such as finance minister Wolfgang Schäuble were discussed. Equally, one can discuss the historic factors that attributed to the problems in the Greek economy, e.g. high levels of tax evasion and the likelihood of success of the proposed economic reform programme. Include arguments about pros and cons of whether Greece should ever have been allowed into the euro.

Another angle would be to widen out the debate to the pros and cons of austerity versus growth with examples of some of the austerity measures and their effects on the real economy. Greek GDP has been cut by around 25%, the largest amount in peace time. This can be illustrated with interviews with public sector workers whose pensions have been cut or an unemployed young person. (According to Eurostat figures, Greece has the highest youth unemployment in the Eurozone with almost 50% of under 25s without a job.)

Figure 8.1 Thessaloniki, Greece, 20 January 2015. Alexis Tsipras, leader of Greece's Syriza main opposition party spoke at a pre-election campaign rally, in Thessaloniki, northern Greece, ahead of Sunday's crucial general elections. Image courtesy of Orhan Tsolak/Alamy.

Austerity

There is now a widespread acceptance that austerity measures alone are not a remedy for Europe's economic problems.[5]

Research published by the IMF itself prompted fierce debate in policy-making circles on the right balance between austerity and growth. The IMF's chief economist Olivier Blanchard and a colleague Daniel Leigh suggested in the October 2012 **World Economic Outlook** that austerity programmes have had a more negative impact on GDP than was previously assumed.[6]

Fiscal multipliers

It is all down to an economic concept known as *fiscal multipliers*. This is the ratio of a change in national income to the change in government spending that causes it. Using data from 28 different economies – G20 and EU member countries for the years 2010 and 2011 – they concluded that since the financial crisis of 2008 there had been a miscalculation of the fiscal multipliers used. Their findings suggest that the damage on the real economy of spending cuts could be more than three times that initially thought.[7]

The Office for Budget Responsibility (OBR) used the IMF's assumptions in their forecasts about the consequences of the government austerity measures. The Trade Union Congress (TUC) estimates that the OBR's use of the IMF values means that they may have under-estimated the economic damage caused by the UK government's austerity policies by £76bn.[8]

As well as huge economic consequences, there are also political ramifications with many European governments facing a public backlash against their austerity programmes.[9] The research added to the growing chorus of criticism of the IMF.

Less controversially, the IMF plays an important role in monitoring and analysing the world economy. It holds meetings in Washington in April and October to assess a number of issues including the world economic outlook, global financial stability, jobs and growth and economic development.

Journalistic practice

Lots of political and financial attention is focused on what forecasts are contained within the World Economic Outlook (WEO) publication. Typically a report would open with a general comment on the IMF's outlook for the world economy as a whole, including the GDP forecast for the current year and the year ahead. Then see if there is a specific factor highlighted in the IMF's commentary that has influenced the forecast, for example, a slowdown in demand in China. Pick out the forecasts for the major economies, adding some comment on what has influenced the forecast. Get a quote from an economist on the IMF's predictions and whether they match market consensus.

The IMF is expecting global growth to pick up in 2017 to 3.4% from 3.1%. However the outlook is subdued given the UK's Brexit vote and weaker than expected US growth. The October 2016 World Economic Outlook said the ultimate impact of Brexit 'remains very unclear. These developments have put further downward pressure on global interest rates'.

Emerging market sentiment is said to have improved, there is less concern about China's near-term economic prospects and there are some strengthening commodity prices. Emerging Asia and India in particular are growing strongly but sub-Saharan Africa is experiencing a sharp slowdown. The IMF says there is a need for 'a broad-based policy response to raise growth and manage vulnerabilities.'[10]

The risk profile of emerging and developing economies has risen in the past few years as their growth rates have slowed down. This is in contrast to developed economies.

In its Global Financial Stability Report published in October 2015, the IMF said company and bank finances were 'stretched thinner in many emerging markets'. Corporate debt in emerging markets quadrupled between 2004 and 2014. China, Thailand, Turkey and Brazil were identified as countries where credit has risen sharply compared with historic trends.[11]

The IMF attracted some criticism for its loans to Ireland during the Eurozone crisis. Ireland is a member of monetary union and there was no balance of payments problem. Some question the suitability of dealing with an insolvent banking system through fiscal adjustment, which will take more resources out of the Irish private sector. Some observers have argued that if the IMF is going to expand its remit to include lending to promote financial stability in the Euro area and the European Union as a whole, then there ought to be a debate on its function.[12]

Box 8.3 Criticisms of the IMF

- Conditions attached to loans increase poverty.
- Currency devaluation and higher taxes often associated with austerity programmes.
- Slow to respond to any crisis.
- IMF policies make it difficult for indebted countries to avoid environmentally damaging projects that generate cash flow.

Over the years the IMF has attracted a great deal of criticism from economists, politicians and NGOs. Amongst some of the fiercest critics have been countries that have been forced to borrow money from the IMF and then sign up to agreements which give them some chance of repaying the loans and solving the problem which originally caused the crisis. Inevitably the reform programme is painful because it involves reducing imports and increasing exports and so reducing the amount of resources available for domestic consumption.

The IMF itself acknowledged that its actions had made a bad situation considerably worse in the case of Argentina, deepening a recession and sparking political chaos throughout the country in 2001. The crisis peaked when the Argentine government defaulted on nearly $100bn in debt to private creditors and had to abandon the convertibility system that pegged the peso to the dollar at a one-to-one rate.[13]

One size patently does not fit all when it comes to assessing the success of IMF interventions. Joseph Stiglitz, the Nobel Prize winning economist was senior vice president and chief economist at the **World Bank** from 1997 to 2000. As such he had a ring-side seat at various financial crises. In his bestselling book *Globalization and Its Discontents*, Professor Stiglitz says 'The economic structures in each of the regions of the world differ markedly: for instance, East Asian firms had high levels of debt, those in Latin America relatively little. Unions are strong in Latin America, relatively weak in much of Asia'.[14]

Some economists argue that conditions attached to financial assistance from the IMF lead to an increase in poverty in recipient countries and are detrimental to social stability.

Currency devaluation and higher taxes are often associated with austerity programmes. In the Euro area the inability to devalue the euro means that even tougher fiscal measures have to be taken which can lead to public unrest as we saw in Greece and Italy during the height of the financial crisis.[15]

The IMF is also said to be slow to respond to any crisis. Failure to prevent repeated crisis culminating in the financial crash of 2008 increased calls for major reform of both the IMF and the World Bank. The IMF recognised it needed to improve risk analysis and strengthen surveillance to respond to a more globalised and interconnected world.[16]

It may be that the IMF is doing the best it can. In his book *Unholy Trinity, the IMF, World Bank and WTO*, Richard Peet suggests that 'the sheer size of the global financial system, where shifts in capital are in the order of trillions of dollars, overwhelms the monetary capabilities of the IMF or the World Bank'.[17]

In *Globalization and Its Discontents*, Joseph Stiglitz says the IMF is pursuing the interests of the financial community over the stability of the global economy or the welfare of the poor countries it is supposed to be helping.[18]

The campaigning journalist George Monbiot claims the IMF does more harm than good by exposing vulnerable countries to harmful foreign corporations.

IMF policies have also been criticised for their impact on people's access to food, particularly in developing countries and for undermining public health systems and the fight against HIV/AIDS in developing countries by forcing countries to cut public spending. Often countries have to reduce subsidies on staples such as wheat flour, sugar and cooking oil as a condition for access to IMF loans.[19]

The environment is also said to have taken second place to financial rectitude, making it difficult for indebted countries to avoid environmentally damaging projects that generate cash flow, in particular oil, coal, forest-destroying lumber and agriculture projects.

The International Monetary Fund and World Bank

Countries don't have to go to the IMF. They could just default, not pay their debts. However, this means that a country is unlikely to be able to borrow again on international markets in the short term. This could bring foreign trade to a virtual halt.

Critics of the IMF say it has drifted too far from its original role in overseeing the international monetary system. It has increasingly become the lender of last resort for countries, especially in Africa, that are very poor and unable to access external funds from international capital markets. The IMF's role has as a consequence increasingly overlapped with the World Bank's **International Development Association** (IDA).[20]

The IMF has its origins in the desire of members of the international community to avoid the economic mistakes of the 1920s and 1930s, namely depression and high unemployment.

An international conference was held at *Bretton Woods*, New Hampshire, in America in July 1944, with representatives of 45 governments agreeing a framework for international economic cooperation. The agreement resulting from the conference led to the establishment of the IMF to administer the post war system of fixed exchange rates. John Maynard Keynes, one of the twentieth century's greatest economic thinkers, helped design the IMF and World Bank.

The IMF has played a major role in shaping the world economy since the end of World War II. The IMF helped countries in the aftermath of the oil price shocks in 1973–1974 and 1979 and assisted countries in the former Soviet bloc in Eastern Europe in their transition from central planning to market-driven economies.[21]

Structure of the IMF

Historically the IMF managing director has been European. Christine Lagarde was appointed MD in July 2011, for a five-year term. She was re-elected unopposed to a second five-year term in February 2016. The managing director has four deputy managing directors.

The IMF's employees come from all over the world and are responsible to the IMF not to the authorities of the countries of which they are citizens.

The Fund is a specialised agency of the United Nations but has its own charter, governing structure and finances. It is an important financial institution with its resources coming mainly from the money that countries pay as their capital subscription when they become members.

It started with 45 members but now has 188 member countries. These include the major trading nations US, Japan, Germany, UK, China, India, Russia and others such as Mexico, Switzerland and Saudi Arabia. The IMF is the third largest official holder of gold in the world, behind the US and Germany, with reserves of 90.5 million ounces, worth around $119bn.

Gold played a central role in the international monetary system until the collapse of the Bretton Woods system of fixed exchange rates in 1973.

Since then, the role of gold has been gradually reduced. However, it is still an important asset in the reserve holdings of a number of countries including the US, Germany, Italy, France and China. It acted as a safe haven at times during the Eurozone crisis and performed a similar role in 2016 with various negative factors buffeting financial markets. It had one of its strongest starts to the year in decades with the gold price rising strongly as investors sought safety.[22]

Box 8.4 IMF quotas

- Each member country has a quota based on its relative position in the world economy.
- A member country's quota determines its maximum financial commitment to the IMF, its voting power and its access to IMF funds.

IMF quotas

The IMF lacks legitimacy in many parts of the world given that up until 2016 its structure still reflected the old industrialised order and failed to adequately reflect the shift in global economic growth eastwards.

A wide range of voices have called for change over the years.

The IMF itself recognised that change was long overdue and proposed changes to give greater influence to the likes of China, India and Brazil. Even so, some critics, such as the Indian Prime Minister Narendra Modi, still feel that the new **quotas** fail to adequately reflect the global economic realities.[23]

Journalistic practice

A comment-type article outlining the case for a change in the representation of the IMF could be illustrated with a table showing the current quotas and the proposed new quotas alongside.

A member's *quota* in the IMF, based broadly on its relative size in the world economy, determines the amount of its subscription, its voting weight, its access to IMF financing and its allocation of **Special Drawing Rights** (SDRs). SDRs can be seen as a line of credit allocated by the IMF to each country in proportion to its quota.

Each member country can draw on its line of credit to obtain convertible currencies from the Fund. The globalisation of international capital markets means that SDRs currently account for a very minor part of world liquidity, or solvency. Responsibility for maintaining levels of national liquidity rests with central banks.

Upon joining the IMF, a country normally pays up to one-quarter of its quota in the form of a widely accepted foreign currency such as the US dollar, euro, yen or sterling. The remaining three-quarters are paid in the country's own currency. Quotas are renewed every five years.

Global governance

Increasingly global economic decisions are taken by the G20, a broader group of the world's largest economies reflecting the shift in world economic power from the west to the east. Historically, since the 1970s decision making has been in the hands of the group of seven major industrialised economies of the US, Japan, Germany, UK, France, Italy and Canada. G20 includes the G7 economies, Brazil China, Russia, and India and others such as Indonesia, South Africa and Saudi Arabia.

Change afoot

Like a super tanker it took time for the IMF to change course. However, bowing to concerted pressure, the Ministers of Finance of the G20, governing most of the IMF member quotas, agreed in principle in December 2010 to reform the IMF with an increase in the quotas of India and China.

Table 8.1 IMF Quota shares (%)

Before reform	After reform
US 17.7	17.398
Japan 6.56	6.46
China 4.0	6.39
Germany 6.12	5.58
UK 4.51	4.225
France 4.51	4.225
Italy 3.31	3.159
India 2.44	2.749
Russia 2.5	2.705
Brazil 1.79	2.3

Christine Lagarde has said the ultimate goal of the revised quota formula was 'reinforcing the legitimacy and effectiveness of the Fund'.

What was agreed in principle was a shift of about 6% of the voting shares to major developing nations and countries with emerging markets. Critics note that Spain's original quota share at 1.69% was close to that of Brazil at 1.79%, despite the fact that the Spanish economy is less than two-thirds of Brazil's. Overall, 54 member countries will receive an increase in their quotas, with China, Korea, India, Brazil and Mexico the largest beneficiaries.

The process got bogged down in the US Congress with Republicans reluctant to give the associated fresh funding to the IMF. Reform of the IMF's quotas could not proceed without the US. However in January 2016, the quota and governance reforms came into effect.[24]

In his book *The BRIC Road to Growth*, Jim O' Neill, said 'we will all benefit from international organisations and governance that reflect the present reality of the global economy, not its distant past'.[25]

The US remains the top member in terms of voting power. However, China will become the third largest member country in the IMF and there will be three other emerging countries, Russia, India and Brazil, among the ten largest shareholders in the fund. The reform package also contained measures to protect the voice of the poorest nations in the IMF and increased the financial strength of the IMF, by doubling its permanent capital resources to SDR 477 billion (about $659bn). 'I commend our members for ratifying these truly historic reforms' said IMF managing director, Christine Lagarde.[26]

Nouriel Roubini and Stephen Mihm, in their book *Crisis Economics*, highlight other reforms that would be beneficial. These include 'providing more liquidity in times of crisis' and 'the IMF can also expand its issue of SDRs, particularly in times of crisis'.[27]

IMF resources

The IMF keeps track of its future ability to lend by monitoring its one-year forward commitment capacity, which gives an indication of resources available for lending. The IMF is the world's traditional lender of last resort. Given the many demands on its funds, it would like to boost its resources.

Christine Lagarde, managing director of the IMF, thinks that increasing the size of the IMF's permanent resources will help improve confidence in the global financial system. However it is unclear how extra money would enable the IMF to anticipate future global shocks. There is a question of whether developing nations should bail out profligate Western industrialised nations.

The IMF is not an aid agency or a development bank, and in theory its loans are not linked to particular projects or activities. The expansion of the IMF's membership, together with changes in the world economy, has required the IMF to adapt in a variety of ways.

When called upon in an emergency, the IMF proceeds in three steps.

First it assesses the situation and makes recommendations to the authorities.

Then comes *conditionality*. An emergency loan is made conditional on the country adopting various policies to correct the problems. The country and the IMF have to agree on the policies before the lending occurs. The interest rate charged on the loan is slightly above the market rate to discourage the Fund being used as a cheap source of money.

Finally, as the loan is being disbursed, typically in several instalments, the IMF monitors the implementation of the agreement and may suspend further disbursements if the country in question is violating its commitments. We have seen this in action in Greece with more concrete evidence of structural reforms sought by the IMF before it lends funds.

The IMF believes that sound macroeconomic policies and public finances are necessary to any long-term solution to a country's problems. Lending is short or medium term. Typically loans have a maturity of 1–4 years. The borrowing country must pay back the IMF on schedule so that the funds are available to other countries.[28]

> **Journalistic practice**
>
> There is ample scope for comment and analysis on the terms and conditions of specific aid packages e.g. Ukraine. Include the views of local economists and/politicians. What is the reaction of the financial markets? How has the local currency reacted to news of the rescue package?

> **Box 8.5** Future issues facing the IMF
>
> - Food and oil price shocks.
> - Impact of increased capital flows for economic policy and the stability of the international financial system.

Food and oil price shocks and the implications of the continued rise of capital flows for economic policy and the stability of the international financial system are just some of the issues that it will have to deal with. In March 2016, the IMF embarked on a study 'to understand the challenges facing the international monetary system, identify the system's shortcomings, and lay the basis for reform'.[29]

At the start of 2016, global food prices were continuing to fall despite concerns about the climate. Increasing demand is putting upward pressure on prices. According to the World Bank, global demand for food is projected to grow in the 15 years to 2030 – including increases of around 60% in sub-Saharan Africa and 30% in South Asia.[30]

The Food and Agriculture Organisation of the United Nations (FAO) measures the monthly change in international prices of a basket of food commodities. The FAO Food Price Index rose for much of 2016 on the back of higher prices for sugar, dairy products, meat and oils. Unfavourable weather conditions in Brazil, the world's largest sugar producer and exporter boosted prices.[31]

Box 8.6 World Bank

- Provides technical and financial assistance to developing countries.
- President of the World Bank is Dr Jim Yong Kim.
- The World Bank Group consists of five organisations.

The World Bank provides technical and financial assistance to developing countries, typically longer term lending. Headquartered in Washington, it was set up after World War II to provide aid to war torn Europe. The President of the World Bank has historically been an American. It is currently Dr Jim Yong Kim, a physician and anthropologist who has previously worked at the World Health Organisation.

Established in 1944, it is made up of five organisations that are owned by 188 member countries. The two organisations you are most likely to come across are The International Bank for Reconstruction and Development (IBRD) and the International Development Association (IDA).

Box 8.7 World Bank Group

- The International Bank for Reconstruction and Development (IBRD)
- The International Development Association (IDA)
- The International Finance Corporation (IFC)
- The Multilateral Investment Guarantee Agency (MIGA)
- International Centre for Settlement of Investment Disputes (ICSID).

Each organisation helps the World Bank in its mission of global poverty reduction and the improvement of living standards.[32] A total of $60bn was lent in 2015.[33] The World Bank also sets the conditions under which further billions in loans and grants flow to the developing world, making it the most important development institution in the world.

The IBRD focuses on middle-income and creditworthy-poor countries, while the IDA focuses on the poorest countries in the world. The International Bank for Reconstruction and Development borrows at low-interest rates by selling bonds in private capital markets in industrialised countries and makes near-market interest loans to creditworthy countries in the developing world.

The International Development Association gives loans to countries that are usually not creditworthy in international financial markets. IDA loans carry no interest, but a 0.75% administration charge is made annually. Since its inception the IDA has supported activities in 108 countries. Funds come from member governments' national budgets.[34]

Since the 1990s, various World Bank Development reports have taken a new holistic approach to development involving poverty, health, education, environment and gender considerations in addition to conventional areas such as increased property rights, trade liberalisation and privatisation.

It has acknowledged the necessity of pursuing more comprehensive strategies that emphasise democratic, equitable and sustainable development.

Journalistic practice

From the mid-1980s, the Bank faced mounting criticism for lending money to projects that cause large scale environmental damage. For example, loans to the Brazilian government for a highway and feeder roads into the Northwest Amazon region.

In his book *Globalization for Development*, Ian Goldin, Professor of Globalisation and Development at Oxford University and a former Vice President of the World Bank (2003–2006), says that in order to support growth and poverty reduction, 'much more aid and higher quality aid is needed'.[35] In addition it needs to be untied 'to ensure it reflects real needs rather than disguised efforts to support domestic enterprises in rich countries'.

Under its modernisation programme, the Bank is aiming to be more open, accountable and focused on results. The World Bank provides low-interest loans, interest-free credit and grants to developing countries in a number of areas including education, health, infrastructure and communications. Its biggest country exposure is to China, Brazil, Turkey, India, Indonesia, Mexico, Colombia and Poland.

Box 8.8 World Bank shareholders

Five largest shareholders are:

- US 16.5%
- Japan 9.72%
- Germany 4.84%
- UK 4.33%
- France 4.33%.

The member countries are represented by a Board of Governors, who generally are member countries' ministers of finance or ministers of development. The governors delegate specific duties to 25 executive directors who work on site at the Bank. The five largest shareholders are the US with 16.5% of the capital shares, Japan (9.72%), Germany (4.84%), France (4.33%) and the UK (4.33%).

Asian Infrastructure Investment Bank

China's growing confidence in playing a role on the global economic stage was exemplified by its involvement in the establishment of the **Asian Infrastructure Investment Bank** (AIIB) in April 2015. Its establishment was widely viewed as very much a wake-up call for the US.[36]

Talk of a BRIC investment bank had been around for a while. Chinese President Xi Jinping first proposed it in October 2013.[37]

Its stated mission is to 'focus on the development of infrastructure and other productive sectors in Asia'. To the annoyance of the US, it attracted 57 founding member countries across the economic spectrum including the UK, Germany, France, Brazil, Taiwan and Norway. The ease with which China managed to attract so many founding members is symptomatic of the direction in which the economic wind is blowing.

The US and Japan declined to be members of the AIIB, but even so the sheer number of major countries on board means it will provide credible competition for the existing players in development banking such as the World Bank.

Journalistic practice

The formation of the AIIB was a major news story across the world. There was straightforward reporting of who was a member, what its mission was and how it would function. At least as much coverage was given to the demonstration yet again of the changing world economic order with China usurping the US at the top table.

There was coverage of the hostility of America towards the bank and the efforts made to persuade its Western allies not to join. There was speculation as to whether China will have preferential access to the fast growing markets of Asia, thereby weakening the US position in those markets. Critics questioned whether the move would embolden China to exert its power in other areas e.g. territorial claims.

Box 8.9 HIPC Initiative

- Launched in 1996 to reduce the debt burdens of the world's poorest countries.
- Reforms often include privatisations of industries.
- 36 countries have programmes under the HIPC initiative.

In 1996, the World Bank and IMF launched the **Heavily-Indebted Poor Countries Initiative (HIPC)** to reduce the debt burdens of the world's poorest countries.[38]

The scheme provides debt relief for low-income countries that have unsustainable debt burdens; most are in Africa including Sierra Leone and Ethiopia. Others include Haiti, Afghanistan and Nicaragua.

In these countries, traditional approaches of debt rescheduling, debt reduction and aid may not allow them to reach a 'sustainable' level of external debt, that is a level of debt that can be serviced comfortably through export earnings, aid and capital inflows, while maintaining an adequate level of imports.

Part of the job of the IMF, working in collaboration with the World Bank, is to help ensure that the resources provided by debt reduction are not wasted. In 2005, to help accelerate progress towards the United Nations **Millennium Development Goals (MDGs)**, the HIPC Initiative was supplemented by the Multilateral Debt Relief Initiative (MDRI). This allows for 100% relief on eligible debts by three multinational institutions – the IMF, the World Bank and the African Development Fund (AfDF) – for countries completing the HIPC Initiative process.

As of September 2015, there were 39 countries that were eligible, potentially eligible or may wish to receive HIPC Initiative Assistance.

Journalistic practice

News stories based on particular aid packages. Give details of the specific aid and include a description of the country's economy. What are the future economic prospects? Include forecast data from the IMF or specialist research organisations.

Another angle could be a look at the work in the specific country of non-government organisations (NGOs). How successful have previous aid packages been? Include interviews with local people on what they see in terms of benefits and the views of local politicians on what they would like to see in future.

Government aid to foreign countries is harder to justify when domestic economic conditions are tough. This is reflected in UK news coverage of critics of the government policy of ring-fencing the foreign aid budget when other spending in departments such as the Ministry of Defence (MOD) is being cut. This is particularly the case when aid is given to the likes of India, whose economy is growing faster than that of the UK. The UK is committed to spending 0.7% of its GDP on foreign aid, equivalent to about £12bn. Controversially, this budget is ring-fenced when other areas of government spending have faced severe cuts.[39] Such stories straddle economics and politics.

The United Nations had a millennium development goal of halving world poverty by 2015.[40] It achieved this three years early, helped by the growth of emerging markets such as India and China. Other goals include reducing child mortality, combating HIV/AIDS, achieving universal primary education and ensuring environmental sustainability. In 2015 United Nations member states replaced the millennium development goals with 17 sustainable development goals including gender equality, climate action and responsible consumption and production. A full list of the 17 goals and summaries of their targets is available at www.un.org/sustainabledevelopment/sustainable-development-goals/.

In any assessment of the World Bank, whilst it is acknowledged that its project lending has produced low-cost housing, clean water supplies and safe sewage disposal where none existed before, critics argue that it fails to adequately address the social, cultural and environmental impacts of its projects and structural adjustment conditions.

Box 8.10 Criticisms of the World Bank

- Fails to address the social, cultural and environmental impacts of its projects.
- Agent of American imperialism imposing faulty development policies on poor third world countries.

In his book *Profit over People*, Noam Chomsky cites the example of Haiti which he says followed the usual World Bank prescription of 'expansion of private enterprises and minimization of social objectives'. This he adds resulted in the usual consequences of 'profits for US manufacturers and the Haitian super-rich, and a decline of 56% in Haitian wages through the 1980s'.[41]

Like the IMF, the World Bank is said by its critics to be an agent of Western and in particular US imperialism, imposing faulty development policies on poor third world countries. The World Bank then becomes part of a set of international institutions designed to keep people of the third world in poverty.

In his book *Unholy Trinity, the IMF, World Bank and WTO*, critic Richard Peet argues that the three global governance institutions run the global economy but they operate undemocratically, aggressively promoting a particular kind of neo-liberal capitalism that seeks to end poverty by increasing inequality.[42]

Writing in the *Daily Telegraph* newspaper, Sir Christopher Meyer, former British Ambassador to the US and Germany, said:

> The authority of the IMF has been hit by its unhappy involvement in the Greek crisis. The World Bank is under challenge from China and its Asian Infrastructure Investment Bank, of which Britain is a founding member. The World Trade Organisation, set up in the forties with the goal of liberalising trade, has not sealed a global deal for over 20 years.[43]

Box 8.11 Poverty reduction successes

- During past 40 years, life expectancy in developing countries has risen by 20 years.
- During past 30 years, adult illiteracy in the developing world has been nearly halved to 25%.
- During past 20 years, the absolute number of people living on less than $1 a day has begun to fall for the first time, even as the world's population has grown by 1.6 billion people.

The global economic crisis had a disproportionate effect on the poor due to job loss. There was a sharp increase in unemployment across the world.[44]

There is still much to be done with around 10% of the global population living in extreme poverty. Research by the World Bank shows a growing concentration of global poverty in sub-Saharan Africa. 'Rapid population growth remains a key factor blunting progress in many countries', it said.[45]

Income inequality is still very much an issue in the world and has risen up the political and economic agenda with the likes of former US President Barack Obama and the OECD expressing their concern.[46] Young people and the poor have fallen further behind. A report published by the charity Oxfam highlighted the fact that the richest 62 people were as wealthy as half of the world's population.[47]

However, there have been some notable successes in poverty reduction in the last 40 years. China has lifted more people out of poverty than anywhere else in the world. Between 2000 and 2010, per capita income rose fivefold from $1,000 to $5,000, moving China into the ranks of middle-income countries.[48]

Beijing now has more billionaires than the US, 100 versus 95, despite the volatility in the Chinese stock market and slower economic growth.[49]

Since 2006, the developing nations have been growing faster than more mature Western industrialised nations, and so hopefully their increased resources will lead to further reductions in poverty in the years ahead.

Assignments

Write a 300 word profile of Christine Lagarde, managing director of the IMF.

Write a detailed report on the IMF's intervention in a chosen country. Why did they go in? Were their actions successful? How is the economy faring now?

Glossary of key terms

Asian Infrastructure Investment Bank (AIIB): established in April 2015 at the behest of the Chinese authorities 'to focus on the development of infrastructure and other productive sectors in Asia'. 57 founder member countries including China, UK, Germany, France, Brazil and Taiwan.

Conditionality: the conditions attached to IMF loan disbursements.

Davos: the annual world economic forum that takes place in January in the Swiss mountain resort of Davos. It attracts a wide range of movers and shakers in the economic, political, business, academic and increasingly show-business world.

Fiscal multipliers: measure the effect of government spending cuts on a country's economic growth.

G20: group of 20 industrialised and emerging market countries.

Heavily-Indebted Poor Countries Initiative (HIPC): debt relief programme for heavily-indebted poor countries who struggle to pay high levels of debt and combat poverty.

Human Development Index (HDI): a United Nations measure of the development of economies based on factors such as life expectancy, schooling, adult literacy rate and income.

International Development Association (IDA): provides interest-free loans – called credits – and grants to governments of the poorest countries.

International Bank for Reconstruction and Development (IBRD): lends to governments of middle-income and creditworthy low-income countries.

International Monetary Fund (IMF): a Washington-based organisation of countries, 'working to foster global monetary cooperation, secure financial stability, facilitate international trade, promote high employment and sustainable economic growth, and reduce poverty'.

Millennium Development Goals (MDGs): development framework of eight goals launched by the United Nations in 2000. They included halving extreme poverty and halting the spread of HIV/AIDS.

Quota: the capital that countries contribute to the IMF's financial resources. This in turn determines the country's maximum financial commitment to the IMF, its voting power and access to IMF financing.

Special Drawing Rights (SDRs): international reserve assets, created by the IMF in 1969 to supplement its member countries' official reserves. Their value is based on a basket of four key international currencies, the euro, Japanese yen, pound sterling and US dollar. SDRs can be exchanged for freely usable currencies.

Sustainable development goals: launched by the United Nations on 25 September 2015, the 17 goals and targets to be achieved by 2030 aim to 'to end poverty, protect the planet and ensure prosperity for all'. The goals include climate change, reduced inequalities, affordable and clean energy and responsible consumption and production.

Troika: committee of the European Commission, European Central Bank and the International Monetary Fund. It came to prominence during the Eurozone crisis and associated national debt.

World Bank: umbrella organisation for the International Bank of Reconstruction and Development (IBRD) and the International Development Association (IDA). Its task is the provision of financial and technical assistance to developing countries around the world with the aim of reducing poverty.

World Economic Outlook (WEO): survey of global economic developments and prospects in the near and medium term produced by IMF economists twice a year. It includes forecasts for a number of economic indicators, such as GDP, for individual countries.

Resource list

IMF website: www.imf.org which includes a blog.
World Bank website: www.worldbank.org.

Recommended reading

'Divided we stand: why inequality keeps rising.' (December 2011). www.oecd.org/els/soc/dividedwestandwhyinequalitykeepsrising.htm

'In it together: why less inequality benefits all.' (21 May 2015). www.oecd.org/els/in-it-together-why-less-inequality-benefits-all-9789264235120-en.htm

Weldon, Duncan (10 October 2012). 'Fiscal multipliers, the IMF and the OBR.' http://touchstoneblog.org.uk/2012/10/fiscal-multipliers-the-imf-the-obr/

Wilkinson, Richard and Pickett, Kate (2010). *The Spirit Level, Why Equality is Better for Everyone*. London: Penguin Books.

Notes

1 'Iceland gets $4.6bn bailout.' (20 November 2008). money.cnn.com/2008/11/20/news/international/iceland/
2 Kabir Chibber (4 October 2011). 'Who are the troika that Greece depends on.' www.bbc.co.uk/news/business-15149626
3 'Greece debt crisis: IMF attacks EU over bailout terms.' (15 July 2015). www.bbc.co.uk/news/business-33531845
4 Larry Elliott, Graeme Wearden and Jill Treanor (21 January 2016). 'IMF demands EU debt relief for Greece before new bailout.' www.theguardian.com/business/2016/jan/21/imf-demands-debt-relief-from-europe-for-greece-before-new-bailout
5 Brad Plumer (12 October 2012). 'IMF: austerity is much worse for the economy than we thought.' www.washingtonpost.com/news/wonk/wp/2012/10/12/imf-austerity-is-much-worse-for-the-economy-than-we-thought/
6 'World Economic Outlook October 2012: coping with high debt and sluggish growth.' (8 October 2012). www.imf.org/external/pubs/cat/longres.aspx?sk=25845
7 Olivier Blanchard and Daniel Leigh (January 2013). 'Growth forecast errors and fiscal multipliers.' IMF Working Paper. www.imf.org/external/pubs/ft/wp/2013/wp1301.pdf
8 Heather Stewart (13 October 2012). 'George Osborne's austerity is costing UK an extra £76bn, says IMF.' www.theguardian.com/business/2012/oct/13/imf-george-osborne-austerity-76bn?
9 Ambrose Evans-Pritchard (13 July 2015). 'Greek deal poisons Europe as backlash mounts against "neo-colonial servitude".' www.telegraph.co.uk/finance/

economics/11737388/Greek-deal-poisons-Europe-as-backlash-mounts-against-neo-colonial-servitude.html
10 World Economic Outlook 2016. 'Subdued Demand: Symptoms and Remedies.' www.imf.org/external/pubs/ft/weo/2016/02
11 'Global Financial Stability Report (GFSR). Vulnerabilities, legacies, and policy challenges. Risks rotating to emerging markets.' (October 2015). www.imf.org/external/pubs/ft/gfsr/2015/02/
12 'IMF approves Euro 22.5 billion loan for Ireland'. (16 December 2010). www.imf.org/external/pubs/ft/survey/so/2010/CAR121610A.htm
13 Paul Blustein (30 July 2004). 'IMF says its policies crippled Argentina. Internal audit finds warnings were ignored.' www.washingtonpost.com/wp-dyn/articles/A25824-2004Jul29.html
14 Joseph Stiglitz (2002). *Globalization and Its Discontents*. London: Penguin Books, p.221.
15 Graeme Wearden (12 November 2015). 'Greek general strike: petrol bombs and teargas during anti-austerity protest – as it happened.' www.theguardian.com/business/live/2015/nov/12/greek-general-strike-against-austerity-measures-business-live
16 'IMF to sharpen assessment of risks facing countries.' (13 October 2008). www.imf.org/external/pubs/ft/survey/so/2008/POL101308A.htm
17 Richard Peet (2009). *Unholy Trinity, the IMF, World Bank and WTO*. London: Zed Books.
18 Joseph Stiglitz (2002). *Globalization and Its Discontents*. London: Penguin Books.
19 Richard Peet (2009). *Unholy Trinity, the IMF, World Bank and WTO*. London: Zed Books.
20 Jonathan Masters (9 October 2013). 'The International Monetary Fund.' CFR Backgrounders. www.cfr.org/europe/international-monetary-fund/p25303
21 'Societal change for Eastern Europe and Asian upheaval (1990–2004).' (n.d.). www.imf.org/external/about/histcomm.htm
22 Elaine Moore (16 March 2016). 'Gold price takes off in early 2016 as a refuge from turmoil.' *Financial Times*.
23 'Indian PM calls for change of IMF quotas to reflect global realities.' (12 March 2016). sputniknews.com/asia/20160312/1036169378/indian-prime-minister-urges-imf-quotas-change-reflect-global-realities.html
24 'Historic quota and governance reforms become effective.' (27 January 2016). www.imf.org/external/np/sec/pr/2016/pr1625a.htm
25 Jim O'Neill (2013). *The BRIC Road to Growth*. London: Publishing Partnership, p.ix.
26 'Historic quota and governance reforms become effective.' (27 January 2016). www.imf.org.en/News/Articles/2015/09/14/01/49/pr1625a
27 Nouriel Roubini and Stephen Mihm (2011). *Crisis Economics. A Crash Course in the Future of Finance*. London: Penguin Books, p.263.
28 A handy factsheet, 'The IMF at a Glance', is available at www.imf.org/external/np/exr/facts/glance.htm
29 'IMF launches debate on future of International Monetary System.' (17 March 2016). www.imf.org/external/pubs/ft/survey/so/2016/POL031716A.htm
30 The World Bank (2016). 'Annual report 2015.' www.worldbank.org/en/about/annual-report/overview
31 'FAO Food Price Index.' (10 November 2016). www.fao.org/worldfoodsituation/foodpricesindex/en/
32 'World Bank Group summary results 2015.' (2016). www.worldbank.org/en/about/annual-report/wbg-summary-results
33 The World Bank (2016). 'Annual report 2015.' www.worldbank.org/en/about/annual-report/overview

34 See www.worldbank.org/ida/results.html.
35 Ian Goldin and Kenneth Reinert (2012). *Globalization for development, meeting new challenges*. Oxford: Oxford University Press (1st edition), p.159.
36 'Why China is creating a new "World Bank" for Asia.' (11 November 2014). www.economist.com/blogs/economist-explains/2014/11/economist-explains-6
37 'History of AIIB.' (2014–2016). Euweb.aiib.org/html/aboutus/introduction/history/?show=0
38 'Debt relief under the Heavily Indebted Poor Countries (HIPC) Initiative.' (17 September 2015). www.imf.org/external/np/exr/facts/hipc.htm
39 'How big is Britain's foreign aid budget and how is it spent?' (18 March 2016). www.theweek.co.uk/63394/how-big-is-britains-foreign-aid-budget-and-how-is-it-spent
40 Achilleas Galatsidas (19 January 2015). 'Sustainable development goals: changing the world in 17 steps.' www.theguardian.com/global-development/ng-interactive/2015/jan/19/sustainable-development-goals-changing-world-17-steps-interactive
41 Noam Chomsky (1999). *Profit over People, Neoliberalism and Global Order*. New York: Seven Stories Press, pp.107 and 108.
42 Richard Peet (2009). *Unholy Trinity, the IMF, World Bank and WTO*. London: Zed Books.
43 Christopher Meyer (25 September 2015). 'When it comes to war and peace, the UN is useless.' www.telegraph.co.uk/news/worldnews/europe/11892162/when-it-comes-to-war-and-peace-the-UN-is-useless.html
44 'Sharp rise in unemployment from global recession.' (2 September 2010). www.imf.org/external/pubs/ft/survey/so/2010/NEW090210A.htm
45 'World Bank forecasts global poverty to fall below 10% for first time; major hurdles remain in goal to end poverty by 2030.' (4 October 2015). www.worldbank.org/en/news/press-release/2015/10/04/world-bank-forecasts-global-poverty-to-fall-below-10-for-first-time-major-hurdles-remain-in-goal-to-end-poverty-by-2030
46 'Divided we stand: why inequality keeps rising.' (December 2011). www.oecd.org/els/soc/dividedwestandwhyinequalitykeepsrising.htm
47 Oxfam International (18 January 2016). '62 people own the same as half the world, reveals Oxfam Davos report.' www.oxfam.org/en/pressroom/pressreleases/2016-01-18/62-people-own-same-half-world-reveals-oxfam-davos-report
48 Elizabeth Stuart (19 August 2015). 'China has almost wiped out urban poverty. Now it must tackle inequality.' www.guardian.com/business/economics-blog/2015/aug/19/china-poverty-inequality-development-goals
49 'Billionaire breakdown.' (5 March 2016). *The Week*, p.49.

9 Residential property markets

Mayfair, Park Lane and Bond Street are some of the most expensive sites on the London version of the Monopoly board game. That is also true in real life and helps to make London one of the world's most expensive cities to live in. Find out why in this chapter along with what factors are boosting prices in some other key global cities.

After reading this chapter you will have a good understanding of key property issues such as prices and affordability and acquire an overview of the US sub-prime housing crisis and its legacy. You'll also learn what measures the UK government is taking to help first time buyers get a foot on the housing ladder.

The movement of many people from rural to urban areas in search of work and higher living standards is a trend that is being seen across the world in both industrialised and developing economies.

Given the restrictions on space and availability of housing this higher demand for City living is feeding through into a relentless rise in the cost of residential property.

In his book *Triumph of the City*, Edward Glaeser concludes that overall, the costs and benefits of developing cities is worthwhile.

> Whether in London's ornate arcades or Rio's fractious favelas, whether in the high-rises of Hong Kong or the dusty workplaces of Dharavi, our culture, our prosperity, and our freedom are all ultimately gifts of people living, working and thinking together – the ultimate triumph of the city.[1]

The top global cities have more in common with each other than with other cities in their home country. Demand for prime property has risen across the world, leading to a sharp upturn in cross-border property investment flows. In recent years there has been strong Asian demand for new-build developments in central London. However from the summer of 2015 there was a noticeable cooling off in demand sparking concern that there is going to be an oversupply of luxury two bedroom flats in skyscraper blocks along the Thames.[2]

Investors have also been active in Asia; with more than 30% of Singapore's prime market purchases going to non-domestic buyers, particularly wealthy Chinese, Malaysians and Indonesians.

However rising local discontent about high prices and the influx of wealthy foreigners prompted the Singapore government to take action to remove the froth from the top end of the market. Foreign buyers are charged an additional tax on top of basic buyer's **Stamp duty land tax** taking the total tax for foreigners to 18%. This has reduced foreign investment in Singapore property.[3]

Box 9.1 The world's ten most important property markets

- London
- New York
- Paris
- Tokyo
- Singapore
- Hong Kong
- Sydney
- Los Angeles
- Chicago
- Dubai.

Source: savills.com "12 Cities" H1 2016

Journalistic practice

Regular features are done on how expensive it is to live in the most popular global cities whether that is Hong Kong, Shanghai or London. In the case of China there is much speculation about the likelihood of a property market crash given the speculative bubble that has arisen there and debate about the actions taken by the authorities to stabilise the market.

News and feature stories are easy to illustrate with graphs of price movements over time, pictures of popular residential locations and interviews with potential home owners and housing market commentators and politicians.

Sub-prime crisis

Problems in the US **sub-prime housing** market triggered the global financial crisis of 2007. Low quality sub-prime borrowers typically have poor credit histories. The US housing bubble burst as interest rates began to rise and house prices in the US fell nationwide for the first time on record. Irresponsible lending by the two major US **mortgage** lenders Fannie Mae and Freddie Mac led to their collapse. They had to be rescued by the US government and were nationalised.

By September 2009, 14% of all US mortgages outstanding were either what's known as delinquent or in foreclosure. Major global financial institutions that had borrowed and invested heavily in mortgage backed securities reported significant losses. Mortgage backed securities are loans bundled together and packaged into bonds which are then sold to investors around the world.

After years in the doldrums the US property market staged a recovery in 2012 on the back of a rebound in the US economy. Prices in many cities such as New York and San Francisco are higher than at their previous peak.[4]

Housing markets in the UK, Australia and Ireland slumped during the financial crisis. In February 2008, the Northern Rock **building society**, the fifth largest mortgage lender in the UK, had to be rescued by the government and was taken into public ownership. This followed its inability to get money market funds during the credit crisis and so it had to borrow money from the Bank of England. This led to what's known as a **bank run** as depositors queued to withdraw their money, the first time this had happened in the UK for 150 years. In November 2011, Virgin Money agreed to buy Northern Rock for £747m.[5]

Figure 9.1 Northern Rock Building Society queues. Image courtesy of Geoffrey Robinson/Alamy.

The negative after-effects of the financial crisis appear to have been shaken off in the Irish and Spanish property markets despite the fact that they both still have a glut of unsold properties.

Both markets are showing the fastest house price growth in the Eurozone, albeit from a low base. This has set the alarm bells ringing with the authorities, worried that there will be a repeat of an unsustainable property boom and subsequent large bank losses when the bubble bursts.[6]

In its economic survey of Ireland in September 2015, the OECD said 'rises in property prices pose risks' to financial stability. It made a number of policy recommendations to help address the developing property market risks.[7]

Spain was very seriously hit by a collapse in its housing market in the wake of the financial crisis, partly due to over development. Large numbers of second homes were built along the coast. The market has stabilised in recent months as the Spanish economy has staged a recovery. However, there is still a large overhang of unsold properties. In addition, although in the three months to September 2016 Spanish unemployment fell to its lowest level in more than six years, an unemployment rate of 18.9% is still the second highest in Europe, after Greece. This will act as a brake on growth in the market.[8]

Mortgages

The purchase of a house is typically your biggest capital outlay. Lucrative tax breaks on mortgages has boosted home ownership in several major western economies. In the UK, home ownership is 65%. In 1953, it was just 32%. Home ownership levels in the US are 64% and 79% in Spain but renting is much more popular in Germany where home ownership levels are 43%.

UK home ownership was boosted during the premiership of Margaret Thatcher in the 1980s when council tenants, those people living in social housing, were given the right to buy the homes they were living in. By 1987, more than one million council houses in Britain had been sold to their tenants.

Table 9.1 Largest mortgage lenders by gross lending market share (%)

Lloyds Banking Group	19.8
Santander	13.5
Nationwide Building Society	13.2
Barclays	10
Royal Bank of Scotland	9.7
HSBC Bank	6.2
Yorkshire Building Society	3.7
Coventry Building Society	3.6

Source: Council of Mortgage Lenders

Whilst that sounds like a good idea in principle it has been a major contributory factor to the shortage of affordable housing and arguably added to the inflation in house prices. This is because many of those who bought their homes at hugely discounted prices were able to then sell them on in the general open market making large profits. New social housing has not been built at a fast enough rate to replace those lost to the private sector.[9]

In 2015, the Conservative Government's announced plans to extend the right to buy policy at discounted rates to housing association tenants. This seems almost certain to exacerbate an already dire shortage of affordable homes.

Shelter, the housing charity says that for decades successive governments have failed to build the homes needed. By the time of the financial crisis in 2008, the number of new homes being built in the UK had fallen to its lowest peacetime level since 1924 – and house building is still well below the levels needed to meet demand.

Some economists think that high levels of home ownership can hinder labour market flexibility, a key concern at a time of high unemployment. Andrew Oswald, Professor of Economics at Warwick University in England, argues that an economy's 'natural rate' of unemployment depends on the ease with which its citizens can move around to find jobs. A key part of the problem is young unemployed people living at home are unable to move out to affordable rental property where there are jobs. Professor Oswald notes that of the major industrialised nations Spain has the highest unemployment, 21% and also the highest rate of home ownership, 79%. In contrast, Switzerland has the lowest unemployment at 3.4% and the lowest rate of home ownership at 40%.[10]

Journalistic practice

Housing market surveys and reports on affordability are often news items with interviews carried out with the research authors such as Simon Rubinsohn, chief economist of the Royal Institution of Chartered Surveyors (RICS). Popular interest can be increased by including video interviews with homeowners such as a young professional living at home with their parents; outlining their difficulties getting on the housing ladder. The views of their parents can also be included.

The housing market is a major driver of economic growth in that a strong and active housing market boosts consumer confidence and spending and creates employment in the important construction sector. The property sector and its attendant services are estimated to represent around 10% of the UK economy.

Housing is important politically as well as economically. It was a major plank of the Chancellor's Autumn Statement in September 2015.[11]

Announcements were made in a number of areas including shared ownership, Help to Buy and stamp duty. Recognising that the high price of London homes puts them increasingly out of reach for all but the very wealthy, a London Help to Buy scheme was launched offering interest-free loans worth up to 40% of the value of a newly built home.

Government coffers will be boosted to the tune of about £1bn by the imposition of a new 3% surcharge on stamp duty for buy-to-let properties and second homes from April 2016. Restrictions on shared ownership were removed and the planning system reformed to deliver more homes.

UK planning environment

There are very strict planning laws in the UK which limit the amount of new building to well below the number needed. For many years, governments of all political persuasions have failed to create and promote an environment in which sufficient new homes are built to meet demand. The Conservative-Liberal Democrat coalition government tried to address this issue with the publication in 2012 of its **National Planning Policy Framework** (NPPF).[12] This overturned existing planning laws in favour of a legal 'presumption in favour of sustainable development' with property developers more likely to get planning permission.

There is strong opposition to the NPPF from the Campaign to Protect Rural England (CPRE) and the National Trust (NT), which protects special places in England, Wales and Northern Ireland. They may have a point given that there are already 200,000 sites with planning permission for new homes and over one million empty properties across Britain.[13]

The CPRE is concerned that since 2010 there has been a noticeable increase in the number of new homes being approved on green belt land. England has 14 green belts, covering 13% of total land. Green belts were established to prevent urban sprawl and stop neighbouring towns merging into one another. In theory, green belt land should only be built on in 'exceptional circumstances'. However the pressure for new housing, particularly in southern England, is prompting local authorities to supply land for development.

Journalistic practice

Interviews can be done with local councils and residents in areas of the UK that are under pressure to build new homes, such as Kent and Hertfordshire. Give the background numbers on the shortage of new homes compared to demand and include photographs or film of the fields under threat.

Housebuilding

Historically, UK governments of all political persuasions have failed to build the number of homes necessary to meet demand, particularly in London and south-east England.[14]

The Housebuilders Federation (HBF) represents member firms who account for around 80% of all new homes built in England and Wales. Government figures show that in the year to June 2016, 139,030 homes were built in England, an increase of 17% on the previous 12 months. However that compares with the government forecast for projected household growth of 240,000 every year from 2013 to 2023. The National Housing Federation estimates that compared with demand, there is a shortfall of more than half a million dwellings.[15]

Budget measures announced in July 2015 reducing rental income for housing associations will lessen their ability to build properties for sale or rent. Housing associations built almost 24,000 homes in 2014.[16]

The housing and homelessness charity Shelter says the housing shortage is 'enormously damaging, socially as well as economically' and is forcing a quarter of those aged under 35 to stay living with their parents.[17]

Former Chancellor George Osborne pledged to take decisive action in his Autumn Statement in November 2015 with plans to build 400,000 homes across England. Shares exposed to the housing market such as housebuilders Taylor Wimpey and Barratt Developments, estate agent Zoopla and Kingfisher, owner of the Homebase DIY chain, responded by rising on the good news.

In January 2016, the government decided to kick-start housebuilding by directly commissioning 13,000 new homes on public land with the government taking responsibility for securing planning permission for development. Smaller developers will be able to buy the sites on condition that 40% of the new homes are 'starter homes' aimed at first time buyers.[18]

The government would like to see 200,000 starter homes built for the under 40s by 2020 with discounted prices of a minimum 20%. Discounts apply to properties worth up to £250,000 outside London or £450,000 in the capital.

A combination of optimistic housebuilders, an improved mortgage climate together with support from government measures, is expected to raise new housing completions. However bottlenecks may arise due to a short supply of bricklayers, carpenters and joiners, many of whom left the industry during the financial crash of 2007–2008.[19]

Skills shortages are driving up construction costs. Housebuilders have been slow off the mark training new tradespeople.

Journalistic practice

The view from the building site can be ascertained by interviewing the bosses of the major housebuilders such as Persimmon, Barratt

Developments and Berkeley on what is holding them back from building more houses. Included in the report can be the size of company land banks and the proposed number of units to be built in the current year.

A local councillor in southern England, where the demand is greatest for new homes, can talk about the dilemmas facing the planning authorities in sensitive areas. The views of politicians can also be included on what they are doing to tackle the housing shortage.

Property prices

Historically, houses have been a good investment with house price growth exceeding UK inflation.

It took over 70 years for house prices to double from their 1900 level, but that feat was matched in the nine years between 1998 and 2007. In the past few years, the attraction of property as an investment in parts of Europe and the US has undoubtedly been boosted by the volatility seen elsewhere in the financial markets.

Location is a key determinant of house prices. The best areas attract the highest prices. Price differentials between London and the rest of the UK have never been greater. Kensington and Chelsea is the UK's most expensive area with houses in Kensington selling for an average of £3.6m.[20] All 17 of the most expensive areas in the UK are London boroughs including Westminster, Camden, Islington and Hackney. Prime areas of London are now more expensive than they were before the financial crash. The north of England, Wales and Northern Ireland contain the least expensive towns in the UK.

Generally, at the top end of the market, a high percentage of cash rich foreign buyers – from countries such as Hong Kong, Malaysia, India, Nigeria and the Middle East – keep demand and prices high in areas such as Mayfair and Knightsbridge. Large numbers of French buyers are attracted to Chelsea and Fulham by the French schools. French and Lebanese buyers are also prominent in Kensington and Knightsbridge.

However a number of negative factors, such as increased UK stamp duty rates, have dampened foreign interest in the London property market. There are fears that thousands of newly built luxury apartments in some parts of London could languish unsold.

The combination of a weak rouble and economic sanctions has depleted the number of Russian buyers in the £3m–£10m price bracket. The slowdown in the Chinese economy has reduced the number of Chinese buyers for high-end London properties.

Despite this, in 2015 overseas buyers accounted for about 20% of all purchases in London's prime markets and over half of purchasers in London's new-build market.[21]

Table 9.2 UK house prices since 1952

1952 Q4 = 100	All Houses (UK) Index	All Houses (UK) Price £	All Houses (UK) Annual Change %	New Houses (UK) Index	New Houses (UK) Price £	New Houses (UK) Annual Change %	Modern Houses (UK) Index	Modern Houses (UK) Price £	Modern Houses (UK) Annual Change %	Older Houses (UK) Index	Older Houses (UK) Price £	Older Houses (UK) Annual Change %
Q4 1952	100.0	1,891		100.0	2,107		100.0	2,020		100.0	1,524	
Q1 1953	100.0	1,891		100.0	2,107		99.1	2,002		101.2	1,542	
Q2 1953	100.0	1,891		100.0	2,107		99.1	2,002		101.2	1,542	
Q3 1953	99.5	1,881		100.5	2,117		99.1	2,002		100.0	1,524	
Q4 1953	99.0	1,872	−1.0	100.5	2,117	0.5	97.8	1,975	−2.2	101.2	1,542	1.2
Q1 1954	98.5	1,863	−1.5	100.5	2,117	0.5	96.9	1,957	−2.2	100.0	1,524	−1.2
Q2 1954	99.0	1,872	−1.0	100.5	2,117	0.5	98.2	1,984	−0.9	99.4	1,515	−1.7
Q3 1954	98.5	1,863	−1.0	101.0	2,127	0.5	96.5	1,948	−2.7	100.0	1,524	0.0
Q4 1954	98.0	1,853	−1.0	101.0	2,127	0.5	96.0	1,939	−1.8	99.4	1,515	−1.7
Q1 1955	100.5	1,900	2.0	102.9	2,167	2.4	98.2	1,984	1.4	102.9	1,569	2.9
Q2 1955	102.5	1,937	3.5	105.3	2,217	4.8	100.9	2,037	2.7	103.5	1,578	4.1
Q3 1955	102.5	1,937	4.0	105.3	2,217	4.3	100.9	2,037	4.6	104.1	1,587	4.1
Q4 1955	102.5	1,937	4.5	105.3	2,217	4.3	100.4	2,029	4.6	104.1	1,587	4.7
Q1 1956	104.4	1,975	3.9	108.1	2,278	5.1	103.1	2,082	5.0	104.7	1,596	1.7
Q2 1956	105.9	2,003	3.4	110.0	2,318	4.5	104.4	2,109	3.5	107.1	1,631	3.4
Q3 1956	105.9	2,003	3.4	110.0	2,318	4.5	104.4	2,109	3.5	107.1	1,631	2.8
Q4 1956	105.9	2,003	3.4	110.5	2,328	5.0	104.0	2,100	3.5	107.1	1,631	2.8
Q1 1957	106.9	2,021	2.4	111.5	2,348	3.1	104.4	2,109	1.3	108.8	1,658	3.9
Q2 1957	106.9	2,021	0.9	112.4	2,369	2.2	104.0	2,100	−0.4	109.4	1,667	2.2
Q3 1957	107.4	2,030	1.4	112.9	2,379	2.6	104.4	2,109	0.0	109.4	1,667	2.2
Q4 1957	107.4	2,030	1.4	113.9	2,399	3.0	104.4	2,109	0.4	109.4	1,667	2.2

Q1 1958	108.4	2,049	1.4	114.4	2,409	2.6	104.9	2,118	0.4	110.6	1,685	1.6
Q2 1958	108.4	2,049	1.4	114.4	2,409	1.7	104.4	2,109	0.4	111.2	1,694	1.6
Q3 1958	108.9	2,058	1.4	114.8	2,419	1.7	105.8	2,136	1.3	111.2	1,694	1.6
Q4 1958	109.4	2,068	1.8	115.3	2,429	1.3	106.2	2,145	1.7	111.8	1,703	2.2
Q1 1959	109.9	2,077	1.4	115.8	2,439	1.3	106.2	2,145	1.3	112.9	1,721	2.1
Q2 1959	111.3	2,105	2.7	116.7	2,459	2.1	107.5	2,172	3.0	114.7	1,748	3.2
Q3 1959	112.3	2,124	3.2	118.2	2,490	2.9	108.4	2,189	2.5	115.3	1,757	3.7
Q4 1959	114.8	2,170	5.0	121.5	2,560	5.4	111.1	2,243	4.6	117.1	1,784	4.7
Q1 1960	115.8	2,189	5.4	123.4	2,600	6.6	111.9	2,261	5.4	118.8	1,811	5.2
Q2 1960	118.2	2,235	6.2	126.3	2,661	8.2	113.7	2,297	5.8	121.8	1,855	6.2
Q3 1960	121.7	2,301	8.3	129.2	2,721	9.3	118.1	2,386	9.0	124.1	1,891	7.7
Q4 1960	123.2	2,328	7.3	131.1	2,762	7.9	119.0	2,404	7.2	126.5	1,927	8.0
Q1 1961	127.1	2,403	9.8	137.3	2,893	11.2	123.0	2,484	9.9	128.8	1,963	8.4
Q2 1961	129.1	2,440	9.2	138.8	2,923	9.8	123.9	2,502	8.9	132.9	2,026	9.2
Q3 1961	130.5	2,468	7.3	139.2	2,933	7.8	124.8	2,520	5.6	135.9	2,071	9.5
Q4 1961	134.5	2,543	9.2	141.1	2,973	7.7	129.6	2,618	8.9	138.8	2,115	9.8
Q1 1962	135.0	2,552	6.2	142.1	2,994	3.5	130.1	2,627	5.8	139.4	2,124	8.2
Q2 1962	137.4	2,599	6.5	146.4	3,084	5.5	131.9	2,663	6.4	142.4	2,169	7.1
Q3 1962	139.9	2,645	7.2	148.3	3,125	6.5	134.1	2,708	7.4	144.7	2,205	6.5
Q4 1962	141.4	2,673	5.1	149.8	3,155	6.1	135.0	2,726	4.1	147.1	2,241	5.9
Q1 1963	145.3	2,748	7.7	151.2	3,185	6.4	140.3	2,833	7.8	150.6	2,295	8.0
Q2 1963	149.3	2,822	8.6	154.5	3,256	5.6	144.7	2,922	9.7	154.7	2,357	8.7
Q3 1963	150.7	2,850	7.7	156.0	3,286	5.2	146.5	2,958	9.2	155.9	2,375	7.7
Q4 1963	155.7	2,943	10.1	157.9	3,326	5.4	152.2	3,074	12.8	161.2	2,456	9.6
Q1 1964	158.6	2,999	9.2	160.3	3,377	6.0	153.5	3,101	9.5	165.9	2,528	10.2
Q2 1964	163.5	3,092	9.6	164.1	3,457	6.2	159.3	3,217	10.1	169.4	2,582	9.5
Q3 1964	166.0	3,139	10.1	169.9	3,578	8.9	160.6	3,244	9.7	172.9	2,635	10.9
Q4 1964	168.5	3,185	8.2	170.8	3,598	8.2	165.0	3,333	8.4	172.9	2,635	7.3

(Continued)

Table 9.2 (Continued)

1952 Q4 = 100	All Houses (UK) Index	All Houses (UK) Price £	All Houses (UK) Annual Change %	New Houses (UK) Index	New Houses (UK) Price £	New Houses (UK) Annual Change %	Modern Houses (UK) Index	Modern Houses (UK) Price £	Modern Houses (UK) Annual Change %	Older Houses (UK) Index	Older Houses (UK) Price £	Older Houses (UK) Annual Change %
Q1 1965	172.9	3,269	9.0	175.6	3,699	9.6	172.1	3,476	12.1	173.5	2,644	4.6
Q2 1965	176.8	3,344	8.1	180.4	3,800	9.9	173.0	3,494	8.6	182.4	2,779	7.6
Q3 1965	178.8	3,381	7.7	182.3	3,840	7.3	173.9	3,512	8.3	184.7	2,815	6.8
Q4 1965	180.8	3,418	7.3	183.3	3,860	7.3	177.9	3,592	7.8	185.3	2,824	7.1
Q1 1966	183.3	3,465	6.0	184.7	3,891	5.2	181.0	3,655	5.1	185.9	2,832	7.1
Q2 1966	188.2	3,558	6.4	189.5	3,991	5.0	184.5	3,726	6.6	194.1	2,958	6.5
Q3 1966	188.2	3,558	5.2	192.8	4,062	5.8	185.8	3,753	6.9	190.0	2,895	2.9
Q4 1966	189.7	3,586	4.9	195.2	4,112	6.5	184.5	3,726	3.7	194.7	2,967	5.1
Q1 1967	192.6	3,642	5.1	198.6	4,183	7.5	188.5	3,807	4.2	196.5	2,994	5.7
Q2 1967	195.6	3,698	3.9	200.5	4,223	5.8	192.0	3,878	4.1	199.4	3,039	2.7
Q3 1967	199.0	3,763	5.8	201.4	4,243	4.5	195.1	3,941	5.0	205.3	3,128	8.0
Q4 1967	203.0	3,837	7.0	205.7	4,334	5.4	198.2	4,003	7.4	210.0	3,200	7.9
Q1 1968	206.4	3,903	7.2	206.2	4,344	3.9	202.2	4,084	7.3	214.7	3,272	9.3
Q2 1968	211.3	3,996	8.1	213.4	4,495	6.4	207.1	4,182	7.8	218.2	3,325	9.4
Q3 1968	214.3	4,052	7.7	218.7	4,606	8.6	208.0	4,200	6.6	222.9	3,397	8.6
Q4 1968	216.3	4,089	6.6	221.1	4,657	7.4	209.7	4,236	5.8	224.7	3,424	7.0
Q1 1969	219.2	4,145	6.2	221.1	4,657	7.2	213.3	4,307	5.5	229.4	3,496	6.8
Q2 1969	222.2	4,201	5.1	223.0	4,697	4.5	216.8	4,379	4.7	231.8	3,532	6.2
Q3 1969	223.6	4,229	4.4	227.8	4,798	4.2	216.4	4,370	4.0	234.7	3,576	5.3
Q4 1969	228.1	4,312	5.5	230.1	4,848	4.1	221.7	4,477	5.7	238.2	3,630	6.0

Q1 1970	231.5	4,378	5.6	234.4	4,939	6.1	223.9	4,522	5.0	243.5	3,711	6.2
Q2 1970	235.5	4,452	6.0	234.9	4,949	5.4	228.8	4,620	5.5	247.6	3,774	6.9
Q3 1970	238.4	4,508	6.6	241.1	5,080	5.9	229.2	4,629	5.9	252.4	3,845	7.5
Q4 1970	242.4	4,582	6.3	245.0	5,161	6.4	233.6	4,718	5.4	256.5	3,908	7.7
Q1 1971	250.7	4,741	8.3	254.1	5,352	8.4	242.0	4,888	8.1	265.3	4,043	8.9
Q2 1971	259.6	4,908	10.3	265.1	5,584	12.8	250.9	5,067	9.7	272.9	4,159	10.2
Q3 1971	277.3	5,244	16.3	280.9	5,916	16.5	267.7	5,406	16.8	293.5	4,473	16.3
Q4 1971	292.6	5,533	20.7	296.2	6,239	20.9	284.5	5,746	21.8	306.5	4,670	19.5
Q1 1972	317.7	6,008	26.7	319.6	6,733	25.8	307.1	6,202	26.9	337.1	5,136	27.1
Q2 1972	346.8	6,557	33.6	345.0	7,267	30.1	338.5	6,836	34.9	362.9	5,531	33.0
Q3 1972	391.1	7,395	41.0	398.6	8,396	41.9	377.9	7,632	41.2	410.6	6,257	39.9
Q4 1972	416.7	7,880	42.4	431.6	9,091	45.7	400.0	8,078	40.6	438.8	6,687	43.2
Q1 1973	444.0	8,396	39.8	467.3	9,844	46.2	423.4	8,551	37.9	469.0	7,147	39.1
Q2 1973	467.1	8,832	34.7	485.7	10,232	40.8	449.0	9,067	32.6	490.5	7,475	35.2
Q3 1973	485.7	9,183	24.2	498.6	10,504	25.1	467.3	9,438	23.7	511.5	7,794	24.6
Q4 1973	516.6	9,767	24.0	526.3	11,088	22.0	486.1	9,817	21.5	548.1	8,353	24.9
Q1 1974	525.1	9,928	18.2	533.6	11,242	14.2	494.5	9,987	16.8	557.5	8,496	18.9
Q2 1974	530.3	10,027	13.5	539.9	11,374	11.2	496.4	10,025	10.6	567.5	8,648	15.7
Q3 1974	536.7	10,148	10.5	543.5	11,450	9.0	500.5	10,109	7.1	579.4	8,829	13.3
Q4 1974	539.9	10,208	4.5	551.9	11,626	4.9	503.4	10,166	3.5	582.5	8,877	6.3
Q1 1975	549.4	10,388	4.6	559.2	11,780	4.8	509.0	10,279	2.9	596.9	9,096	7.1
Q2 1975	567.4	10,728	7.0	582.2	12,265	7.8	526.2	10,626	6.0	612.5	9,334	7.9
Q3 1975	580.6	10,978	8.2	599.4	12,627	10.3	538.3	10,872	7.5	625.7	9,534	8.0
Q4 1975	597.0	11,288	10.6	624.0	13,144	13.1	554.6	11,201	10.2	638.2	9,725	9.6
Q1 1976	609.2	11,519	10.9	639.1	13,463	14.3	565.3	11,417	11.1	651.3	9,924	9.1
Q2 1976	620.9	11,739	9.4	654.8	13,793	12.5	573.7	11,586	9.0	665.7	10,144	8.7
Q3 1976	634.6	11,999	9.3	671.0	14,134	11.9	590.0	11,916	9.6	673.2	10,258	7.6
Q4 1976	645.7	12,209	8.2	688.7	14,508	10.4	597.0	12,057	7.6	686.9	10,468	7.6

(Continued)

Table 9.2 (Continued)

1952 Q4 = 100	All Houses (UK) Index	All Houses (UK) Price £	All Houses (UK) Annual Change %	New Houses (UK) Index	New Houses (UK) Price £	New Houses (UK) Annual Change %	Modern Houses (UK) Index	Modern Houses (UK) Price £	Modern Houses (UK) Annual Change %	Older Houses (UK) Index	Older Houses (UK) Price £	Older Houses (UK) Annual Change %
Q1 1977	656.3	12,409	7.7	703.3	14,816	10.1	605.9	12,236	7.2	699.4	10,658	7.4
Q2 1977	671.1	12,689	8.1	724.8	15,267	10.7	618.5	12,490	7.8	712.5	10,858	7.0
Q3 1977	686.0	12,970	8.1	742.5	15,641	10.7	631.1	12,745	7.0	729.4	11,115	8.4
Q4 1977	695.5	13,150	7.7	765.5	16,125	11.1	639.0	12,905	7.0	735.0	11,200	7.0
Q1 1978	730.9	13,820	11.4	799.9	16,851	13.7	672.0	13,573	10.9	773.8	11,791	10.6
Q2 1978	766.4	14,491	14.2	834.4	17,577	15.1	705.6	14,251	14.1	811.9	12,372	13.9
Q3 1978	841.6	15,912	22.7	912.2	19,216	22.9	783.4	15,822	24.1	883.8	13,467	21.2
Q4 1978	889.7	16,823	27.9	962.8	20,283	25.8	828.6	16,735	29.7	938.2	14,296	27.6
Q1 1979	941.1	17,793	28.7	1028.1	21,658	28.5	872.5	17,620	29.8	998.2	15,210	29.0
Q2 1979	1008.9	19,075	31.6	1088.2	22,923	30.4	935.8	18,900	32.6	1077.6	16,420	32.7
Q3 1979	1083.5	20,485	28.7	1173.3	24,716	28.6	999.2	20,180	27.5	1168.2	17,801	32.2
Q4 1979	1161.8	21,966	30.6	1240.1	26,124	28.8	1076.1	21,733	29.9	1256.3	19,144	33.9
Q1 1980	1199.4	22,677	27.4	1321.5	27,839	28.5	1142.2	23,067	30.9	1286.6	19,605	28.9
Q2 1980	1234.8	23,348	22.4	1368.6	28,830	25.8	1138.1	22,986	21.6	1327.0	20,220	23.1
Q3 1980	1249.7	23,628	15.3	1391.5	29,314	18.6	1150.2	23,230	15.1	1345.1	20,497	15.1
Q4 1980	1242.8	23,497	7.0	1398.9	29,468	12.8	1142.3	23,070	6.1	1337.0	20,373	6.4
Q1 1981	1255.1	23,730	4.6	1447.0	30,481	9.5	1163.0	23,488	1.8	1341.6	20,444	4.3
Q2 1981	1274.5	24,098	3.2	1470.9	30,985	7.5	1179.1	23,814	3.6	1365.1	20,801	2.9
Q3 1981	1279.3	24,188	2.4	1465.7	30,875	5.3	1190.3	24,040	3.5	1366.3	20,820	1.6
Q4 1981	1258.7	23,798	1.3	1498.0	31,557	7.1	1167.5	23,578	2.2	1334.4	20,334	−0.2

Q1 1982	1278.7	24,177	1.9	1524.1	32,107	5.3	1178.7	23,805	1.3	1359.4	20,715	1.3
Q2 1982	1305.2	24,679	2.4	1539.3	32,426	4.7	1212.2	24,482	2.8	1392.0	21,211	2.0
Q3 1982	1320.6	24,969	3.2	1553.4	32,724	6.0	1235.0	24,943	3.8	1405.7	21,420	2.9
Q4 1982	1352.9	25,580	7.5	1588.9	33,471	6.1	1264.4	25,537	8.3	1445.7	22,030	8.3
Q1 1983	1391.4	26,307	8.8	1607.8	33,868	5.5	1303.8	26,332	10.6	1487.4	22,665	9.4
Q2 1983	1448.4	27,386	11.0	1676.9	35,324	8.9	1354.7	27,359	11.8	1548.4	23,594	11.2
Q3 1983	1490.2	28,175	12.8	1715.4	36,137	10.4	1396.4	28,202	13.1	1594.5	24,297	13.4
Q4 1983	1513.9	28,623	11.9	1760.5	37,085	10.8	1414.7	28,571	11.9	1613.8	24,591	11.6
Q1 1984	1569.5	29,675	12.8	1808.7	38,101	12.5	1469.4	29,677	12.7	1691.2	25,770	13.7
Q2 1984	1630.7	30,833	12.6	1861.8	39,219	11.0	1529.4	30,887	12.9	1764.0	26,880	13.9
Q3 1984	1653.0	31,254	10.9	1873.0	39,455	9.2	1556.7	31,440	11.5	1796.7	27,379	12.7
Q4 1984	1721.2	32,543	13.7	1943.7	40,946	10.4	1615.4	32,626	14.2	1862.2	28,376	15.4
Q1 1985	1755.9	33,200	11.9	2009.7	42,334	11.1	1636.3	33,046	11.4	1900.9	28,966	12.4
Q2 1985	1807.4	34,174	10.8	2045.1	43,080	9.8	1685.8	34,047	10.2	1961.8	29,895	11.2
Q3 1985	1835.3	34,700	11.0	2088.5	43,994	11.5	1711.9	34,574	10.0	1991.6	30,348	10.8
Q4 1985	1874.2	35,436	8.9	2156.0	45,417	10.9	1741.9	35,180	7.8	2036.2	31,028	9.3
Q1 1986	1885.3	35,647	7.4	2159.2	45,485	7.4	1747.1	35,285	6.8	2058.5	31,368	8.3
Q2 1986	1957.7	37,015	8.3	2226.7	46,907	8.9	1816.2	36,681	7.7	2144.8	32,682	9.3
Q3 1986	2023.1	38,251	10.2	2310.3	48,668	10.6	1874.9	37,866	9.5	2214.7	33,748	11.2
Q4 1986	2094.1	39,593	11.7	2392.3	50,395	11.0	1949.2	39,366	11.9	2293.6	34,949	12.6
Q1 1987	2162.2	40,882	14.7	2416.4	50,903	11.9	2004.0	40,472	14.7	2393.2	36,467	16.3
Q2 1987	2273.5	42,987	16.1	2525.8	53,206	13.4	2104.4	42,500	15.9	2518.1	38,371	17.4
Q3 1987	2350.1	44,434	16.2	2607.7	54,933	12.9	2174.8	43,922	16.0	2611.8	39,799	17.9
Q4 1987	2345.9	44,355	12.0	2628.7	55,374	9.9	2160.4	43,632	10.8	2602.9	39,663	13.5
Q1 1988	2384.8	45,091	10.3	2644.7	55,713	9.4	2210.0	44,633	10.3	2611.8	39,799	9.1
Q2 1988	2588.0	48,932	13.8	2863.4	60,318	13.4	2403.0	48,530	14.2	2827.5	43,086	12.3
Q3 1988	2874.6	54,352	22.3	3168.8	66,753	21.5	2696.3	54,455	24.0	3114.5	47,460	19.2
Q4 1988	3027.7	57,245	29.1	3371.4	71,021	28.3	2855.4	57,667	32.2	3270.7	49,840	25.7

(Continued)

Table 9.2 (Continued)

1952 Q4 = 100	All Houses (UK) Index	All Houses (UK) Price £	All Houses (UK) Annual Change %	New Houses (UK) Index	New Houses (UK) Price £	New Houses (UK) Annual Change %	Modern Houses (UK) Index	Modern Houses (UK) Price £	Modern Houses (UK) Annual Change %	Older Houses (UK) Index	Older Houses (UK) Price £	Older Houses (UK) Annual Change %
Q1 1989	3148.7	59,534	32.0	3393.9	71,495	28.3	2944.0	59,458	33.2	3476.0	52,967	33.1
Q2 1989	3292.0	62,244	27.2	3451.8	72,714	20.6	3072.9	62,060	27.9	3648.6	55,598	29.0
Q3 1989	3320.5	62,782	15.5	3435.3	72,366	8.4	3047.7	61,551	13.0	3726.5	56,785	19.6
Q4 1989	3252.4	61,495	7.4	3394.9	71,515	0.7	3003.9	60,666	5.2	3663.5	55,824	12.0
Q1 1990	3151.5	59,587	0.1	3296.9	69,452	−2.9	2923.3	59,038	−0.7	3566.0	54,338	2.6
Q2 1990	3119.5	58,982	−5.2	3239.6	68,243	−6.1	2897.0	58,509	−5.7	3547.4	54,055	−2.8
Q3 1990	3027.7	57,245	−8.8	3194.6	67,296	−7.0	2843.2	57,422	−6.7	3434.4	52,333	−7.8
Q4 1990	2904.6	54,919	−10.7	3084.2	64,971	−9.2	2761.3	55,768	−8.1	3274.8	49,902	−10.6
Q1 1991	2885.0	54,547	−8.5	3057.0	64,397	−7.3	2768.8	55,918	−5.3	3228.5	49,197	−9.5
Q2 1991	2931.0	55,418	−6.0	3121.0	65,746	−3.7	2762.6	55,793	−4.6	3344.2	50,960	−5.7
Q3 1991	2903.8	54,903	−4.1	3088.1	65,052	−3.3	2779.7	56,139	−2.2	3286.8	50,085	−4.3
Q4 1991	2836.7	53,635	−2.3	3018.2	63,580	−2.1	2712.9	54,790	−1.8	3220.5	49,074	−1.7
Q1 1992	2760.1	52,187	−4.3	3033.9	63,911	−0.8	2653.6	53,593	−4.2	3092.5	47,124	−4.2
Q2 1992	2785.3	52,663	−5.0	3014.8	63,509	−3.4	2658.4	53,689	−3.8	3151.8	48,028	−5.8
Q3 1992	2763.1	52,243	−4.8	2998.0	63,154	−2.9	2633.2	53,179	−5.3	3138.3	47,822	−4.5
Q4 1992	2653.4	50,168	−6.5	2899.1	61,071	−3.9	2526.9	51,034	−6.9	2996.8	45,665	−6.9
Q1 1993	2651.3	50,128	−3.9	2925.2	61,621	−3.6	2552.2	51,544	−3.8	2928.1	44,619	−5.3
Q2 1993	2745.9	51,918	−1.4	2987.4	62,931	−0.9	2608.0	52,672	−1.9	3108.1	47,362	−1.4
Q3 1993	2736.8	51,746	−1.0	2922.4	61,562	−2.5	2587.6	52,260	−1.7	3153.2	48,049	0.5
Q4 1993	2700.0	51,050	1.8	2848.6	60,008	−1.7	2576.6	52,038	2.0	3096.4	47,183	3.3
Q1 1994	2714.6	51,327	2.4	2947.2	62,084	0.8	2592.7	52,363	1.6	3084.2	46,997	5.3
Q2 1994	2716.5	51,362	−1.1	2805.6	59,102	−6.1	2598.4	52,477	−0.4	3110.9	47,404	0.1
Q3 1994	2736.0	51,731	0.0	2786.0	58,687	−4.7	2614.8	52,808	1.0	3135.9	47,786	−0.5
Q4 1994	2756.3	52,114	2.1	2923.5	61,586	2.6	2609.6	52,703	1.3	3137.6	47,811	1.3

Q1 1995	2701.8	51,084	−0.5	2954.7	62,243	0.3	2567.1	51,845	−1.0	3104.1	47,300	0.6
Q2 1995	2730.8	51,633	0.5	2944.2	62,020	4.9	2597.1	52,452	0.0	3140.2	47,850	0.9
Q3 1995	2715.0	51,334	−0.8	3005.0	63,301	7.9	2595.3	52,415	−0.7	3078.4	46,909	−1.8
Q4 1995	2693.7	50,930	−2.3	2979.8	62,772	1.9	2552.2	51,545	−2.2	3071.3	46,801	−2.1
Q1 1996	2716.8	51,367	0.6	2957.5	62,302	0.1	2579.6	52,097	0.5	3093.3	47,136	−0.3
Q2 1996	2804.8	53,032	2.7	3110.8	65,530	5.7	2655.2	53,624	2.2	3077.5	46,895	−2.0
Q3 1996	2856.4	54,008	5.2	3257.1	68,613	8.4	2701.3	54,555	4.1	3234.9	49,293	5.1
Q4 1996	2917.9	55,169	8.3	3332.9	70,210	11.8	2743.5	55,408	7.5	3315.4	50,520	7.9
Q1 1997	2951.8	55,810	8.6	3349.0	70,549	13.2	2792.6	56,399	8.3	3343.5	50,948	8.1
Q2 1997	3088.9	58,403	10.1	3412.8	71,892	9.7	2904.1	58,651	9.4	3530.8	53,802	14.7
Q3 1997	3213.2	60,754	12.5	3478.9	73,284	6.8	3001.5	60,618	11.1	3717.8	56,653	14.9
Q4 1997	3270.1	61,830	12.1	3582.3	75,462	7.5	3042.3	61,443	10.9	3790.7	57,763	14.3
Q1 1998	3326.9	62,903	12.7	3553.3	74,853	6.1	3110.4	62,817	11.4	3863.1	58,867	15.5
Q2 1998	3449.5	65,221	11.7	3589.7	75,618	5.2	3230.0	65,234	11.2	4021.9	61,286	13.9
Q3 1998	3510.1	66,366	9.2	3719.5	78,354	6.9	3260.8	65,856	8.6	4113.7	62,685	10.6
Q4 1998	3507.2	66,313	7.3	3740.9	78,804	4.4	3266.1	65,962	7.4	4106.0	62,568	8.3
Q1 1999	3568.8	67,478	7.3	3781.1	79,650	6.4	3326.5	67,183	6.9	4183.6	63,751	8.3
Q2 1999	3702.8	70,010	7.3	3839.7	80,886	7.0	3445.4	69,583	6.7	4367.9	66,559	8.6
Q3 1999	3827.2	72,362	9.0	3983.6	83,917	7.1	3557.9	71,855	9.1	4529.3	69,018	10.1
Q4 1999	3947.5	74,638	12.6	4089.2	86,141	9.3	3678.1	74,283	12.6	4669.1	71,149	13.7
Q1 2000	4109.4	77,698	15.1	4225.6	89,015	11.8	3822.9	77,208	14.9	4875.0	74,285	16.5
Q2 2000	4294.7	81,202	16.0	4290.6	90,383	11.7	4005.4	80,893	16.3	5106.2	77,808	16.9
Q3 2000	4280.6	80,935	11.8	4377.2	92,207	9.9	3998.6	80,756	12.4	5114.2	77,930	12.9
Q4 2000	4317.3	81,628	9.4	4412.4	92,950	7.9	4039.4	81,580	9.8	5121.0	78,035	9.7
Q1 2001	4441.5	83,976	8.1	4540.2	95,641	7.4	4124.4	83,297	7.9	5293.1	80,656	8.6
Q2 2001	4635.1	87,638	7.9	4630.0	97,534	7.9	4331.6	87,482	8.1	5543.5	84,472	8.6
Q3 2001	4815.5	91,049	12.5	4809.4	101,312	9.9	4488.9	90,659	12.3	5746.3	87,562	12.4
Q4 2001	4894.0	92,533	13.4	4958.9	104,462	12.4	4577.6	92,450	13.3	5818.0	88,656	13.6

(Continued)

Table 9.2 (Continued)

1952 Q4 = 100	All Houses (UK) Index	All Houses (UK) Price £	All Houses (UK) Annual Change %	New Houses (UK) Index	New Houses (UK) Price £	New Houses (UK) Annual Change %	Modern Houses (UK) Index	Modern Houses (UK) Price £	Modern Houses (UK) Annual Change %	Older Houses (UK) Index	Older Houses (UK) Price £	Older Houses (UK) Annual Change %
Q1 2002	5043.3	95,356	13.6	5066.8	106,735	11.6	4745.9	95,849	15.1	6000.8	91,441	13.4
Q2 2002	5474.1	103,501	18.1	5402.2	113,801	16.7	5116.6	103,335	18.1	6533.8	99,562	17.9
Q3 2002	5861.7	110,830	21.7	5673.2	119,508	18.0	5491.2	110,900	22.3	7021.0	106,987	22.2
Q4 2002	6132.0	115,940	25.3	5978.4	125,937	20.6	5782.7	116,789	26.3	7384.6	112,528	26.9
Q1 2003	6343.4	119,938	25.8	6204.7	130,705	22.5	6006.3	121,304	26.6	7656.8	116,676	27.6
Q2 2003	6631.4	125,382	21.1	6347.4	133,711	17.5	6253.3	126,292	22.2	8040.3	122,520	23.1
Q3 2003	6863.0	129,761	17.1	6457.4	136,027	13.8	6441.3	130,090	17.3	8306.9	126,581	18.3
Q4 2003	7082.0	133,903	15.5	6688.3	140,892	11.9	6649.9	134,302	15.0	8573.1	130,638	16.1
Q1 2004	7416.4	140,225	16.9	6997.9	147,415	12.8	6934.3	140,045	15.4	8971.6	136,710	17.2
Q2 2004	7852.1	148,462	18.4	7353.6	154,907	15.9	7374.3	148,931	17.9	9622.1	146,623	19.7
Q3 2004	8117.6	153,482	18.3	7729.0	162,816	19.7	7624.0	153,976	18.4	9941.1	151,484	19.7
Q4 2004	8063.7	152,464	13.9	7711.7	162,451	15.3	7562.6	152,735	13.7	9931.5	151,337	15.8
Q1 2005	8081.0	152,790	9.0	7669.7	161,567	9.6	7589.6	153,281	9.5	9959.8	151,768	11.0
Q2 2005	8329.8	157,494	6.1	7801.5	164,342	6.1	7742.3	156,364	5.0	10272.3	156,530	6.8
Q3 2005	8336.8	157,627	2.7	7846.2	165,284	1.5	7699.0	155,491	1.0	10174.4	155,038	2.3
Q4 2005	8324.1	157,387	3.2	7926.7	166,980	2.8	7689.4	155,297	1.7	10118.9	154,193	1.9
Q1 2006	8479.2	160,319	4.9	7920.9	166,857	3.3	7838.3	158,303	3.3	10354.9	157,789	4.0
Q2 2006	8728.6	165,035	4.8	8197.7	172,688	5.1	8038.2	162,340	3.8	10713.2	163,249	4.3
Q3 2006	8909.7	168,460	6.9	8325.7	175,386	6.1	8214.8	165,907	6.7	10920.1	166,402	7.3
Q4 2006	9100.4	172,065	9.3	8590.5	180,964	8.4	8371.2	169,066	8.9	11176.0	170,302	10.4
Q1 2007	9284.9	175,554	9.5	8754.8	184,424	10.5	8528.7	172,247	8.8	11457.5	174,591	10.6
Q2 2007	9615.8	181,810	10.2	9029.6	190,214	10.1	8415.8	169,967	4.7	11897.9	181,302	11.1
Q3 2007	9738.6	184,131	9.3	9042.1	190,476	8.6	8536.2	172,398	3.9	12021.5	183,185	10.1
Q4 2007	9729.5	183,959	6.9	9127.2	192,268	6.2	8504.2	171,753	1.6	12048.7	183,599	7.8

Q1 2008	9486.4	179,363	2.2	9057.4	190,798	3.5	8309.1	167,812	−2.6	11721.8	178,618	2.3
Q2 2008	9230.0	174,514	−4.0	8854.9	186,533	−1.9	8091.5	163,416	−3.9	11412.7	173,908	−4.1
Q3 2008	8736.7	165,188	−10.3	8336.1	175,604	−7.8	7645.3	154,405	−10.4	10807.2	164,682	−10.1
Q4 2008	8294.5	156,828	−14.7	7807.0	164,457	−14.5	7254.5	146,512	−14.7	10251.7	156,217	−14.9
Q1 2009	7918.0	149,709	−16.5	7580.7	159,691	−16.3	6930.0	139,958	−16.6	9682.1	147,537	−17.4
Q2 2009	8148.5	154,066	−11.7	7497.3	157,934	−15.3	7106.9	143,532	−12.2	10084.7	153,671	−11.6
Q3 2009	8470.7	160,159	−3.0	7763.1	163,534	−6.9	7383.0	149,108	−3.4	10474.7	159,615	−3.1
Q4 2009	8574.2	162,116	3.4	7805.8	164,433	0.0	7464.1	150,746	2.9	10670.8	162,602	4.1
Q1 2010	8615.0	162,887	8.8	7991.5	168,346	5.4	7507.4	151,620	8.3	10663.9	162,498	10.1
Q2 2010	8923.4	168,719	9.5	8027.3	169,098	7.1	7745.7	156,433	9.0	11161.5	170,080	10.7
Q3 2010	8851.2	167,354	4.5	8160.4	171,904	5.1	7664.5	154,793	3.8	11118.3	169,421	6.1
Q4 2010	8619.4	162,971	0.5	7946.4	167,395	1.8	7518.3	151,840	0.7	10689.8	162,892	0.2
Q1 2011	8588.1	162,379	−0.3	7964.6	167,779	−0.3	7485.4	151,177	−0.3	10663.5	162,491	0.0
Q2 2011	8820.0	166,764	−1.2	8140.0	171,473	1.4	7648.5	154,469	−1.3	11043.2	168,278	−1.1
Q3 2011	8811.2	166,597	−0.5	8082.5	170,263	−1.0	7630.3	154,103	−0.4	11083.7	168,895	−0.3
Q4 2011	8715.4	164,785	1.1	8198.5	172,707	3.2	7547.6	152,432	0.4	10900.8	166,107	2.0
Q1 2012	8606.3	162,722	0.2	8214.6	173,045	3.1	7453.5	150,532	−0.4	10752.0	163,840	0.8
Q2 2012	8724.4	164,955	−1.1	8340.5	175,697	2.5	7529.1	152,059	−1.6	10987.1	167,423	−0.5
Q3 2012	8669.1	163,910	−1.6	8167.5	172,052	1.1	7494.5	151,360	−1.8	10916.8	166,351	−1.5
Q4 2012	8616.9	162,924	−1.1	8228.5	173,337	0.4	7442.1	150,302	−1.4	10846.2	165,276	−0.5
Q1 2013	8623.9	163,056	0.2	8263.0	174,064	0.6	7478.1	151,028	0.3	10789.1	164,406	0.3
Q2 2013	8848.1	167,294	1.4	8327.3	175,419	−0.2	7659.7	154,696	1.7	11130.0	169,600	1.3
Q3 2013	9039.7	170,918	4.3	8505.1	179,164	4.1	7805.4	157,639	4.1	11409.3	173,856	4.5
Q4 2013	9226.3	174,444	7.1	8704.5	183,364	5.8	7951.8	160,595	6.8	11685.3	178,062	7.7
Q1 2014	9420.9	178,124	9.2	8982.9	189,228	8.7	8106.9	163,729	8.4	11967.4	182,361	10.9
Q2 2014	9866.2	186,544	11.5	9021.9	190,051	8.3	8500.7	171,680	11.0	12616.5	192,251	13.4
Q3 2014	9986.1	188,810	10.5	9181.3	193,409	8.0	8611.5	173,918	10.3	12819.5	195,345	12.4
Q4 2014	9996.2	189,002	8.3	9310.8	196,136	7.0	8649.3	174,683	8.8	12702.0	193,554	8.7

(Continued)

Table 9.2 (Continued)

1952 Q4 = 100	All Houses (UK)			New Houses (UK)			Modern Houses (UK)			Older Houses (UK)		
	Index	Price £	Annual Change %	Index	Price £	Annual Change %	Index	Price £	Annual Change %	Index	Price £	Annual Change %
Q1 2015	9973.1	188,566	5.9	9135.0	192,434	1.7	8618.2	174,053	6.3	12742.9	194,178	6.5
Q2 2015	10274.2	194,258	4.1	9233.6	194,511	2.3	8880.8	179,358	4.5	13191.1	201,008	4.6
Q3 2015	10352.2	195,733	3.7	9601.0	202,250	4.6	Series discontinued			Series discontinued		
Q4 2015	10421.5	197,044	4.3	9642.4	203,122	3.6						
Q1 2016	10501.9	198,564	5.3	9973.3	210,093	9.2						
Q2 2016	10802.0	204,238	5.1	10205.6	214,987	10.5						

The Nationwide house price methodology has developed over time and this needs to be considered when interpreting the long run series of house prices. Maintenance in terms of updating weights for the mix-adjustment process is carried out at regular intervals. Significant developments include:

- 1952 – 1959 Q4 – Simple average of purchase price.
- 1960 Q1 – 1973 Q4 – Weighted average using floor area (thus allowing for the influence of house size).
- 1974 Q1 – 1982 Q4 – Weighted averages using floor area, region and property type.
- 1983 Q1 – Development of new house price methodology. A statistical 'regression' technique was introduced under guidance of 'Fleming and Nellis' (Loughborough University and Cranfield Institute of Technology). This was introduced in 1989 but data was revised back to 1983 Q1.
- 1993 – Information about neighbourhood classification (ACORN) used in the model were significantly updated following Census 1991 publication – regular updates since but typically for new postcodes.

Source: Nationwide

City bonuses also play a role, albeit on a smaller scale, in boosting demand and prices for properties in prime central London. Some observers think it is a good thing that British buyers are becoming more of a feature in the prime central London market. Indeed there are calls from both ends of the political spectrum for action to make it tougher for foreign buyers to buy homes in London for investment.[22]

> **Journalistic practice**
>
> There are regular reports on queuing buy-to-let investors, many from overseas, at the launch of high profile new developments in the east of London. This is often accompanied with comment on the lack of affordability for local people.
>
> Features can be produced on the impact of the slowdown in the Chinese economy and collapse in the value of some emerging market currencies on demand for London properties. Pictures of white stucco mansions in Kensington and Chelsea can be included in these reports.
>
> Changes announced in the Autumn Statement and Budget affecting buy-to-let investments also generate a lot of coverage because many middle-aged people have bought such properties as a source of retirement income.
>
> There is regular coverage of the high prices of flats in the exclusive One Hyde Park apartment block, opposite Harvey Nichols in Knightsbridge. In June 2015, a five bedroom flat was put up for sale at £75m, the most expensive flat ever put on the market.

Factors driving up UK house prices

> **Box 9.2** Factors boosting number of UK households
>
> - Migration
> - Almost half of marriages end in divorce
> - Growth in the buy-to-let market
> - People are living longer.

There has been an increase in the number of households due to people living longer, a large rise in the number of people living alone as almost half of all marriages end in divorce and high levels of migration from overseas.

Buy-to-let investors and speculators have been very active in the market in the belief that prices will continue to rise. However, the Chancellor's 2015 Autumn Statement lessened the attractions of investing in the UK buy-to-let market.[23]

208 Residential property markets

The Bank of England's programme of quantitative easing has undoubtedly boosted the housing market. Its large scale buying of bonds has depressed yields and hence lowered borrowing costs. In principle this should lead to cheaper mortgages.

There is a limited stock of housing as new homes have not been built at a rate fast enough to match demand.

House prices (along with schools) are a popular topic of conversation in the UK. Given the high level of home ownership in the UK that is perhaps not surprising. However it is a relatively recent phenomenon says Neil Monnery in his book *Safe as Houses? A Historical Analysis of Property Prices*:

> Before 1960 the major themes were slum clearance, improved sanitation, overcrowding, housebuilding programmes, the rise of building societies to facilitate house purchases by working people, and movements in construction costs.
>
> The story of our lifetimes, on the other hand, has introduced the idea of houses being a wealth generating asset and the financial benefits of getting onto the housing ladder.[24]

Journalistic practice

House price stories can always guarantee a spot in news media. The problems facing young people getting on the housing ladder, regional differences in property prices and prospects for future prices are all angles that are regularly explored.

Affordability

In the 40 years preceding the financial crisis of 2007/2008, rising real incomes (incomes after inflation has been taken into account) made home ownership affordable for more people. However since then UK house prices have soared and affordability has declined.[25] This has led to a reduction in home ownership from 73% in 2007 to 65% in 2015.

In 1979, house prices were less than four times average incomes. In 2015, the gap was a gaping hole with house prices at six times median incomes and 12 times in London. Subsequently, the average age of first time buyers has risen steadily. It was 21 in 1988 and 37 in 2014. In 1996, 55% of people under 30 owned their own home; in 2016 it is expected to be 30%.[26]

This is having a knock-on effect on wealth inequality. A survey by the Office for National Statistics in December 2015 showed the first rise in wealth inequality in almost a decade mainly on the back of rapid rises in house prices in London and south-east England. Older householders were the main beneficiaries.[27]

A survey published in November 2016 by the Royal Institution of Chartered Surveyors (RICS) showed price rises nationally, but further falls in central London. 'The dire shortage of available housing across the UK is continuing to push prices upwards, regardless of the uncertainty linked to the ongoing discussions surrounding Brexit.'[28]

Real wages only started to increase in 2015 after many years of stagnation following the financial crisis. In addition, compared with older home owners, young people have student loans to repay and it is harder to secure mortgage finance. The government has imposed stricter lending requirements on mortgage providers in an attempt to prevent a repeat of the problems that occurred during the financial crisis.

These negative factors have led to a decline in the volume of housing transactions in the UK. The volume of transactions is well down on its long-term average with the record low seen in 2009 when 848,000 homes ere sold – the lowest since modern transaction records began in 1978. RICS is expecting transactions to edge up to between 1.25 and 1.3 million in 2016, compared to 1.22 million in 2015. The prospect of gradual interest rate rises and ongoing mortgage market regulation will continue to make it difficult for first time buyers to get a foot on the housing ladder.

London has tended to outperform other geographic locations in the UK. It is popular with both locals and foreigners.[29]

Box 9.3 Why London is attractive to foreign buyers

- It is one of the world's major financial centres.
- It has a large multicultural population.
- It has a recognised and trusted legal system. Several high profile Russian legal battles have been fought out in the London courts.
- Positive quality of life factors such as good schools, shopping, cultural activities, and easy access to the countryside.
- Relative to other countries there is political and financial security. This has led to a steady stream of wealthy individuals of various nationalities making London their home, most recently Greeks and French seeking to avoid the fallout from the financial crisis in the form of higher taxes in their home countries.[30]

Several key markets were unaffected by the aftermath of the financial crisis and their property markets have continued to move ahead. This has been the case in Switzerland, Canada and Australia. The latter boosted by its proximity to the fast growing Asian economies and, up until 2015, strong demand for its commodities. Investors from around the world are attracted to

Switzerland's position at the centre of Europe but outside the Eurozone, its economic stability, favourable tax policies and natural beauty.

Asian property markets

Asian markets have boomed in recent years reflecting their growing economic importance in the world. This is notably the case in China where prices have risen to a level that is widely seen as unsustainable prompting intervention by the Chinese authorities to try to dampen the market. This has taken the form of interest rate rises, the introduction of a property tax in Shanghai and Chongqing and local restrictions on the acquisition of second and third homes in an effort to make homes more affordable. Many economists have warned that a bursting of the property bubble is the biggest risk facing the world's second-largest economy in the medium to long term.[31]

Hong Kong is one of the world's major financial centres. Mainland Chinese investors have boosted demand on the island, propelling it to top slot in the list of the world's most expensive places to buy a residential property. Hong Kong authorities are trying to increase land supply but this is a slow process. Given the growing numbers of middle class people in China, demand is likely to continue to exceed supply in Hong Kong. In common with Singapore, Hong Kong levies an additional 15% stamp duty on foreign residential property purchasers.

Back in the West, New York remains a perennial favourite with local and overseas buyers reflecting its pre-eminent position in the world economy. It is attracting wealthy overseas buyers from the emerging markets of Russia, China, Brazil and Argentina.

Mortgages

In the UK, most people have a *mortgage* which is a loan provided to purchase a property over a certain period of time. Mortgage lending is the primary mechanism used in many countries to finance private ownership of residential and commercial property.

If you want the certainty of knowing what your monthly interest payments will be then you can take out a *fixed* rate mortgage (FRM). The interest rate remains constant for a fixed period, typically 2, 3, 4, 5 or 10 years. In America, fixed rate mortgages are standard.

Adjustable rate mortgages (ARM), also known as floating rate or variable rate mortgages, have interest rates that vary according to money market rates. These are the rates that lenders will have to pay to borrow money themselves. (Bank base rate is a short-term interest rate set by the Bank of England. It is the main interest rate around which the main UK banks fix their lending and borrowing rates.)

A tracker mortgage is a variable rate mortgage that is linked directly to the base rate of the Bank of England. There is undoubtedly scope for innovation within the mortgage market with different products for different life stages, for example, a traditional mortgage early in life ending up with equity release later in life when there might be a desire to downsize to a smaller property. Prohibitive costs associated with such a move have caused many older home owners to stay in large houses they would rather sell, adding to the shortage of properties available to buy. People are living longer. Around 30% of mortgages are due to mature for people over the age of 60.

Record low interest rates in the UK, 0.25%, have not all been passed through to borrowers. In principle low mortgage rates should be encouraging house buying but stricter lending policies following the global financial crisis of 2008 meant that many potential first time buyers could not get a foot on the property ladder because they could not save enough for a deposit.

New types of lenders such as LendInvest, the peer-to-peer (P2P) mortgage company, are taking market share from established mortgage providers. Increasingly, fintech companies are attracting tech savvy consumers.[32]

Help to Buy

The UK government has launched a number of initiatives to try to boost home ownership with a particular focus on helping first time buyers. The most successful of these have been two Help to Buy schemes which have transformed the ability of first time buyers to step onto the housing ladder.[33]

There is a mortgage guarantee scheme assisting potential buyers who can afford mortgage payments but cannot raise the sizeable deposits required to secure a mortgage. This scheme requires a deposit of just 5% of the purchase price. It is open to first time buyers and home movers for new-build and older homes in the UK with a purchase price up to £600,000. The Help to Buy mortgage guarantee scheme is due to end on 31 December 2016.[34]

There is also an equity loan scheme for new owner-occupier homes in England. Both first time buyers and home movers are eligible for the scheme. A deposit contribution of at least 5% of the property price is required. The government will provide a loan of up to 20% of the price. A mortgage of up to 75% will be needed to cover the rest of the payment. The equity loan part of Help to Buy is available until 2020.[35]

The Help to Buy schemes led to a 60% rise in the number of first time buyers across the UK. However it was less used in London because the very high prices were out of reach for almost all first time buyers.[36] Recognising this, the government announced a special equity loan scheme for London in the 2015 Autumn Statement. The scheme is available to those buying a new-build property that have a 5% deposit. A loan of up to 40% of the value of the home will be provided interest-free for five years.[37]

Journalistic practice

Customer stories featuring happy first time buyers being interviewed in their new home are easy to compile. Their journey to becoming first time buyers can be detailed along with their thoughts for the future.

House builders such as Barratt can be interviewed on what impact Help to Buy has had on their sales.

Details of government assistance schemes are reported with forecasts on the likely impact on the overall market in terms of transactions and prices. Longer reports can include historic analysis of affordability and mortgage lending. Government help for first time buyers is not without its critics.[38] There are worries that the taxpayer would have to foot a sizeable bill if there was a housing market crash.

The question is regularly posed as to the desirability of such high levels of home ownership in the UK relative to overseas countries.[39] Concern is also often expressed about the possibility of a house price bubble forming with prices boosted by the scheme.

In 2014 more than 300,000 buyers purchased their first home, the largest number since 2007. Aggregate gross lending in 2014 was 14% higher than the previous year at £203bn but that was still way down on the peak lending total of £357bn seen in 2007. The fragility of the market was demonstrated by a dip in the numbers of first time buyers in 2015.

In 2014–2015, there were 564,000 first time buyers in England, well down on the 815,000 in 2004–2005 with the biggest decline in buyers outside London.[40] However the various government assistance schemes mean that fewer first time buyers need help with their deposit from parents, the so-called *bank of mum and dad*.

Loan to value ratios

Mortgage lenders typically offer first time buyers an average loan of three times their salary. The bigger the deposit you can put down the better the mortgage deal you will get as lenders will view the loan as less risky. The **loan to value ratio** (LTV) is the size of loan relative to the value of the property. A mortgage loan in which the purchaser has made a deposit of 20% has a loan to value ratio of 80%. The LTV is an important indicator of the riskiness of the mortgage loan. The higher the LTV, the greater the risk that the value of the property (in case of repossession or foreclosure) will be insufficient to cover the remaining loan.

Even before the introduction of the government's Help to Buy schemes, in some parts of the UK such as north-east England, places like Durham and Sunderland, and Scotland, there were a high percentage of first time buyers with mortgages of 90% loan to value or more. This reflects a number of factors including lower income levels, less availability of parents able to help out with deposits and, in some cases such as Hull, extra mortgage incentives to buyers of ex-council housing.

Areas of high loan to value mortgages, stagnant incomes, high unemployment and falling house prices are likely to be particularly vulnerable to repossession if the economy goes into recession or interest rates rise.

However, recovery in the volume of housing transactions will only come about if first time buyers are given greater access to high loan-to-value lending. This was the view espoused in a report 'Bricks and mortar in a digital world: 15 years of the property market', published in May 2016 by the conveyancer My Home Move. If such lending occurred then the number of property transactions could 'rise by over a fifth in five years to reach almost 1.5 million in 2020'. Doug Crawford, chief executive of My Home Move, said 'We need more lending to those with smaller deposits so that average deposit sizes for first time buyers fall to 10%'.[41]

> **Journalistic practice**
>
> Any change in interest rates and thereby mortgage rates is a big news story that can expect to top news bulletins on the day. Include the size of any likely change in mortgage rates, what difference it will make to the average monthly mortgage payment and include comment from a housing market economist on the likely impact on the market and the prospect for future changes in mortgage rates.
>
> Monthly mortgage lending data from the Council of Mortgage Lenders (CML) is often reported as an illustrator of the strength of consumer confidence generally and the housing market in particular.

Property taxation

Stamp duty land tax (SDLT) is paid on increasing portions of a UK residential property price above £125,000.[42]

Chancellor George Osborne introduced changes to the structure of stamp duty in 2014 which has had a depressing effect on the market in prime central London. There is much less demand for houses above £2m because of the hefty increase in the associated tax bill. This has affected demand in areas such as Mayfair, Chelsea, Knightsbridge and Kensington with property price falls in some cases.

In the past, stamp duty was paid on the whole value of the property, not just the amount over the threshold, which made it an unpopular tax. Higher thresholds failed to keep pace with rampant house price inflation particularly for those buying homes in London and south-east England.

> **Box 9.4** Stamp duty land tax in England and Wales
>
> - Up to £125,000: zero tax
> - From £125,001 to £250,000: 2%
> - From 250,001 to £925,000: 5%
> - From 925,001 to £1.5m: 10%
> - The portion above £1.5m: 12%
> - From 1 April, 2016 an additional 3% on top of the normal tax is levied on second homes.

Mansion tax

Ahead of the UK general election in 2015, the opposition Labour Party and the Liberal Democrat members of the coalition government proposed the introduction of an annual mansion tax.[43]

It was estimated that around £1.2bn a year would be raised by imposing the tax on property worth £2m or more. The money was earmarked for the National Health Service.

Around 100,000 properties would have been affected predominantly in London and south-east England. A third of properties in London above the £2m threshold have been in the same ownership for more than 10 years. Just 12 properties were thought to be eligible in Wales compared to almost a third of households in Kensington. Those with homes between £2m and £3m would pay £3,000 per year and owners of affected homes on low incomes would be able to defer the tax payments until their property was sold. The threshold would rise over time in line with the average increase in high value property prices.

Journalistic practice

The possible introduction of a mansion tax generated much press coverage. There were many angles taken. These included: a focus on whom would be eligible to pay, whether it was fair that it would hit many elderly people on modest incomes who happened to have lived in houses in London for a long time, how the tax could practically be introduced and how much revenue would be raised from it. In addition, there was commentary on the impact of the tax on the overall housing market, how people would seek to avoid paying the tax and discussion of whether its introduction reflected the politics of envy. Added to the mix were interviews with indignant 'celebrities' threatening to move elsewhere and experts warning of the potential loss of foreign investment.

In May 2015, a similar mansion tax on homes over $1.7m was proposed by the mayor of New York as part of a programme to increase the amount of affordable housing across the city.

Building societies

In the UK, **building societies**, such as Nationwide, are financial institutions owned by their members that offer banking and other financial services, especially mortgage lending. In 2016, there were 45 societies, compared to over 100 in the 1920s. Most major towns had a building society named after that town. Nationwide is the largest building society with around £200m of group assets. Over the years, the share of the new mortgage loans market held by building societies has declined. In 1977, building societies accounted for 96% of new mortgage loans.

Lloyds Banking group, which includes the brands Lloyds Bank, Halifax, Bank of Scotland and Scottish Widows, is the biggest mortgage lender with around 20% of the market. Better technology, marketing, extensive branch networks and access to cheaper international sources of funds for lending have all benefited the banks over building societies.

However in recent years, building societies such as the Nationwide, Yorkshire and Coventry have featured in the top ten list of mortgage lenders by gross lending. They have achieved this by offering attractive products for first time buyers, the often overlooked second steppers, self-builders and older borrowers. Up until recently these sectors of the market have tended to be ignored by banks, still highly risk averse in the aftermath of the financial crisis.

House prices indices

The Nationwide and Halifax produce house price indices. These are closely followed by the media and economists as a guide to the state of the market. The Nationwide and Halifax base their indices on their own mortgage approvals which mean that they can only give a snapshot of the market.[44]

> **Journalistic practice**
>
> Reports should include the monthly percentage change in average house prices and the total average price. This should be compared to the price a year ago. Quarterly figures, a less volatile measure of house price movement, are also often quoted. Give an indication of the underlying trend. Were there any noticeable regional differences? Include a quote from a housing economist on the prospects for prices and a graph showing the annual change in house prices.

Prospects for residential property prices

A combination of slower world economic growth coupled with specific government measures to cool overheated markets has led to a slowdown in Eastern markets. However as the world economic axis has decidedly shifted eastwards, Shanghai, Singapore, Hong Kong, Mumbai, and to a lesser extent Moscow, can expect to figure strongly in future league tables of the most important global property markets.

Singapore, an established market with transparent processes, is expected to continue to attract international investment particularly from Asian buyers attracted by a familiar language and culture. Global property consultants Savills say the number of Chinese buyers has tripled since 2007, as they seek to diversify their investments abroad.

Property in cities such as New York, long established as safe havens for international wealth, should continue to be in demand. Savills predicts that successful future investment will be in second-tier cities and resorts in Asia catering to its ageing wealthy inhabitants. 'Singapore is an established market with transparent processes. As such, it is expected to continue to attract international investment particularly from Asian buyers attracted by a familiar language and culture'.[45]

Following Britain's referendum decision in June 2016 to leave the European Union, estate agents and analysts were quick to forecast an abrupt end to the UK's house price boom. Political and economic uncertainty were cited as reasons for buyers delaying purchases leading to a drop in the volume of transactions. Job losses in financial services if foreign banks move some of their operations to other European cities will reduce demand for housing in central London, the City and Canary Wharf. In a best-case scenario overall house prices are expected to be flat in 2016 with small falls of 3–5% in both 2017 and 2018.[46]

However, the trajectory of long-term house prices is likely to remain upward due to the underlying inflationary pressures created by an undersupply of the homes people want in the places people want them. The volume of transactions may be depressed by historic standards due to the relative lack of first time buyers in the market and the relatively low level of existing properties offered for sale.

Renting

The difficulties in buying a property in the UK, coupled with a shrinking number of affordable houses, is prompting a substantial shift towards private renting. Over one million families rent in the UK. According to the English Housing Survey, in 2004–2005, 24% of 25–34 year olds lived in the private rented sector. By 2014–2015 this had increased to 46%.[47] There are predictions that by 2025, more than half of people aged under 40 will be living in private rented accommodation.[48]

However renting is also expensive and increased tenant demand is pushing up rents. The average cost of renting a home in the UK was £1,000 a month in August 2016. A RICS survey published in December 2015 forecast that rental growth could outstrip house price growth as landlords seek to pass on higher costs to tenants. Rents could increase by 5% a year which is higher than people's income growth making buying and renting unaffordable for large numbers of people.[49]

There is already an affordability gap. Figures from the housing charity Shelter show that in the year to October 2015, one in five working adults aged 20–34 moved back home with their parents. A further 15% have never moved out.

The biggest review of the UK housing market in more than a decade was launched in February 2016. The Redfern review – led by Pete Redfern, chief executive of builder Taylor Wimpey – will look at supply, first time buyers and planning issues.[50]

> **Journalistic practice**
>
> As more people rent, so media coverage of the rented sector has increased with regular reports on the high cost of renting for the so-called '**Generation Rent**', who previously might have been home owners. Publication of research by organisations such as the Resolution Foundation think tank and charities such as Shelter often provide news stories. Government promotion of the fledgling build-to-rent market is also covered, often in association with reporting on infrastructure measures in the Budget.

A gap between London and the regions of England is also evident in the prime rental markets. In addition, more than 1.8m households are on social housing waiting lists in England, an 81% increase since 1997.

Research by the Royal Institution of Chartered Surveyors suggests that home ownership in England has been falling since 2003 and has also fallen in other places including the US, Australia, Austria, Finland and the Irish Republic. If current trends were projected forward, then by 2025 the percentage of home ownership could be below 60% – lower than most other European countries. In the third quarter of 2016, the US homeownership rate remained near its lowest level in three decades at 63.5%. It has been steadily declining for a decade.[51]

Buy-to-let

A combination of favourable tax treatment and low returns on other investments prompted a surge in the buy-to-let market in the five years to the end of 2015. The government's relaxation of the pension rules, allowing people to withdraw large cash sums further boosted the market. However, the market was dealt what David Cox of the Association of Residential Letting Agents described as a 'catastrophic' blow in the Chancellor's 2015 Autumn Statement.

From April 2016, buy-to-let landlords and second home owners have had to pay an additional 3% stamp duty, adding a sizeable extra cost to property buying. The measure will add up to £7,500 to the cost of a £250,000 property. Some industry watchers think the higher tax could push up rents. Alex Chesterman, founder and chief executive of Zoopla, the property portal, thinks the 3% surcharge on buy-to-let properties could have 'negative repercussions' for tenants. Landlords could sell up, limiting supply and pushing up prices.[52]

Alarm bells have been ringing in both the Treasury and Bank of England as figures show buy-to-let lending close to its pre-crisis peaks. New loans to landlords are expected to be around £38bn in 2016 compared to £45.7bn in 2007. Lenders are less rigorous in their lending policies for buy-to-let investors relative to owner-occupiers. For example, lenders accepted smaller deposits of just 20% to secure loans.

Bank of England governor Mark Carney has expressed his concern on several occasions about the threat to the UK's financial stability posed by the high levels of lending to landlords.[53]

Around 16% by value of all outstanding mortgages are buy-to-let mortgages. Mr Carney is also concerned that were house prices to start falling then landlords could try to sell at the same time, amplifying the downward trend. From 1 January 2017, buy-to-let borrowers will have to have higher levels of rent relative to their mortgage costs. Lenders will have to stress-test all new mortgages at a rate of 5.5%.

Negative factors for the buy-to-let market

- Stricter mortgage lending criteria.
- Tighter regulation of the buy-to-let market.
- 3% higher stamp duty taxation on purchase of buy-to-let properties from April 2016.
- Lower tax relief for wear and tear on properties.
- Likelihood of a rise in UK interest rates following moves by the US Federal Reserve.

Reflecting these negative headwinds, the Council of Mortgage Lenders (CML) predicts that purchases of investment properties will decline from around 116,000 in 2015 to 90,000 by 2017. However, in the first couple of months after the tax changes property auctions saw strong demand from investors, particularly for London properties. Landlords know what the extra costs are and property is still seen as a good investment given the huge numbers of people who have to rent because they cannot afford to buy.[54]

Journalistic practice

The Chancellor's surprise move on higher stamp duty for investors was much debated in the press with speculation on what it might mean for the market. Interviews were conducted with small and large private landlords, estate agents and industry experts such as the Council of Mortgage Lenders.

Build-to-rent

In contrast to the US and Germany, the private rented sector in the UK is not regulated with professional landlords. In the past the bad image of the private landlords deterred large property developers from entering the market and developing a build-to-let sector of high quality properties. However this is slowly changing.

A Build-to-Rent scheme was launched in 2012 as part of a UK government push to increase the supply of high quality homes available for market rent in the private sector. Several local authority pension schemes are investing in Build-to-Rent because it is delivering affordable homes for key workers such as nurses and other important groups that are critical to their local economies. It is not just happening in London and south-east England but in cities with strong rental demand such as Liverpool, Manchester, Birmingham and Sheffield.

In January 2016, the large British insurance firm Legal & General announced that it was forming a partnership with a Dutch fund manager to build and rent out 3,000 new UK homes. This is part of a £600m 'build-to-rent' plan. Once built, Legal & General will be the landlord and will use the rental income to pay pensions. Other insurance companies have been investing in private rental housing, attracted by the stable, long-term rental yields.[55]

The British Property Federation estimates that building 10,000 homes each year will add about £1.2bn to the UK economy and create 11,000 jobs.

Assignments

Write a 250 word summary of the US sub-prime crisis.
Produce a report on one particular country's residential property market.

Glossary of key terms

Building society: a UK financial institution owned by its members that offers mortgage lending and other financial services. The largest is the Nationwide building society.
Bank run: when investors lose confidence in a bank and en masse seek to withdraw their funds.

Funding for Lending Scheme (FLS): launched on 13 July 2012 by the Bank of England and UK Treasury with the aim of increasing lending to businesses and non-financial companies. It provides funding to banks and building societies for an extended period with the pricing and quantity of funds linked to their lending performance.

Generation Rent: the large number of young adults who faced with rising property prices and a shortage of affordable housing are forced to rent.

Loan to value ratio (LTV): the size of the loan relative to the value of the property.

Mortgage: a loan provided to purchase a property over a certain period of time.

National Planning Policy Framework (NPPF): sets out the government's planning policies for England. It aims to make the planning system less complex.

Stamp duty: a tax payable when you buy a property or land over a certain price in England, Wales and Northern Ireland.

Sub-prime housing: housing financed by loans to people who may have difficulty making repayments.

Resource list

Housebuilders Federation: www.hbf.co.uk
Housing and homelessness charity Shelter: www.shelter.org.uk
Resolution Foundation: www.resolutionfoundation.org
Halifax Building Society, the largest provider of residential mortgages: www.halifax.co.uk
Nationwide Building Society: www.nationwide.co.uk
Savills: www.savills.co.uk
Knight Frank: www.knightfrank.com
Royal Institution of Chartered Surveyors: www.rics.org
National Trust: www.nationaltrust.org.uk
Council of Mortgage Lenders (CML) is the UK trade association for the residential mortgage lending industry: www.cml.org.uk
Building Society Association: www.bsa.org.uk
English Housing Survey: www.gov.uk/government/statistics/english-housing-survey-2014-to-2015-headline-report
Eurostat provides detailed statistics on EU and candidate countries: www.ec.europa.eu/eurostat.
The official government site with details of the various Help to Buy schemes and customer stories: www.helptobuy.gov.uk

Notes

1 Edward Glaeser (2011). *Triumph of the City.* London: Macmillan, p.270. The book was shortlisted for the FT/Goldman Sachs Business Book of the Year 2011.

2 Hilary Osborne (7 March 2016). 'Glut of new-build properties leads to falling premiums in central London.' www.theguardian.com/money/2016/mar/07/glut-new-build-properties-falling-premiums-central-london-oversupply
3 'Singapore and Hong Kong are most expensive for foreign property investors.' (12 January 2015). www.propertywire.com/news/europe/foreign-buyers-most-expensive-2015011210028.html
4 Megan Cassella (26 August 2015). 'US housing market seen strong enough to handle Fed rate hikes: Reuters poll.' www.reuters.com/article/2015/08/26/us-property-poll-usa-idUSKCN0QV11020150826
5 'The rise and fall of Northern Rock.' (14 August 2014). www.telegraph.co.uk/finance/newsbysector/banksandfinance/11032772/The-rise-and-fall-of-Northern-Rock.html
6 Mehreen Khan (15 September 2015). 'Ireland's blistering property market threatens new bubble.' www.telegraph.co.uk/finance/economics/11865721/Irelands-blistering-property-market-threatens-new-bubble.html
7 'Economic survey of Ireland 2015.' (15 September 2015). www.oecd.org/economy/economic-survey-ireland.htm
8 'Spanish property prices up and down according to location, latest index suggests.' (4 February 2016). www.propertywire.com/news/europe/spain-real-estate-markets-2016020411523.html
9 Dawn Foster (7 December 2015). 'Right to buy: a history of Margaret Thatcher's controversial policy.' www.theguardian.com/housing-network/2015/dec/07/housing-right-to-buy-margaret-thatcher-data
10 Andrew J. Oswald, (May 1999). 'The housing market and Europe's unemployment: a non-technical paper.' www.andrewoswald.com/docs/homesnt.pdf
11 Jill Treanor and Rowena Mason (25 November 2015). 'Autumn Statement and spending review – the key points at a glance.' www.theguardian.com/uk-news/2015/nov/25/autumn-statement-spending-review-2015-george-osborne-key-points-live
12 Gov.UK. (27 March 2012). 'National planning policy framework.' www.gov.uk/government/publications/national-planning-policy-framework--2
13 'Planning reforms putting rural England under siege.' (24 March 2014). www.cpre.org.uk/media-centre/news-release-archive/item/3568-planning-reforms-putting-rural-england-under-siege
14 Isabelle Fraser (28 January 2016). 'Fewer homes being built in London as UK house building falls 25pc short of target.' www.telegraph.co.uk/finance/property/news/12127141/Fewer-homes-being-built-in-London-as-UK-house-building-falls-25pc-short-of-target.html
15 Tom De Castella (13 January 2015). 'Why can't the UK build 240,000 houses a year?' www.bbc.co.uk/news/magazine-30776306
16 Jon Stone (8 July 2015). 'Budget 2015: George Osborne's new housing policy will cut affordable house building by 14,000.' www.independent.co.uk/news/uk/politics/budget-2015-live-george-osborne-s-new-housing-policy-will-cut-affordable-house-building-by-14000
17 'Why can't Britain build enough homes to meet demand?' (11 August 2015). www.bbc.com/news/business-33539816
18 Gov.UK (4 January 2016). 'PM: the government will directly build affordable homes.' www.gov.uk/government/news/pm-the-government-will-directly-build-affordable-homes
19 Hilary Osborne (14 January 2016). 'UK housebuilding held up by lack of bricklayers, says report.' www.theguardian.com/business/2016/jan/14/uk-house building-held-up-lack-bricklayers-report-rics
20 Foxtons (n.d.). 'Kensington house prices. What does the Kensington property market look like today?' www.foxtons.co.uk/living-in/kensington/house-prices/

222 Residential property markets

21 Robert Booth and Tim Clark (15 January 2015). 'Foreign investors buy 80% of homes in Thameside developments.' www.theguardian.com/society/2015/jan/15/foreign-investors-buy-80-per-cent-developments
22 Patrick Collinson (21 November 2015). 'Is it time to close the door to foreign buyers of British property?' www.theguardian.com/money/blog/2015/nov/21/foreign-buyers-british-property
23 Lee Boyce (26 November 2015). 'The death knell for buy-to-let? Stamp duty bill on a £275k home is more than trebled as Chancellor targets landlords.' www.thisismoney.co.uk/money/mortgageshome/article-3333549/Chancellor-trebles-stamp-duty-bill-275k-buy-let-second-home.html
24 Neil Monnery (2011). *Safe as Houses? A Historical Analysis of Property Prices.* London Publishing Partnership, p.158.
25 Shelter England (2016). 'The shortage of affordable homes.' england.shelter.org.uk/campaigns_/why_we_campaign/the_housing_crisis
26 Andrew Sentence (10 October 2015). 'The housing ladder is broken for the younger generation.' *The Daily Telegraph*, p.40.
27 Heather Stewart (18 December 2015). 'Almost half of Britain's private wealth owned by top 10% of households.' www.theguardian.com/money/2015/dec/18/britain-private-wealth-owned-by-top-10-of-households
28 (10 November 2016). 'House hunters return, but struggle to find affordable homes.' www.rics.org/uk/news/news-insight/press-releases/perspective-house-hunters-return-to-the-market-but-struggle-to-find-available-homes
29 Stuart Farquhar (5 January 2016). 'Unstoppable foreign investors are the real drivers of London property.' www.property-report.com/foreign-territory/
30 Yolande Barnes (16 July 2015). 'The world and London – 2015, top of the league.' www.savills.co.uk/research_articles/188294/189972-0
31 Xiaoyi Shao and Clare Jim (18 January 2016). 'Strong China property data masks big problem: unsold homes.' www.reuters.com/article/us-china-economy-property-idUSKCN0UW178
32 William Turvill (14 March 2016). 'Skype's founder just invested £17m in this mortgage lender.' www.cityam.com/236655/peer-to-peer-mortgage-company-lendinvest-announces-17m-investment-from-skype-founders-company
33 'Help to Buy.' (2016). www.helptobuy.gov.uk/
34 Kevin Peachey (28 May 2014). 'Q & A: Help to Buy mortgage scheme.' www.bbc.co.uk/news/business-24447335
35 Laura Howard (n.d.). 'Help to Buy scheme explained.' www.moneysupermarket.com/mortgages/hubs/first-time-buyers-help-to-buy-scheme/
36 Clear Barrett (13 February 2016). 'Help to Buy? More like Help to Cry for London's first-time buyers.' www.ft.com/cms/s/0/0989bc0c-d0b0-11e5-831d-09f7778e7377.html
37 'Help to Buy: what has changed and who qualifies?' (2 December 2015). www.theweek.co.uk/house-prices/55455/help-to-buy-how-it-works-and-who-should-apply
38 Christopher Middleton (8 October 2013). 'Help to Buy: is it really a bad idea?' www.telegraph.co.uk/finance/property/property-market/10363191/help-to-buy-is-it-really-a-bad-idea.html
39 Heather Stewart (1 December 2015). 'George Osborne's property-owning drive criticised by housing expert.' www.theguardian.com/society/2015/dec/01/osbornes-property-owning-criticised-housing-expert-kate-barker
40 'English Housing Survey 2014 to 2015: headline report.' (18 February 2016). www.gov.uk/government/statistics/english-housing-survey-2014-to-2015-headline-report
41 My Home Move (18 May 2016). 'Bricks and mortar in a digital world: 15 years of the property market.' www.myhomemove.com/news/uk-housing-transactions-set-to-jump-by-a-fifth-by-2020-but-recovery-dependent-on-first-time-buyers

42 Gov.UK (8 August 2016). 'Stamp duty land tax.' www.gov.uk/stamp-duty-land-tax/residential-property-rates
43 Steven Swinford (19 April 2015). 'Ed Miliband's mansion tax will force 120,000 to revalue their homes.' www.telegraph.co.uk/news/politics/ed-miliband/11548295/Ed-Milibands-mansion-tax-will-force-120000-to-revalue-their-homes.html
44 'Nationwide house price index.' (2016). www.nationwide.co.uk/about/house-price-index/headlines
45 'Mapped: the cities where HNWIS will buy, hold and sell real estate.' (22 December 2015). http://www.savills.com/blog/article/197861/us-articles/mapped-the-cities-where-hnwis-will-buy-hold-and-sell-real-estate.aspx
46 Judith Evans (25 June 2016). 'EU exit expected to end UK house price boom.' www.ft.com/cms/s/0/f17916f0-39da-11e6-9a0s-82a9b15a8ee7.html
47 Gov.UK (18 February 2016). 'English Housing Survey headline report 2014 to 2015.' www.gov.uk/government/statistics/english-housing-survey-2014-to-2015-headline-report
48 Hilary Osborne (17 November 2015). 'Generation rent: only 26% of young adults will be on the housing ladder by 2025.' www.theguardian.com/money/2015/nov/17/generation-rent-young-adults-housing-ladder-2025
49 Brian Milligan (22 December 2015). 'Rent rises could soon outpace house prices, warn surveyors.' www.bbc.co.uk/news/business-35154420
50 Isabelle Fraser (4 February 2016). 'UK kicks off biggest housing review in more than a decade.' www.telegraph.co.uk/finance/newsbysector/constructionandproperty/12138852/Government-launches-biggest-housing-review-in-more-than-a-decade
51 Ed Monk (25 February 2015). 'Homeownership falls to lowest level for 29 years as high prices lock out the young.' www.thisismoney.co.uk/money/article-2968673/Homeownership-England-falls-2-hit-lowest-level-29-years-high-house-prices-lock-young.html
52 Kathryn Hopkins and Tom Knowles (3 December 2015). 'Osborne's buy-to-let levy could backfire'. *The Times*, p.51.
53 'Carney promises action on buy-to-let property market.' (16 December 2015). www.bbc.co.uk/news/business-35108952
54 Rosie Taylor (28 May 2016), 'Undeterred: buy-to-let investors adopt new strategies'.www.telegraph.co.uk/property/buy/undeterred-buy-to-let-investors-adopt-new-strategies/
55 Julia Kollewe (27 January 2016). 'Legal & General to build and rent out 3,000 new UK homes.' www.theguardian.com/business/2016/jan/27/legal-general-to-build-and-rent-out-3000-new-uk-homes

10 Surveys

After reading this chapter you will know how to interpret some key economic surveys. These include those produced by: the CBI, Nationwide House Price Index, Society of Motor Manufacturers and Traders, Manpower Employment reports and the Purchasing Managers' Index (PMI) published by Markit. You'll also be able to discuss what these surveys can tell us about the state of the economy and what trends to look out for in following months.

As the financial services sector has grown so has the coverage of economic matters. Traditional City analysts have been joined by a plethora of think tanks, trade bodies and consultancies specialising in sectors such as housing and employment.

Reports published by some of these organisations such as the **Confederation of British Industry (CBI)** are regularly used as the basis for news stories in their own right or as a basis for comment and analysis of a specific issue. Such reports often set that day's agenda for the broadcast media.

Financial reporters typically have some structure built into their monthly journalism tasks from the timetable for official economic announcements. Often a useful indicator to what these figures may show comes from sector-specific surveys that are also published regularly. These are closely followed by City analysts and policy makers.

Box 10.1 Confederation of British Industry (CBI)

- UK's top business lobbying organisation with 240,000 members across all sectors.
- Industrial Trends Survey conducted on a monthly and quarterly basis.
- What does it say about output growth and export orders?
- What are future growth prospects?

There are some key surveys that journalists almost always cover. An example of this would be the highly regarded **CBI Industrial Trends Survey**.[1]

It provides a useful snapshot of the health of UK PLC. UK governments of all political colours are keen to rebalance the economy away from financial services and property to manufacturing and exports.

The CBI is the UK's largest business lobbying organisation, speaking for around 240,000 businesses that together employ around a third of the private sector workforce.

Members include companies of all sizes from large FTSE 100 companies through to small family-owned businesses and start-ups. The survey is conducted on a monthly and quarterly basis and covers 38 sectors of UK manufacturing industry. It is often more useful to look at the three month rather than one month time horizon for a more representative guide to business confidence.

> **Journalistic practice**
>
> In terms of reporting the survey, questions to address in one's report are: Have total manufacturing orders increased or decreased? What is the split between exports and imports?
>
> What are the underlying factors behind the trend? For example, has the strength of the pound and weak demand in the Eurozone, Britain's single biggest trading partner, depressed exports?
>
> How is manufacturing investment faring? In reports include quotes from the CBI's director general and/or a UK economist on manufacturing output and the outlook in the following months.

By looking at such factors an informed view can be made about the industrial outlook. Analysts will extrapolate from this what it might mean in terms of the timing and direction of any change in UK interest rates. Declining export orders coupled with weaker investment intentions suggest a softening in the economy. The Bank of England is less likely to raise interest rates against such a negative backdrop. This is in turn is likely to lead to a sell-off in the pound versus the dollar, at least in the short term.

There are many multinational and national research organisations compiling regular surveys on the health of specific economies. The biannual **World Economic Outlook** published by the International Monetary Fund (IMF) is probably the most authoritative of these reports and is widely covered in the financial press.[2] More detail on the WEO can be found in Chapter 8 on the IMF and World Bank.

Economic forecasts and surveys by the well-respected **Organisation for Economic Co-operation and Development (OECD)** are often reported. The OECD produces very useful economic surveys of specific countries.[3]

Journalistic practice

Country-specific features and comment pieces can be illustrated by the research findings of the OECD. It analyses a wide range of data including incomes and productivity, employment trends and government debt.

Economic surveys published by the **EY ITEM Club** regularly provide the backbone for economic news reports.[4] ITEM, in the EY ITEM Club, stands for Independent Treasury Economic Model. The model is used by the Treasury for its policy analysis. The business and financial advisory firm Ernst & Young has sponsored the ITEM club for many years. The club is the only non-governmental forecasting group to use the Treasury's model of the UK economy. The reports provide a detailed economic analysis and forecast of economic activity for the period ahead.

Journalistic practice

In structuring a news report, journalists should include the EY ITEM Club's forecasts made for UK GDP and CPI inflation, together with commentary on the overall outlook for the economy as a whole, reflecting the impact of any changes in oil and other commodity prices and the Euro/sterling currency rate.

The *EY ITEM Club* often makes observations on consumer confidence and retail sales and the labour market, which might provide the basis for a news report. Reports should include a quote from the Club's chief economic advisor.

Given the uncertainty surrounding the depth and sustainability of the world economic recovery, any guidance on trends in trade is keenly followed. Manufacturing industry's share of the UK economy has declined over the years as production has switched to lower cost production sites in the East such as China and Vietnam.

However one UK manufacturing bright spot is motors, which plays an important role in the UK's balance of payments. The UK is now a net exporter of cars. The automotive sector has an annual turnover of £40bn and a workforce of over 700,000.

In recent years, sales have grown strongly in emerging markets such as China and Turkey but have suffered in Continental Europe in countries such as Spain and France due to recession.

> **Box 10.2** Society of Motor Manufacturers and Traders
>
> - The SMMT publishes regular updates on new car sales known as registrations.
> - The UK is a net exporter of cars.
> - The automotive sector accounts for 9% of UK's total exports.

The **Society of Motor Manufacturers and Traders (SMMT)** publishes regular updates on new car sales, known as registrations. These are always picked up by the press.[5]

> **Journalistic practice**
>
> Reports should include the monthly change in new car registrations and a geographic breakdown of sales. Other factors such as the split between the domestic and fleet market may be noteworthy if they illustrate business confidence. Inclusion of a quote from the SMMT's chief executive on the outlook is also desirable. February is typically the weakest sales month as consumers postpone buying ahead of the registration plate change in March.
>
> Any new investment in car production facilities is a major news story as they are major local employers. Such a news item can generate colourful feature reports including the view from the assembly line.
>
> Other possible news or feature ideas emanating from new car registration figures are the trend towards smaller, more energy efficient models. More general features on Britain's membership of the European Union or technology, skills and innovation are often illustrated with examples from the motor industry, for example ultra-low emission vehicles and connectivity, otherwise known as customer intelligence.
>
> Reports can be illustrated with a graph of new car registrations over a chosen timeframe, or by tables of best-selling models. Ford Fiesta usually tops the UK bestseller list.

In March 2016, it was announced that two of the world's largest market data companies, IHS and Markit, were to merge, creating a powerhouse in economic, corporate and debt data and analysis.[6]

Markit Economics is an independent provider of the influential **Purchasing Managers' Index** (PMI) survey.[7] Central banks use the data to help guide interest rate decisions. PMIs are based on monthly surveys of carefully selected companies.

They provide an advance indication of what is really happening in the private sector economy by tracking variables such as output, new orders, stock levels, employment and prices across the manufacturing, construction, retail and services sectors. The surveys also give a useful illustration of the variance in economic performance geographically.

The PMI has been a useful indicator of both economic recession and recovery. A PMI level below 50 suggests economic contraction. Publication of such a figure tends to lead to a fall in the respective stock market, generating market news stories. A run of falling PMIs indicates an economic slowdown and prompts commentators to ask what measures the authorities might take to halt the decline, such as lowering lending rates or boosting infrastructure spending on items such as railways and public housing.

This is particularly the case when looking at the Chinese economy given its growth to be the world's second largest economy. It is seen as a bellwether to the general health of the developing economies.

Journalistic practice

Publication of the monthly PMI data for the major economies, notably US and China, is a major financial news story. Reports should headline the index itself and what it implied about the state of the economy in question. Was the headline figure in line with market expectations? What does the figure indicate and how does it compare with previous months? Might there be a policy response from the authorities?

In PMI news reports, any exceptional factors distorting the monthly index should be highlighted such as lunar New Year holidays in China and exceptionally bad weather conditions such as heavy snowfall on the east coast of America, which in the past has disrupted transportation and adversely impacted trade. Chinese street scenes or snow-covered highways could be used to illustrate aspects of the PMI story.

When analysing the PMI for the Eurozone it is always interesting to note how the major constituent economies are faring, namely Germany and France.

A news report on the PMI is usually accompanied by details of the response of the stock, bond and currency markets to the data release. The expectation of rising domestic interest rates should boost the local currency and depress local bonds. Include a response to the data from a City economist.

Box 10.3 Markit PMI

- Monthly economic surveys of carefully selected companies.
- Used by central banks to help make interest rate decisions and by financial analysts to forecast official economic data.
- Produced ahead of comparable official data series.

Around three million people are employed in the retail sector making it the UK's largest private sector jobs provider. The retail sector generates around 5% of UK GDP.

Whilst Britain may no longer be a nation of shopkeepers it is certainly a nation of shoppers, so there is always interest in these stories. Retail sales account for about one-tenth of the UK economy.

Journalistic practice

The trading results of major high street retailers such as Marks & Spencer and Tesco are usually reported in the financial press. What are the headline figures in terms of profits or loss? Were the results as expected? Are there any notable features e.g. lower sales of a particular category such as womenswear in the case of M&S, and if so why? Include opinion from a retail analyst on the current results and the outlook for the year. Include the share price movement if it was noticeable.

Much has already been written about the death of the high street in the UK with the growth of online retailing and out of town superstores. The business model of many store groups has not kept pace with changing shopping trends and they have too many shops on expensive high streets.

Feature articles can be produced in a number of areas. For example, an interview can be done with the owner of a small independent shop that has bucked the trend and prospered despite competition from larger players. How have they achieved it, what are their future prospects? The report can be illustrated by pictures of the shop frontage, its products and the owner.

Another feature can focus on the changing nature of retail with interviews with a company executive, e.g. managing director of John Lewis on their multi-platform retail offer. Why they have done it, what investments they are making and what trends they expect to see in the future? A retail analyst can be quoted giving their opinion on the company's performance and/or a customer can be asked about which shopping experience they prefer and why. Such a feature can be illustrated with photographs of the shops and warehouses.

The **British Retail Consortium (BRC)** speaks for a wide range of retailers from the large multiples and department stores through to independents. It produces monthly retail sales reports.[8] Retail stories are regularly the subject of both news and feature reports. They are relatively easy to explain and illustrate.

Journalistic practice

The BRC is good for industry comment on issues such as the changing nature of retailing with the decline in traditional high street shopping in favour of shopping online via mobile devices.

It is also vocal on retailers' rising costs in areas such as business rates, the apprenticeship levy and national living wage.

Competition is ferocious on the UK high street, no more so than in food retailing. The surging popularity of discounters such as Aldi and Lidl has put serious downward pressure on the margins of the major food retailers such as Tesco, Sainsbury's and Morrisons. The issue of food deflation, falling shop prices for food and also for non-food items, can be illustrated with data from the BRC.

The change in the nature in UK retailing has been striking since 2010. Retailers keen to at least maintain, if not grow, their market share have had to resort to offering discounted prices to attract customers. An estimated three-quarters of goods are thought to be the subject of some sort of promotion at any one time.

Lower oil prices in the commodity markets mean that retailers' costs are down and that is reflected in cheaper petrol prices which together with food deflation means the consumer is able to enjoy a lower cost of living. This feeds through to positive economic growth on the back of an upturn in consumer spending in other areas.

Ahead of the publication of the UK Government's annual Budget, the BRC are often vocal in their lobbying on business rates. These are non-domestic rates, charged on most commercial properties including shops, offices and factories.

Retailers pay around £145bn in rent every year for their premises. BRC continues to campaign for a reduction in the face of a decline in the number of high street shoppers.

The John Lewis Partnership (www.johnlewispartnership.co.uk/), which includes the John Lewis department stores and Waitrose food shops, is very much viewed as a bellwether stock. It produces weekly sales figures that are closely followed by retail analysts, given the Partnership's presence on the High Street and online.

It proved to be resilient through the recession with consumers trusting its quality and service. Its online sales continue to grow as a percentage of the total with a big increase coming from tablet and smartphone users. Click and collect sales, where you order online and then collect the items from one of their stores, are around a third of all sales on johnlewis.com.

The structure of the John Lewis Partnership is often cited as an example of the favourable benefits of mutual corporate ownership. The Partnership employs around 94,000 permanent staff who are all Partners and own the 43

John Lewis shops across the UK, 338 Waitrose supermarkets (www.waitrose.com), an online and catalogue business (www.johnlewis.com), a production unit and a farm. The business has annual gross sales of over £10bn. Partners share in the profits.

> **Journalistic practice**
>
> John Lewis' weekly sales figures can be treated as a news report in their own right if they demonstrate a particular trend in the market place, e.g. lower sales of furniture and other expensive – what's known in the trade as large ticket – items.
>
> In features on food retailing, Waitrose is often cited as an upmarket example compared to the discounters Lidl and Aldi. Journalists can then discuss the polarisation in the market and the adverse impact this is having on companies such as Tesco.

The CBI produces a monthly *distributive trades survey* which is always closely analysed.[9] Firms responding are responsible for a third of employment in retailing. The retail results constitute the UK component of the European Commission survey of retail trades.

> **Journalistic practice**
>
> In reporting the survey, note should be made of the annual sales trend, future outlook and internet sales volumes. Is there anything of interest to report in the wholesale data? For example, a big jump in building sales indicates a strong recovery in the property and building industries.

Box 10.4 Retail sector

- British Retail Consortium, trade body for a wide range of retailers.
- John Lewis Partnership includes John Lewis Department Stores and Waitrose supermarkets.
- *CBI Distributive Trades Survey* gives a monthly snapshot of retailing. Firms responding are responsible for a third of retail employment.

Labour market trends are often picked up by the surveys carried out by **Manpower**, the global recruitment company. Employment and unemployment figures are important economically and politically.

Manpower's quarterly *Employment Outlook survey* gives an indication of employers' hiring intentions in 41 countries, including the world's major labour markets. The survey includes a useful breakdown of hiring intentions in specific sectors. These include retail, finance and business services, utilities, agriculture and construction. This latter sector was severely hit by the fall-out from the recession but it is hiring again as major property markets recover in the UK and US.[10]

Journalistic practice

When writing a news report on any of the Manpower surveys, the opening paragraph should summarise the survey findings. For example, UK employers expect to grow staffing levels across most industry sectors in the second quarter. Useful statistics to include in news reports are the net employment outlook. For example, +7% means that 7% more employers expect to increase total employment. Mention the time frame and highlight any notable features within specific sectors or countries.

In a labour market feature, key facts from the Employment Outlook can be illustrated by maps, graphs and charts. The Outlook is particularly useful when comparing the differential scale and speed of economic recovery within countries. An example could be an analysis of the recovery in the Eurozone economies that suffered most in the financial crisis, namely Greece, Spain and Ireland.

Other topics that can be illustrated by Manpower data include reports on sectoral and regional UK skill shortages, for example, employers in north-east and north-west England struggling to find talented staff in a number of sectors including information technology (IT), engineering and finance and even finding it hard to fill vacancies for entry level jobs.

The London-based **Chartered Institute of Personnel and Development** (CIPD) is the professional body for human resource management. It has over 135,000 members internationally working in the private, public and voluntary sectors.[11]

CIPD produces survey reports on topical human resource issues as reward management as well as general people management and development themes. The changing nature of work and how best to deal with it is a perennial preoccupation of policy makers.

Journalistic practice

Many of the CIPD reports provide useful material for features and opinion pieces. Past surveys have looked at gender diversity in the boardroom, managing an age-diverse workforce and the impact of social media and technology on the world of work. Within an article on the general economic outlook, information on the recruitment intentions and pay policies of employers can be gleaned from the CIPD.

Box 10.5 Employment

- Manpower is a global recruitment company.
- Quarterly Employment Outlook survey of 2,100 UK employers shows:
  - What is the net employment outlook?
  - Any regional difference in employers intentions?
  - Which are the most optimistic sectors?

Box 10.6 Royal Institution of Chartered Surveyors (RICS)

- What does latest residential market survey show?
- What is the picture in sales and prices?
- Are there any regional differences?
- What are the expectations for annual price and sales growth?

There is always a lot of interest in coverage of the housing market given the high number of owner-occupiers in many major industrialised countries.

Problems in the sub-prime housing market in America, which has a high number of owner-occupiers, were largely to blame for the financial crisis of 2008. The problem has not been entirely solved and so the state of the US housing market continues to attract media coverage.

In the UK, around two-thirds of the population own their own home. Discussion of house prices has become almost a national pastime. Monthly house price statistics are produced by the Halifax and Nationwide building societies based on their mortgage business.[12]

Together they account for around a quarter of the UK mortgage market. The Halifax House Price Index is the UK's longest running monthly house price series with data covering the whole country going back to January 1983. It has developed into a widely used benchmark for the housing market.

Journalistic practice

Shortages of affordable housing in many major global cities, planning regulations and development are just a couple of the newsworthy topics in property. The sale of the Halifax House Price Index – owned by the Lloyds Banking Group – to the Markit financial data company for an undisclosed sum was itself a news story in March 2015.

News reports on the monthly UK house price indices should start with the headline monthly trend in house prices, i.e. how much prices grew or fell in the specific month in question. The price change compared to a year ago should be included and, if relevant, a comparison with the peak of the housing market in 2007. Include any noteworthy geographic features, for example, house prices in prime central London falling when stamp duty rose in 2016.

In compiling news reports, note if there any specific reasons for the monthly change in average house prices such as a better economic outlook, unemployment falling faster than expected, improvements in consumer confidence or low interest rates. The news story should include a quote from a housing market economist or other expert opinion such as that from Shelter, the homelessness charity.

In theory over the medium and longer term, upward pressure on prices should be reduced if there is a revival in house building that helps bring supply and demand into better balance.

A broad sweep of the global property sector both residential and commercial is regularly provided by RICS, the **Royal Institution of Chartered Surveyors (RICS)**. It is an international organisation with over 100,000 members working in the land, property and construction sectors. Its surveys cover a wide range of topics looking at specific sectors of the market and localities e.g. Hong Kong residential and global construction markets.

Journalistic practice

The content of the RICS survey can provide the anchor for news stories such as house price inflation due to the shortage of property for sale. Its surveyors on the ground are well placed to reflect the realities of the property market.

Regular surveys are also carried out by global property groups *Savills* and *Knight Frank*. These look at aspects of the local market such as purchase prices, most popular locations, the rental market, etc. See the chapter on global property markets for more detailed discussion of their research output.

The Building Societies Association (BSA) represents all 44 UK building societies. Its members hold almost £240bn of retail deposits, accounting for 18% of all such deposits in the UK. The BSA regularly comments and carries out surveys on housing-related matters.

Box 10.7 Federation of Small Business (FSB)

- Speaks for the self-employed and owners of small businesses with 200,000 members.
- Small businesses employ more than half of all private sector workers and contribute 50% of UK GDP.
- The FSB Small Business Index shows how businesses feel about issues such as confidence, employment and credit conditions.

The **Federation of Small Business (FSB)** is a UK campaigning pressure group for the self-employed and owners of small firms. Formed in 1974, it has 200,000 members and has almost 7,000 businesses in its 'Voice of Small Business' survey panel.

Small businesses employ more than half of all private sector workers and contribute around 50% of UK GDP.

Journalistic practice

Financial reporting of the *FSB Small Business Index* should include a general comment on the mood of small business. Are they confident about their own growth prospects and planning to create jobs in the months ahead? How is access to finance?

A news report can be produced on the back of the publication of net lending figures from the Bank of England. Include the amount of lending and compare the figure with the same period in the previous year. Explain the trend and look ahead to the prospects for the months ahead. Conclude the report with a quote from a bank official on the data.

The issue of lack of credit availability was a major factor in the aftermath of the financial crisis with small firms repeatedly criticising the lack of financial support from the banking sector. The issue is regularly covered in the financial press and prompted the Bank of England to alter the terms of its Funding for Lending Scheme (FLS) to favour small business lending over that to households.

> **Box 10.8** Bank of England agents
>
> - The Bank has 12 agencies around the UK.
> - Main function to assess economic conditions affecting businesses in their area.
> - Monthly agents' summary covers a number of areas including employment intentions, housing market activity, construction output, the cost of credit, output price inflation and capacity utilisation.

A guide to overall business conditions in the UK can be found from reports from Bank of England agents. The Bank of England has 12 agencies located in different parts of the UK whose main function is to assess economic conditions affecting businesses in their area.

The agents provide a monthly summary of business conditions covering a number of areas. These include manufacturing output, credit availability and investment intentions. Such summaries can provide the backdrop to general financial reports on business conditions.[13]

Arguably, the biggest survey of all is that of public opinion in a general election. In addition to copious amounts of political coverage there is also demand for reports on the financial implications of the election. Financial markets dislike uncertainty, which is reflected in volatility in the stock market and currency markets ahead of news of the election outcome.

The surprise Conservative Party majority secured in the May 2015 general election prompted the pound to surge to its highest level in six years. The news was also welcomed in the UK government bond market as yields on 10-year gilts, which move inversely to prices, fell. The benchmark FTSE 100 index of leading shares and FTSE 250, which has more exposure to the UK economy, moved higher on the election result.

Any associated financial news reports should include some examples of shares that move noticeably. In this instance, shares in house builders, banks, betting companies and Centrica energy company were in demand. The latter two had been overshadowed by the prospect of adverse regulation by an incoming Labour government. An extension of the 'Right to Buy' housing programme was supportive to the housebuilding sector.

The UK general election outcome was seen as supportive for both consumers and businesses. In addition financial markets assumed the existing accommodative policy stance would continue with deficit reduction measures and low interest rates.

Uncertainty surrounding the outcome of an election can weigh heavily on the financial markets and prompt both businesses and consumers to postpone investment decisions until the political landscape becomes clearer. This was evidenced ahead of the outcome of the Scottish independence referendum in 2015 when concern about the possible break-up of the United Kingdom prompted some investors to withdraw funds from Scottish banks.

Uncertainty about possible future tax and business policies depressed the share prices of companies with large exposure to the Scottish economy such as Royal Bank of Scotland, gas company BG group, drinks company Diageo and defence company BAE Systems.

Speculation ahead of the pivotal Greek parliamentary election in 2015 saw a heavy sell-off in European financial markets, worried that the left wing Syriza party would renege on its debt payments to international creditors, prompting a Greek exit from the European Union (EU).

Shares in Greek companies, particularly the banks, were sold heavily and yields on Greek 10-year government bonds spiked up. Following the election, reports focused on the protracted debt renegotiations with the international creditor group known as the **Troika**. This group is made up of the European Commission, European Central Bank (ECB) and International Monetary Fund (IMF). Press coverage analysed the likely impact of a Greek exit ('Grexit') from the EU.

Journalistic practice

Once an election result is known, news reports can focus on the likely financial market reaction notably in bonds and the currency market. Note can also be made about the political stability of the country in question post-election and if a factor, mention can be made of any upturn in capital flight from the country as investors seek a more stable environment for their money.

Ahead of the referendum on EU membership, the pros and cons of Britain remaining within the European Union were extensively covered in the media. There were interviews with spokespeople for both sides. The view from particular industry sectors such as the City, property, retail and farming were sought. The implications for trade and business were analysed and the uncertainty surrounding the outcome of the referendum was reported with reference to the financial markets, specifically, changes in the value of the pound, shares and bonds.

Key issues checklist

Trade: Will President Trump introduce protectionist trade policies? UK Brexit negotiations with the EU, scale of new UK inward investment and progress of UK export push to the BRICs.

Labour market: Real wage growth, youth unemployment, skills gap.

GDP: Monitor Trump's economic stimulus programme of tax cuts and higher infrastructure spending. China slowdown and progress of Abenomics.

Monetary policy: Speed and scale of US rate rises, when will UK rates rise, impact on emerging market currencies and bonds. End of QE?

Inflation: Threat of higher UK inflation due to Brexit, and in the US due to Trump's growth programme. Threat of deflation in Europe.

UK property market: How is the London market faring post-Brexit? What actions are being taken to improve housing supply and affordability and what's happening in the buy-to-let market?

BRICs: Monitor slowdown in Chinese economy. Impact on emerging markets–particularly China–of US protectionism. What political factors are impacting on Russian, South African and Brazilian economies?

Currencies: Likely to be volatility in the £/$ exchange rate due to worries about free trade and progress of Brexit negotiations.

Bonds: Prices down and yields up reflecting rising inflation and interest rates.

Fiscal policy: Has Trump vote triggered the end of global austerity?

Shares: Focus on economic growth and government spending should boost stock markets.

Interest rates: Faster growth suggests higher inflation and rising interest rates.

Assignments

Write a 300 word news story on employment prospects outside the UK based on the latest Manpower Employment Outlook.

Produce a feature report on the prospects for the UK high street. This should include commentary on consumer confidence, the trading performance of some large retailers such as John Lewis and Tesco and some comment on the general economic background in the months ahead.

Glossary of key terms

British Retail Consortium (BRC): trade association for the UK retail industry.

CBI Industrial Trends Survey: a bellwether for UK manufacturing with questions on items such as optimism, export orders, employment and investment.

Chartered Institute of Personnel and Development (CIPD): professional body focused on human resource issues.

Confederation of British Industry (CBI): lobby group for 190,000 businesses of all sizes.

EY ITEM Club: only non-governmental economic forecasting group using HM Treasury model of the UK economy.

Federation of Small Business (FSB): promotes the interests of the self-employed and the small business sector.

Leading indicators: data releases which usually lead (pre-date) turning points in the economy.

Manpower: global employment agency and consultancy.

Organisation for Economic Co-operation and Development (OECD): organisation of 34 countries established in 1961. It aims to help governments foster sustainable economic growth policies and fight poverty.

Purchasing Managers' Index (PMI): indicator of health of the manufacturing sector, includes new orders and inventory levels.

Royal Institution of Chartered Surveyors (RICS): professional body that accredits professionals within land, property and the construction sectors.

Society of Motor Manufacturers and Traders (SMMT): trade body for the UK automotive industry.
Troika: group of three international organisations – European Commission, International Monetary Fund and European Central Bank – that set conditions for Eurozone bailouts during the financial crisis.
World Economic Outlook: biannual survey of economic developments and prospects for the near and medium term produced by IMF economists.

Resource list

Confederation of British Industry: www.cbi.org.uk
Society of Motor Manufacturers & Traders (SMMT): www.smmt.co.uk
OECD: www.oecd.org
EY ITEM Club: www.ey.com
British Retail Consortium: www.brc.org.uk
Manpower: www.manpowergroup.com
Savills: www.savills.com
Knight Frank: www.knightfrank.com
Halifax: www.lloydsbankinggroup.com/media/economic-insight/halifax-house-price-index/
Nationwide: www.nationwide.co.uk/about/house-price-index/headlines
Royal Institution of Chartered Surveyors: www.rics.org.uk

Notes

1 *CBI Industrial Trends Survey.* (24 October 2016). www.cbi.org.uk/news/exports-rise-as-manufacturers-benefit-from-weaker-pound
2 *World Economic Outlook Reports.* (2016). www.imf.org/external/ns/cs.aspx?id=29
3 See www.oecd.org/eco/surveys/
4 See www.ey.com/UK/en/Issues/Business-environment/Financial-markets-and-economy/Economic-Outlook
5 'SMMT new car registrations.' (2016). www.smmt.co.uk/2016/02/uk-new-car-market-starts-2016-on-a-high-with-best-january-in-11-years/
6 Nick Goodway (22 March, 2016). 'Merger of HSI and Markit creates global data powerhouse.' www.independent.co.uk/news/business/news/merger-of-ihs-and-markit-creates-global-data-powerhouse-a6945271.html
7 See www.markiteconomics.com/public
8 BRC-KPMG retail sales monitor October 2016. (8 November 2016). 'Improved growth across categories in best month since January.' brc.org.uk/news/2016/improved-growth-across-categories-in-best-month-since-january
9 See www.cbi.org.uk/business-issues/economy/business-surveys/distributive-trades-survey
10 *Manpower Employment Outlook Survey* (Q4 2016). www.manpowergroup.co.uk/the-word-on-work/meos-q416
11 See www.cipd.co.uk/research/default.aspx
12 Nationwide House Price Index (October 2016). 'Annual house price growth slowed in October.' www.nationwide.co.uk/about/house-price-index/headlines
13 *Bank of England Agents' Summary of Business Conditions* (2016). www.bankofengland.co.uk/publications/Pages/agentssummary/2016/sep.aspx

Index

Locators for figures and tables are in *italic*. Locators for glossary entries are suffixed '(g)'.

Abenomics 13–14, 20, 20(g), 41–2, 131
adjustable rate mortgages (ARM) 210
aerospace industry 128, 163
affordable housing 192, 194, 208, 234
Africa: corruption 160; emerging economies 150–2, 159–61; Heavily-Indebted Poor Countries Initiative 180–1; Tripartite Free Trade Area 139
African Development Fund (AfDF) 181
agflation 32, 42(g)
agriculture: commodity prices 32; Common Agricultural Policy 133; fair trade 135–6; food inflation 33, 35; protectionism 133, 134
aid 177, 179, 181
air passenger duty (APD) 111, 113(g)
alcohol taxation 107, 112
annual investment allowance 110
anti-austerity 12–13, 108
apprenticeships 91–2
Arab Spring 78
Argentine 171–2
artificial intelligence 92
Asia: emerging markets 151; housing markets 189, 210; trade 138; *see also individually named countries*
Asian Infrastructure Investment Bank (AIIB) 138, 180, 183–4(g)
asset purchase facility (APF), Bank of England 10
asset purchasing, Japan 13–14
Association of South-East Nations (ASEAN) 138–9, 141(g)
asylum seekers 88
austerity 113(g); anti-austerity 12–13, 108; fiscal policy 172; Greece 168–9; IMF 169; public spending 4, 98

automobile industry 121–3, 129, 161, 226–7
Autumn Statement, UK 106–8, 113(g), 192–3
aviation sector, China 163

bailouts 100, 167–8
balance of payments 38, 123, 124–5, 141(g)
balance of trade 124–5
banana wars 134–4
bank base rate 1, 15–16, 19, 21(g)
bank levy 107, 114(g)
Bank of England 21(g); Funding for Lending 4–5; inflation reports 6, 30–3; inflation target 6–7, 27, 29–30; loans from 111; monetary policy 1–2; quantitative easing 10, 11, 208; surveys 236
Bank of Japan (BOJ): Abenomics 13–14, 41–2; Brexit 20
bank of mum and dad 212
bank run, financial crash (2008/2009) 190, 219(g)
banking sector: lending 4; shadow economy 113; sub-prime crisis 189–91, 233
base rate 1, 15–16, 19, 21(g)
basket of goods 28–9
Bean, Charlie 10
benefits 86, 92–3
Bernanke, Ben 103
Blinder, Alan 18–19
Bolton, Anthony 164
bond yields 15, 21(g), 99
bonds 21(g); European Central Bank 15; quantitative easing 9

boom (economic cycles) 68
borrowing costs 37; *see also* lending; mortgages; national debt
borrowing requirement 114(g)
BP 64
Brazil: currency valuations 149; as emerging market 158–9; quantitative easing 9, 12–13
Bretton Woods conference 173–4
Brexit: car industry 121; currencies 131–2; economic growth 45–6, 56–7; emerging economies 149; global context 19–20, 45–6, 47–9; housing markets 216; inequality 132; trade 135; US 50
BRICs 146, 164(g); consumer markets 161–3; investment bank 180; investment funds 163–4; key issues checklist 238; membership of African countries 160; *see also* Brazil; China; India; Russia
British Property Federation 219
British Retail Consortium (BRC) 229–31, 238(g)
Broadbent, Ben 40
budget, UK 114(g); Autumn Statement 107–8, 192–3; fiscal policy 105–6, 110–12; housing 192–3, 207; Institute for Fiscal Studies 108–9; surplus budget aim 102, 105, 108
budget deficit 98, 100–2, 105, 106, 108, 109, 113, 114(g)
budget surplus 102, 105, 109, 114(g)
building societies 190, 215, 219(g), 235
Building Societies Association (BSA) 235
build-to-rent 219
Burberry 162–3
bureaucracy, minimum wage 85
business: Ease of Doing Business Index 155, 158; FTSE 100 index 45, 225; small and medium-sized enterprises 4–5, 110, 235; surveys 236; UK/China trade 126–7; *see also* Confederation of British Industry; small and medium-sized enterprises
business confidence 38
business rates 110, 114(g)
buy-to-let 207, 217–19

Cameron, David: migration 90–1; trade 126, 127, 156
Campaign to Protect Rural England (CPRE) 193
capital flight 157

capital gains tax 106, 114(g)
capital markets, financial crash (2008/2009) 99
car industry 121–3, 129, 161, 226–7
carbon tax 110
Carlsberg 148
Carney, Mark: appointment 19, 20; Brexit 47; buy-to-let 218; forward guidance 16
CBI *see* Confederation of British Industry
central bank governors 7–8
central bankers, monetary policy 18–20
Centre for Cities 87
Chancellor of the Exchequer's role 6, 105, 106; *see also* Osborne, George
Chartered Institute of Personnel and Development 232–3, 238(g)
childcare measures 110
China: Asian Infrastructure Investment Bank 180; commodity prices 32; consumption 52, 54, 161–2; currency 48, 54, 131, 147; economic growth 47, 49, 52–5; as emerging market 147, 152–3; employment/unemployment 81; housing markets 210, 216; infrastructure investment 59–60; PMI survey 228; pollution 150; population 88, 152–3; poverty 183; shadow economy 113, 154; trade 126–9, 138–9, 153; UK trade 126–9, 153
China Media Capital (CMC) 129
Chomsky, Noam 182
cities: housing markets 188–9, 190, 216; migration in China 152–3; migration in India 154–5; UK labour market 85, 86–8
claimant count (benefits) 76, 93(g)
commodity prices 31–3
commodity supercycles 31–2, 42(g)
Common Agricultural Policy (CAP) 133, 141(g)
comparative advantage 124, 141(g)
conditionality 176, 184(g)
Confederation of British Industry (CBI) 238(g); Brexit 46; distributive trades survey 231; Industrial Trends Survey 37, 224–5; surveys 224–5
confidence *see* business confidence; consumer confidence
Conservative government UK: apprenticeships 91–2; general election 236; right-to-buy 192
Conservative-Liberal Democrat coalition government, UK: benefits 93; Brexit 47, 57; credit rating 100; housebuilding

194; housing 193, 214; National Living Wage 83; quantitative easing 10; stamp duty 213–14, 219; surplus budget aim 102, 105, 109; UK/China 127, 153; Work Programme 79
construction industry 194
consumer confidence 5, 57, 110
consumer markets, emerging economies 161–3
Consumer Price Index (CPI) 27, 42(g)
consumer price inflation 6
Consumer Prices Index Housing (CPIH) 27
consumption: China 52, 54, 161–2; emerging economies 161–2
consumption tax 98, 114(g)
Corbyn, Jeremy 12, 108
corn 35; 'corn belt' 32
corporation tax 98, 105, 109, 121
corruption 148, 154, 160
corruption index 148
cost of living crisis 4, 69, 82
cost-pull inflation 31
council housing 191–2
Council of Mortgage Lenders (CML) 218
credit ratings: Brexit 46–7; financial crash (2008/2009) 100; UK 100; US 104
cultural industries, UK 129
culture, China 129
currencies: Brazil 158–9; Brexit 45–6; central bankers 20; China 48, 54, 131–2; euro 14; inflation 38; Japan 13–14, 131; Special Drawing Rights 174–5; trade 131–2
currency valuations 149
current account, balance of payments 123, 124, 125–6
current transfers 124
customer service, artificial intelligence 92
cyclical unemployment 92–3, 93(g)

Dale, Spencer 10
data: employment/unemployment 5–6, 75, 76–7; house prices 195, *196–206*, 207–10, 208–9; India 156; key issues checklist 238; trade 119–20; *see also* Office for National Statistics; surveys
Davos 184(g)
debt *see* mortgages; national debt
Debt Management Office (DMO) 10, 114(g)
debt service 98, 114(g)
deficit, national debt 98, 100–2, 105, 106, 108, 109, 113, 114(g)

deflation 39, 40, 42(g)
demand, technological developments 66–7
demand-pull inflation 31
demographics: emerging economies 151; housing 207; workforce 88–9; youth unemployment 77–80, 92; *see also* population
deposits, house purchase 212–13
depreciation 131, 141(g)
development: and environment 179; globalisation 140; millennium development goals 181–2; World Bank 179, 181
direct taxes 110
discrimination, employment 89
distributive trades survey 231
Doha Round of trade talks 134
Dolphin, Tony 80
Draghi, Mario 14, 15, 41
dumping 86, 141(g)
duty 106, 112, 114(g); *see also* Air Passenger Duty; stamp duty
duty-free 134

Ease of Doing Business Index 155, 158
economic cycles 68
economic data *see* data
economic growth 45–50; BRICs *146*; China 47, 49, 52–5; emerging markets 150–1; Europe 55–6; financial crash (2008/2009) 8–9, 10; glossary 69–70; growth promoters 63; infrastructure 59–60; Japan 61, 131; oil 63–9; productivity 58–9; shadow economy 62–3; South Africa 160; trade 126; UK 56–60, 67, 105; US 50–2
economic surveys *see* surveys
economics of happiness 69
EDF energy 60
education, development of skills 91–2
El Niño 35
elections 236–7
emerging markets 146–8, 164(g); Africa 150–2, 159–61; Brazil 158–9; China 152–3; concerns 148–52; consumer markets 161–3; forecasts 170–1; glossary 164; IMF 174, 175–6; India 154–7; investment 147–8, 153–4, 163–4; millennium development goals 181–2; Russia 157–8; South Africa 159–61
employment law 89
employment/unemployment 74–5; base rate 15–16; Brexit 57; data 5–6, 75,

76–7; economic growth 57–8; Europe 80–1; flexibility 89; glossary 93–4; home ownership 192; key issues checklist 237; labour market issues 88–9; measuring 76–7; migration 90–1; Natural Rate of Unemployment 92–3, 192; Northern powerhouse 87–8; productivity 58–9; shadow economy 62–3, 93; skill shortages 91–2; surveys 231–3; taxation 67; types of unemployment 86–7; youth unemployment 77–80; *see also* income
energy: carbon tax 110; economic growth 51–2; India 155; investment 60; Japan 130; Russia 157; South Africa 161; UK/China 128
Engineering Employers Federation (EEF) 110
environment: and development 179; housing 193; IMF 172; pollution 150
equity loans 211
Ethiopia 150–1
euro: Brexit 45–6, 47; European Central Bank 14–15; Germany 129; Greece 168, 172; Swiss National Bank 20
Europe: agriculture 35, 133–4; Brexit 45–6, 48–9; economic growth 55–6; employment/unemployment 80–1
European Central Bank (ECB) 21(g); anti-austerity protests 12; IMF 168; inflation 15, 40–1, 55; monetary policy 14–15
European Economic Area (EEA) 90–1, 137
European Union: agriculture 133, 134; Consumer Price Index 27; employment law 89; IMF 171; single market 137; youth unemployment 78; *see also* Brexit; Grexit
exchange rates *see* currencies
Exchange Traded Funds (ETFs) 36
exports: China 53–5; European Union 137; UK current account 125; UK/China 126–8, 153; *see also* balance of payments
EY ITEM Club 226, 238(g)

factory gate prices 37
fair trade 135–6, 141(g)
Federal Open Market Committee (FOMC) 8, 21(g)
Federal Reserve 21(g); Brexit 20; monetary policy 7–9; quantitative easing 11; unemployment rate 81

Federation of Small Business 235, 238(g)
fertility rates 88–9
film industry 58
Finance Bill 114(g)
financial crash (2008/2009): capital markets 99; China 52; economic growth 8–9; employment/unemployment 74; forward guidance 15–16; globalisation 132; housing markets 189–91, 210; IMF 172; income 4, 74; inflation 39–40; monetary policy 1; poverty 183; productivity 58, 59; public spending 98; sub-prime crisis 189–91; *see also* austerity
financial services 123, 125
first time buyers 194, 208, 211–13, 217
fiscal cliff 103, 114(g)
fiscal multipliers 170–3, 184(g)
fiscal policy 98–104, 114(g); austerity 172; global perspectives 113; glossary 113–15; Institute for Fiscal Studies 108–9; Office for Budget Responsibility 104–5; spending review 106–8; UK budget 105–6, 110–12
flexibility, employment 89
floating rate mortgages 210
food: banana wars 134–5; commodity prices 32; emerging markets 163; fair trade 135–6; IMF 177; inflation 33–6; retail sector 230, 231
Food & Agriculture Organisation (FAO) 177
Food Price Index 34, 42(g)
Ford 121
forecasts: BRICs *146*; debt 105; economic growth 47–9, 51–2, 56; emerging markets 170–1; employment/unemployment 84; forward guidance 15–18; globalisation 140; housing markets 216; after quantitative easing 11; uncertainty 236–7; World Economic Outlook 170
foreign aid 177, 179, 181
foreign direct investment (FDI) 153
foreign investment, Brexit 46
forward guidance 15–18, 21(g); *see also* forecasts
fracking 50
France, economic growth 55–6
free trade: China 54; global perspectives 137–40; World Trade Organisation 133–4
frictional unemployment 86, 93(g)
FTSE 100 index 45, 225

fuel pricing 111
Funding for Lending 4–6, 21(g), 235

G20 175, 184(g)
gas: Japan 130; Russia 157; UK/China 128
GATT 133, 141(g)
GDP *see* gross domestic product
gender: consumer confidence 5; employment/unemployment 81
General Agreement on Tariffs and Trade (GATT) 133, 141(g)
general elections 236–7
generation rent 217, 220(g)
geographic mobility of workforce 87
Germany: economic growth 48–9, 55–6; minimum wage 84; trade 129–30; unemployment 80
Glaeser, Edward 188
global context: Brexit 19–20, 45–6, 47–9; currencies 131–2; debt 113; food prices 33–4; forward guidance 17–18; house prices 216; oil 64–5; quantitative easing 9, 12–13; youth unemployment 78
Global Financial Stability Report 171
global governance 175
globalisation 141(g); inflation 41; Special Drawing Rights 174–5; tourism 140–1; trade 120, 132, 137–40
Globalization and Its Discontents (Stiglitz) 140, 172
gold: Bretton Woods system 173–4; inflation 36–9
Goldin, Ian 179
goods: basket of 28–9; commodity prices 31–3; inflation 25–6; trade 123
Google 154
Graphene 67
Greece: debt 99–100, 103; general election 237; Grexit 103, 168, 237; IMF 168–9, 177; shadow economy 62; Syriza party 12, 99, 237; unemployment 80; youth unemployment 74
green belts 193
Green Budget 109
greenhouse gas emissions 110
Greenspan, Alan 8
Grexit 103, 168, 237
gross domestic product 69(g); China 53; Japan 61; key issues checklist 237
growth *see* economic growth

Haiti 182
Haldane, Andy 29
Halifax House Price Index 215, 233, 234
Hammond, Philip 105
happiness, economics of 69
Happy Planet Index (HPI) 69, 69(g)
Hawes, Mike 122
health care, China 128–9
Heavily-Indebted Poor Countries Initiative (HIPC) 180–1, 184(g)
Help to Buy 193, 211–12
hidden economy *see* shadow economy
high street retail 229–30
home ownership 40, 191, 208, 217
Hong Kong, housing market 210
house prices: affordability 208–9; China 54; global perspectives 216; indices 215; inflation 26; monetary policy 3–4; surveys 233; UK trends 195, *196–206*, 207–10
Housebuilders Federation (HBF) 194
housebuilding 194–5, 219
housing associations 194
housing markets 188–9; annual investment allowance 110; Asia 189, 210; building societies 190, 215; build-to-rent 219; buy-to-let 207, 217–19; glossary 219–20; Help to Buy 211–12; housebuilding 194–5; key issues checklist 238; loan to value ratios 212–13; London 157–8, 188, 193, 195, 207, 209; mansion tax 214–15; mortgages 191–3, 210–11; planning laws 193; renting 216–17; stamp duty 111, 189, 193, 195, 213–14, 219; sub-prime crisis 189–91, 233; surveys 233–4; UK trends 195, *196–206*, 207–10
HSBC 107
Human Development Index 184(g)
human rights, China 153
hyperinflation 39–40, 42(g)

IHS (data company) 227
illegal activities 62
IMF *see* International Monetary Fund
imperialism, of World Bank 182
imports: current account 125; food 33–4; UK/China 127–8; *see also* balance of payments
income *see* wages
income (national) 124
income tax, UK budget 110–11
Independent Treasury Economic Model (ITEM) 226

India: as emerging market 154–7; employment/unemployment 81; pollution 150
indirect taxes 110
Indonesia, as emerging market 150
industry *see* manufacturing
inequality: Brexit 132; house prices 208–9; minimum wage 84–5; World Bank initiatives 183
inflation 25–6, 42(g); basket of goods 28–9; Consumer Price Index 27; definitions 39–42; European Central Bank 15, 40–1, 55; food 33–6; glossary 42–3; gold 36–9; key issues checklist 238; monetary policy 1–2, 3, 39, 40; Retail Price Index 28
inflation hedge 26, 42(g)
inflation rate 25, 42(g)
inflation reports 6, 30–3
inflation target 43(g); Bank of England 6–7, 27, 29–30; European Central Bank 15; forward guidance 16; US 17
informal economy *see* shadow economy
information technology (IT) products 135
infrastructure investment: India 155; pension funds 111; UK/China 59–60
inheritance tax 114(g)
input prices 37
Institute for Fiscal Studies 108–9, 114(g)
Institute for Public Policy Research (IPPR) 78–9, 92
intangible services 124
interest rates: forward guidance 17–18; and inflation target 29–30; Japan 113; monetary policy 1–3, 40; mortgages 211; oil 65; quantitative easing 12; savers 38; sub-prime crisis 190; UK budget 111; US 17–18, 50
International Bank for Reconstruction and Development (IBRD) 178, 184(g)
International Development Association (IDA) 178, 184(g)
International Energy Agency (IEA) 65–6
International Labour Organisation (ILO) 76–7
International Monetary Fund (IMF) 167–9, 184(g); assessment of debt 102, 104; austerity 169; Autumn Statement, UK 106; changes to 175–6; criticisms of 170–2; economic growth 48, 57; employment/unemployment 77; fiscal multipliers 170–3; food 35–6; Heavily-Indebted Poor Countries Initiative 180–1; quantitative easing 11; quotas 174–5; resources 176–7; structure of 173–4; World Economic Outlook 47–8, 169, 225
investment: economic growth 58; emerging markets 147–8, 153–4, 158, 163–4; infrastructure 59–60; oil 65; scientific research 111–12
investment allowance 110
invisibles 124, 125, 141(g)
Iran, oil 64
Ireland: housing markets 191; IMF loans 171
Italy, shadow economy 62

Jacques, Martin 54
Jaguar Land Rover 121, *122*, 127
Japan: Abenomics 13–14, 20, 41–2, 131; debt 13, 14, 98–9, 113; economic growth 61; quantitative easing 13; trade 130–2
job centres 76
John Lewis Partnership 229, 230–1

Keynes, John Maynard 173
Kim, Jim Yong 178
Klein, Naomi 140
knowledge-based capital 66

labour *see* employment/unemployment
Labour Force Survey (LFS) 16, 76, 93(g)
Labour Party UK: air passenger duty 111; Bank of England loans 111; Brexit 46; budget 107–8; Corbyn election 12, 108; cost of living crisis 4, 69, 82; mansion tax 214
Lagarde, Christine: Brexit 46; economic growth 57; quotas 175, 176; structure of IMF 173
landlords, buy-to-let 217–19
Latin American, shadow economy 62
leading indicators 238(g)
Leeds, Northern powerhouse 87–8
left wing parties, anti-austerity protests 12
Legal & General 219
legal issues: China 154; employment 89
lending: borrowing costs 37; Funding for Lending 4–5, 235; IMF 171–2, 173, 176–7; shadow banking 113; sub-prime crisis 189–90; World Bank 179; *see also* mortgages; national debt
LendInvest 211
life sciences, China 128–9
Liverpool, Northern powerhouse 87–8
living costs crisis 4, 69, 82

living standards, unemployment 85
Lloyds Banking group 215, 234
loan to value ratios (mortgages) 212–13, 220(g)
loans *see* lending; mortgages; national debt
lobbying 46, 107, 225
London: employment/unemployment 87; financial services 125; housing market 157–8, 188, 193, 195, 207, 209
low growth 49–50
Low Pay Commission 85

M4 corridor 87
Mac, Freddie 190
Mae, Fannie 190
Manchester, Northern powerhouse 87–8
Mann, Catherine 49, 98
Manpower 231–2, 233, 238(g)
mansion tax 214–15
Mantega, Guido 9
manufacturing: car industry 121–3, 129, 161, 226–7; China 53–4, 55; Europe 55; labour market 86; North Sea oil 63–4; Producer Price Index 37; productivity 58; surveys 225, 226; trade 123; youth unemployment 78–9
marine trade 128
market volatility: Brexit 47, 49; China 52–3; emerging economies 147, 163–4; gold 36; housing 195; stock markets 32
Markit 227, 228
Marks & Spencer 229
May, Theresa: China 127; India 156
McDonnell, John 6
measurement, unemployment 76–7; *see also* data
Mercedes 163
Mercosur 139, 141(g)
Merkel, Angela 88, 129, 168
Mexico: as emerging market 150; migration 124
Meyer, Christopher 182
Middle East and North Africa (MENA) 78
migration: balance of payments 124; economic growth 58–9; employment/unemployment 67–8; labour market 90–1
Migration Advisory Committee (MAC) 90–1
Mihm, Stephen 176
millennium development goals 181–2, 184(g)

minimum wage 82–6
mining industry, South Africa 161
MINT countries 150, 164(g)
mobility of workforce 87
monetary policy 1–2, 21(g); Abenomics 13–14; anti-austerity protests 12–13; central bankers 18–20; European Central Bank 14–15; Federal Reserve 7–9; forward guidance 15–18; Funding for Lending 4–6; glossary 20–1; house prices 3–4; inflation 1–2, 3, 6–7, 39, 40; key issues checklist 237; quantitative easing 9–11
Monetary Policy Committee 21(g); economic data 5–6; forward guidance 15–16; purpose of 2–3; quantitative easing 10
money supply 21(g), 40
Monbiot, George 172
Monnery, Neil 208
Monsoon 83
mortgages 21(g), 191–3, 210–11; buy-to-let 217–18; help-to-buy 211–12; loan to value ratios 212–13; monetary policy 1; sub-prime crisis 189–91, 233
Multilateral Debt Relief Initiative (MDRI) 181
multinational organisations 167; glossary 183–5; *see also* International Monetary Fund; World Bank; World Trade Organisation
My Home Move 213

national debt: Brazil 159; definition 109; financial crash (2008/2009) 99–100; fiscal policy 98; Heavily-Indebted Poor Countries Initiative 180–1; to IMF 171–2, 173; inflation 39; Japan 13, 14, 98–9, 113; surplus budget aim 102, 105, 108, 109; UK 101–3, 112; US 103–4; *see also* lending
National Living Wage 83–6
National Minimum Wage 82, 83
National Planning Policy Framework (NPPF) 193, 220(g)
National Trust 193
Nationwide 215
natural gas 50
Natural Rate of Unemployment (Nairu) 92–3, 93(g), 192
natural resources, economic growth 63
NEET (not in education, employment or training) 78, 93(g)
Nene, Nhlanhla 159

net migration 91, 94(g)
New Zealand, inflation target 29
Newcastle, employment 85
Nigeria, as emerging market 150, 152
Nike 140
Nissan 121
North Sea oil 63–4
Northern powerhouse 87–8, 94(g)
Northern Rock 190, *190*
north/south divide (UK) 87
not in education, employment or training (NEET) 78, 93(g)
nuclear power stations: Japan 130; UK/China 60, 127

Obstfeld, Maurice 47–8
OECD *see* Organisation for Cooperation and Development
Office for Budget Responsibility (OBR) 83, 85, 104–5, 114(g), 170
Office for National Statistics (ONS) 115(g); basket of goods 28–9; borrowing 112; zero hours contracts 89
official economy 62–3
oil: agriculture 35; economic growth 63–9; emerging economies 149; IMF 177; inflation 33; price of 63–6, 177; retail sector 230; Russia 157; UK/China 128
Old Lady of Threadneedle Street 1
'one child' policy, China 88
O'Neill, Jim 176
OPEC (Organization of the Petroleum Exporting Countries) 65–6
Organisation for Cooperation and Development (OECD) 69(g); economic growth 48, 49; surveys 225–6
Organization of the Petroleum Exporting Countries (OPEC) 65–6
Osborne, George *101*; Brexit 47, 57; credit rating 100; housebuilding 194; National Living Wage 83; quantitative easing 10; stamp duty 213–14, 219; surplus budget aim 102, 105, 109; UK/China 127, 153
Oswald, Andrew 192
output gap 4, 21(g)
output prices 37
outsourcing 86
outward direct investment (ODI) 153
overheating economy 68

parallel economy *see* shadow economy
pay rises 38, 57, 83–4; *see also* income

peer-to-peer (P2P) mortgages 211
Peet, Richard 182
pensions: Retail Price Index 28; UK budget 111
personal finances, consumer confidence 5
petrol 33
Piketty, Thomas 108
planning laws, housing 193
plenum 69(g)
PMI survey 227–8, 238(g)
policymaking: inflation target 6–7; youth unemployment 79–80
political context: anti-austerity protests 12; Brexit 46; general elections 236–7
political risk 148
pollution 150
population: China 88, 152–3; employment/unemployment 88–9; India 154–5, 156; Japan 61; *see also* demographics
poverty 80–1, 183
Praet, Peter 15
prices: food 32, 33–6, 177; IMF 177; oil 63–6, 177; stability 1–2, 14–15; *see also* inflation
Producer Price Index (PPI) 37
productivity 21(g); base rate 19; economic growth 58–9; emerging markets 150–1
Productivity Plan 58
property markets *see* house prices; housing markets
protectionism 133–4, 141(g)
public opinion surveys 236–7
public sector employment 82
public spending: austerity 4, 98; central banks 41
Purchasing Managers' Index (PMI) survey 227–8, 238(g)
purchasing power 37
Putin, Vladimir 103

quantitative easing 21(g); emerging markets 148–9; European Central Bank 15; global impacts 12–13; housing markets 208; inflation 41; monetary policy 9–11
quotas 141(g); IMF 174–5, 184(g); trade 133, 134

railways 60
ratings agencies 46, 100, 115(g)
raw materials 123
Reading, employment/unemployment 87

real (Brazilian currency) 158–9, *159*, 164(g)
real exchange rate 149
recessions 70(g); Brazil 158; economic cycles 68–9; economic growth 45–6; emerging markets 149; *see also* financial crash (2008/2009)
recovery, economic cycles 68
recruitment 83
Redfern, Pete 217
redistributive effect, inflation 38
referendum vote *see* Brexit
regional differences, UK: house prices 3–4; labour market 86–8; London housing market 157–8, 188, 193, 195, 207, 209
regional trade blocs 120, 136, 137–40
remittances 124, 142(g)
renewable energy 128
renminbi 48, 54, 70(g), 131, 147
renting 216–17, 219
research: China 128–9; Institute for Fiscal Studies 108–9; investment in 111–12
residential housing *see* housing markets
Resolution Foundation 84
resource gap 124
resources, IMF 176–7
Retail Price Index 28, 43(g)
retail sector: China 54, 161–3; emerging markets 161–3; surveys 229–31; *see also* commodity prices
retirement age 89
retraining 87
rice 32
right-to-buy schemes 191–2
risk premiums 37
Roubini, Nouriel 176
Royal Institution of Chartered Surveyors 233, 234, 238(g)
rural-urban migration, emerging economies 152–3, 154–5
Russia: action in Ukraine 33, 148, 157; currency 148; as emerging market 157–8; fiscal policy 103; inflation 33

Saudi Arabia, oil 64
Saul, John Ralston 132
savers, rate of return 37–8
Savills and Knight Frank 234
Schäuble, Wolfgang 168
scientific research: China 128–9; investment 111–12
Scottish independence referendum 236–7
seasonal unemployment 86, 94(g)

self-assessment 112
semi-manufactured goods 123
service sector: China 53–4; trade 123–4; UK 58, 125; youth unemployment 78–9
shadow economy 115(g); banking sector 113; China 113, 154; economic growth 62–3; employment/unemployment 93
shale gas 50
shares, emerging markets 148
Sheffield, Northern powerhouse 87–8
Shell 64
Shelter 194, 217
ship building 128
Singapore housing 189, 210, 216
single markets 137–8
skills, workforce: construction industry 194; demographics 88–9; economic growth 67–8; migration 90; shortages 80, 91–2; youth 80
small and medium-sized enterprises: Federation of Small Business 235; Funding for Lending 4–5, 235; UK budget 110
Small Business Index 235
smog 150
social care industry 83
social housing 191–2
social problems, unemployment 85
Society of Motor Manufacturers and Traders (SMMT) 121–2, 227, 239(g)
South Africa: as emerging market 150, *151*, 159–61; quantitative easing 12–13
South America, Mercosur 139
sovereign debt 99, 115(g)
space technologies 67
Spain: economic growth 55; housing markets 191; unemployment 80
Special Drawing Rights (SDRs) 174–5, 184(g)
spending review, UK 106–8, 115(g)
'squeezed middle' 4, 69
stability, and economic growth 49–50
stagflation 39, 43(g)
stamp duty land tax 111, 189, 193, 195, 213–14, 219, 220(g)
starter homes 194
statistics *see* data
steel industry 86
Stiglitz, Joseph 108, 140, 172
stock markets: Brexit 45; China 152; Japan 14; oil 65; volatility 32
structural deficit 109, 115(g)
structural unemployment 86, 94(g)

sub-prime crisis 189–91, 220(g), 233
subsidies 133, 134
supermarkets 230, 231
surveys 224; British Retail Consortium 229–31; Building Societies Association 235; business 236; Charted Institute of Personnel and Development 232–3; Confederation of British Industry 37, 224–5, 231; EY ITEM Club 226; Federation of Small Business 235; general elections 236–7; glossary 238–9; housing markets 233–4; key issues checklist 237–8; labour force survey 16, 76, 93(g); Manpower 231–2, 233; Organisation for Cooperation and Development (OECD) 225–6; Purchasing Managers' Index (PMI) survey. 227–8; retail sector 229–31; Royal Institution of Chartered Surveyors 233, 234; Society of Motor Manufacturers and Traders 227; World Economic Outlook 47–8, 169, 225
sustainable development goals 77, 182, 184(g)
Sweden, migration 124
Swiss National Bank (SNB) 20
synthetic biology 111–12, 115(g)
Syriza party, Greece 12, 99, 237

tariffs 121, 133, 134, 135, 142(g)
Tata 121, 156
taxation: buy-to-let 217–18; carbon tax 110; employment market 67; mansion tax 214–15; recessions 69; shadow economy 62, 63; stamp duty 111, 189, 193, 195, 213–14, 219; UK budget 105–6, 107, 110–11; unemployment 86
technology industry: artificial intelligence 92; basket of goods 29; economic growth 66–7; financial services 125; M4 corridor 87; scientific research 111–12; tariffs 135
textiles industry 134
Thatcher, Margaret 191–2
tourism: from China 161–2, 163; trade 140–1; UK 125, 161–2
tracker mortgages 211
trade 119–26; banana wars 134–4; Brexit 135; China 126–9, 138–9, 153; Doha Round of trade talks 134; fair trade 135–6; Germany 129–30; globalisation 120, 132, 137–40; glossary 141–2; India 156; Japan 130–2; key issues checklist 237; regional trade blocs 120, 136, 137–40; tech tariffs 135; tourism 140–1; UK 120–1, 126–9; World Trade Organisation 133–5; *see also* free trade
trade deficit 124
trade surplus 124
Trade Union Congress (TUC) 170
trading groups/partnerships 136–9
training: apprenticeships 91–2; labour market 87
Transatlantic Trade and Investment Partnership (TTIP) 138, 142(g)
Trans-Pacific Partnership (TPP) 137–8, 142(g)
transport, railways 60
transport services trade 123–4
Tripartite Free Trade Area (TFTA) 139, 142(g)
TROIKA 184(g), 237
Trump, Donald 138
Tsipras, Alexis 100, *169*
Turkey: as emerging market 150; migration 124

UK: car industry 121–3, 226–7; credit rating 100; current account 125–6; economic growth 56–60, 67, 105; house prices 3–4, 195, *196–206*, 207–10; labour market 86–8; national debt 101–3, 112; trade 120–1, 126–9; trade with China 126–9, 153; *see also* Bank of England; Brexit; budget; *named governments e.g. Conservative-Liberal Democrat coalition government*
UK Trade & Investment (UKTI) 126–7, 142(g)
Ukraine 33, 148, 157
uncertainty 236–7
underground economy *see* shadow economy
unemployment *see* employment/ unemployment
unemployment rate 76, 81
United Kingdom *see* UK
United Nations: employment/unemployment 77; IMF 173; millennium development goals 181–2; sustainable development goals 77, 182, 184(g)
urbanisation, emerging economies 152–3, 154–5
US: currencies 131–2; economic growth 50–2; employment/unemployment 81; fiscal policy 103–4; forward guidance 16–18; IMF 176; inflation 41; PMI

survey 228; quantitative easing 12; sub-prime crisis 190; Trans-Pacific Partnership 137–8
US Federal Reserve *see* Federal Reserve

Value Added Tax (VAT) 111, 115(g)
variable rate mortgages 210–11
Varoufakis, Yanis 99
VAT 111, 115(g)
Venezuela, oil 64
visas 162
visibles 123, 142(g)
volatility *see* market volatility
Volkswagen 56, 122–3

wages: cost of living crisis 4, 69, 82; economics of happiness 69; financial crash (2008/2009) 4, 74, 81–2; income tax 110–11; migration 90–1; National Living Wage 83–6; National Minimum Wage 82, 83; pay rises 38, 57, 83–4; percentage spend on food 33–4
Watson, Richard 140
weather 35
WEO (World Economic Outlook) 47–8, 169, 225
wheat 32

White, William 11
'winners and losers' 9, 120
Work Programme 79
workfare programme 79–80
workforce: geographic mobility 87; size 76; training 87; *see also* skills
World Bank 184(g); criticisms of 182–3; Heavily-Indebted Poor Countries Initiative 180–1; purpose of 178–9
World Bank Development reports 178–9
World Economic Outlook (WEO) 47–8, 169, 184(g), 225
World Trade Organisation (WTO) 133–5, 142(g)

Xi Jinping 126, 153

Yellen, Janet: appointment at Fed 7, 7–8; interest rates 17–18, 50
yield, quantitative easing 9
youth contract 79
Youth Employment Initiative (YEI) 78
youth unemployment 77–80, 92
yuan (renminbi) 48, 54, 70(g), 131, 147

zero hours contracts 89
Zuma, Jacob 159